The Caring General

The Life and Letters of Major General Sir Harold Goodeve Ruggles-Brise, KCMG, CB, MVO

James Barker-McCardle & Alan Ogden

Foreword by General the Lord Dannatt GCB, CBE, MC, DL

 Helion & Company Limited

Helion & Company Limited
Unit 8 Amherst Business Centre
Budbrooke Road
Warwick
CV34 5WE
England
Tel. 01926 499 619
Email: info@helion.co.uk
Website: www.helion.co.uk
Twitter: @helionbooks
Visit our blog at blog.helion.co.uk

Published by Helion & Company 2023
Designed and typeset by Mary Woolley (www.battlefield-design.co.uk)
Cover designed by Paul Hewitt, Battlefield Design (www.battlefield-design.co.uk)
Printed by Short Run Press, Exeter, Devon

ISBN 978-1-804514-89-4

British Library Cataloguing-in-Publication Data.
A catalogue record for this book is available from the British Library.

For details of other military history titles published by Helion & Company Limited
contact the above address, or visit our website: http://www.helion.co.uk.

We always welcome receiving book proposals from prospective authors.

Dedication

For Sir Timothy and Lady Ruggles-Brise without whose friendship, generosity and considerable patience this remarkable story would have gone largely untold.

"Such was our Divisional General (Ruggles-Brise), a man of justice, a soldier who inspired in all ranks a feeling of confidence and loyalty and not merely a picturesque figurehead, unknown and misunderstood. A man whose personality breathed kindness but never weakness, and lastly a soldier who, whilst he showed us that he understood our difficulties, made us feel that they were there to be overcome at all costs."

Captain Eric Whitworth, 12th South Wales Borderers

Contents

Acknowledgements

This volume would never have come about without the encouragement, kindness and incredible patience of Tim and Rosemary Ruggles-Brise. My gratitude also goes to the two fabulous archivists at Blair Castle, Jane Anderson and Keren Guthrie, who provided access to considerable correspondence and hosted my two visits as well as to Sarah Troughton and the Trustees at Blair for granting permission to publish material from their archives.

Further thanks go to Suzanne Foster at Winchester College for hosting a fascinating visit and for granting access to their archives which shed valuable light on Harold's early years. I am also most grateful to Captain Alan Ogden, the Grenadier Guards Regimental Historian for his help, patience and proof reading concerning all matters pertaining to the Grenadiers.

My wife, Joy, who accompanied me on both trips to Perthshire and Winchester College, has helped with much of the research and the transcribing of very many faded pencil written letters. Lastly my thanks go to my daughter, Sarah, who has done much of the typing and unlike her father has the technical skills to format a book.

This has been a happy journey …

James Barker-McCardle

Foreword

Growing up in Essex not far from Finchingfield, I was very much aware of the high regard in which Sir John Ruggles-Brise, then Lord-Lieutenant of Essex, was held. He was known as a man who took a deep and genuine interest in all those with whom he came into contact whether in his village of Finchingfield or more widely across the county of Essex. At the time I did not give much thought as to where Sir John might have gained these caring instincts nor indeed did I have a personal connection to the Ruggles-Brise family. At least that was until I met and married Philippa Gurney whose grandmother Pleasance was a Ruggles-Brise of Spains Hall, Finchingfield.

Having been given the privilege of writing a foreword to this outstanding biography of Major General Sir Harold Ruggles-Brise, many of the pieces of a previously unsolved jigsaw have fallen into place. I am now convinced that the Sir John Ruggles-Brise that I knew and respected as a boy was very likely to have been deeply influenced by his great uncle, Major General Sir Harold Ruggles-Brise, with whom he sometimes stayed in London after the First World War. Dying in 1927, self-evidently I never knew Sir Harold but having married into the wider Ruggles-Brise family, I got to know his great nephew, Sir John, quite well. Now, in reading Jim Barker-McCardle's manuscript, I can see that the deep tradition of caring runs right through the family and continues to this day – mostly recently in dedicated service to the Lieutenancy and Shrievalty in Essex and in my wife as the current Lord-Lieutenant of Norfolk. The example set by Major General Sir Harold Goodeve Ruggles-Brise KCMG CB MVO as the caring General has been lovingly followed down the generations.

It is no surprise to me to learn that Harold Ruggles-Brise routinely wore a pair of cufflinks, engraved with the motto of Sandhurst "Serve to Lead." The concept of serving those whom you aspire to lead is the value that underpinned the officer training that Harold went through, culminating in his commissioning into the Grenadier Guards in 1885, and still is the guiding ethos of Sandhurst today. His regimental service and studies at the Army Staff College prepared Harold well for the war in South Africa and his first staff appointment as Brigade Major of the Guards Brigade in 1899.

The pages of this volume with their narrative sections and carefully arranged sequence of letters tell the story of Harold's involvement in the bitter fight against the Boers and then the subsequent years of peace before the outbreak of the Great War. It was during these times that Harold realised the importance of valuing those under his command as men who will fight better as soldiers if their individual needs and worries are properly addressed. And he was rigorous in overseeing the best training possible, exemplified by his highly successful tenure as Commandant of the School of Musketry at Hythe. It was here that the excellence of marksmanship with the rifle and the steadfastness of the British infantry was forged into the British Expeditionary Force that deployed to France and Belgium in August 1914.

While in peacetime to have been Commandant of Sandhurst would have provided Harold with the opportunity to influence the development of many young leaders, he was relieved to be appointed instead as the commander of the newly formed 20th Brigade as part of the 7th Division. This new Division was the first reinforcement to the original BEF that had fought so gallantly from Mons to the Marne, blunting the German Army's attempt to encircle Paris and end the war with a rapid knockout. By mid-October 1914, the lines of trenches from Switzerland to the Channel had formed and Harold's 20th Brigade entered the line at Ypres. So, the stage was set for the defining chapters of Harold's military career.

In the years following the end of the Great War, politicians, poets and historians did not treat the Generals kindly, too often and unfairly lampooning them for seeming to command from the comfort of distant chateaux. This was certainly not Harold's experience either as a brigade or divisional commander on the Western Front. "Serve to Lead" was too deeply ingrained in him for that. Harold was forward in the combat areas as much as possible to share the harsh conditions with his troops and lead by example. After the initial battle fought by his brigade with very heavy casualties, Harold had to order his men back into the line after a very short period of recuperation. It is typical of the man about whom the Brigade Chaplain wrote "…the Brigadier (Ruggles-Brise) gave the order in a voice which was broken with emotion, for he knew full well the desperate nature of the task he was setting his men."

That was the voice of the caring General that this volume so brilliantly describes but sharing the hardships with his men meant that he had to share their wounds as well. Harold was severely injured on 2nd November 1914 by shellfire. However, the experience of injury and recovery put him into position to fight another battle on behalf of others, this time with the War Office who sought to place wounded senior officers on half pay in their substantive, invariably lower rank. In a spirit that I know and recognise he took the fight into the political arena and won! This was not a selfish battle but one that was standing up for decency and respect – another example of his caring.

The exchanges of letters between Harold and his beloved wife, Dertha, continue the narrative through the rest of the Great War – sufficient recovery from his wounds to command 40th Division back on the Western Front then appointment as Military Secretary to the Commander in Chief – an appointment that necessitated Harold removing an Army Commander from his appointment at the height of the German Spring Offensive of 1918.

With the Allies victorious and an armistice signed on 11th November that year, it was with very mixed feelings that Harold received the news that the War Office had concluded that he could not be offered another Major General's appointment and was to be retired on full pension on 9th March 1920. But for the caring General, as one door closed, another opened. The needs of retired officers and soldiers, especially the wounded, gave rise in 1921 to the formation of what is now the Royal British Legion. Typically, Harold played a significant role in the establishment of this much needed institution which has just celebrated its centenary. Like the compassion of Bryn Parry who founded Help for Heroes after the Iraq and Afghanistan campaigns in recent years, it was the compassion and care of men like Harold Ruggles-Brise who forged the Legion into being the organisation that has looked after so many men and women whose service for Sovereign and Country had placed them in dire need.

Struck down by pneumonia in 1927, Harold's death deprived our nation prematurely of the services of this most caring of men. It is a tribute to him and his family that in 1929 The Ruggles-Brise Holiday Homes Fund for ex-soldiers was set up in his memory. In Finchingfield Church, his memorial plaque includes the words:

> I have fought a good fight – I have finished my course

Strictly speaking, this inscription is true, but Jim Barker-McCardle's inspiring volume ensures that the spirit and memory of Major General Sir Harold Ruggles-Brise lives on. His commitment to his men and his devotion to his wife and family are an inspiration and shining example to future generations. If ever a General deserved the accolade of being "The Caring General", it was Sir Harold Ruggles-Brise.

Richard Dannatt
General The Lord Dannatt GCB CBE MC DL

Introduction

A hundred or more years ago it was not uncommon for families with a rural estate that the eldest son would inherit and younger sons would go into politics, the civil service, a profession or the Army or Navy.

Harold was the youngest of five bothers. The eldest Archie inherited Spains Hall Estate, Evelyn entered the Home Office and is remembered as a visionary Prison Reformer, in particular for the creation of the Borstal system which segregated young offenders from adults. Another brother Cecil also joined the Army but was accidentally shot whilst training in Canada. In addition to his brothers Harold had seven sisters for such a large family was not unusual in Victorian times.

Harold chose the Army and this is his story, one of a brave, compassionate and highly respected soldier told from personal records covering both his military and his private lives.

The genesis of this biography began in May 2011 when my wife Rosemary was hosting a dinner as High Sheriff of Essex for the Judges and other county notables including Jim Barker - McCardle who was our Chief Constable at the time. Little did we know what would ensue from that evening

"It was his eyes" Jim said when I asked him what in particular had caught his attention when he first saw Harold's portrait that evening. Painted after his sudden death from pneumonia in 1927, judging by family photographs, it was a good likeness.

"I immediately sensed that here was a compassionate and kindly man, the very antithesis of the Blackadder First World general".

After Jim retired from the Police, he was able to devote much of his time to furthering his interest in military history becoming a professional guide to the European battlefields of both World Wars. It was perhaps not surprising therefore that he should express an interest in finding out more about Harold from the family.

Fortunately, the family hold a considerable collection of correspondence and memorabilia relating to Harold's career in the Army from commissioning into the Grenadier Guards in 1885 to his appointment as Military Secretary to Field Marshal Lord Haig in 1918, an appointment requiring considerable sensitivity and tact not least when he had to inform an officer senior to himself and a friend that he had been relieved of his command.

The collection was expanded in the early 1990s when my brother Jimmie and our Uncle Sir John extracted everything held in the Essex Records Office and spent many hours sifting through letters including those written when Harold was serving in the Second Anglo-Boer War right through to his retirement, collating them along with an impressive collection of memorabilia. I am most grateful to both for all the time and effort they devoted to this task and I know that our uncle who died in 2007 would have been overjoyed that a Biography of Harold would emerge from his endeavours.

In 1895 Harold married Lady Dorothea Stewart-Murray, eldest daughter of the 7th Duke of Atholl who was affectionately known as "Dertha". So the second major source of material for Jim was in the Blair Castle archives.

The immediate family have been unbelievably fortunate in war time. Harold and his three nephews Edward, Ralph and Evelyn all served in the Great War and survived, although apart from Evelyn they were all wounded. Less fortunate was Evelyn's wife, Mildred (née Cubitt) who lost two brothers on the same day at Gallipoli, and another at Gaza, Palestine. Subsequently, Mildred went to Northern France in 1915 to work as a nurse in the Anglo-French Hospital in Tréport. However, during the Second World war their son Oliver was killed in action at Caen in July 1944 aged 21.

As part of his research for this biography, Jim arranged for Rosemary and me to visit the Western Front on three occasions. On the first visit we were taken to Herenthage Wood, Ypres where Harold was severely wounded during the First Battle of Ypres in November 1914. Anecdotally, I understand that as he was being carried off the field of battle presumed dead an eagle-eyed orderly noticed him lift his hand slightly. This may well have saved his life.

We next visited Frezenberg Ridge where my grandfather Edward won his MC when serving with The Essex Yeomanry in the Second Battle of Ypres. Of the 70 who set out under his command that day, only 12 returned uninjured. As Jim later observed, "a lot of Essex blood was shed that day". Edward was later wounded at Loos in 1915 but had a lucky escape when a bullet hit him in the chest and was only stopped by the coins in the pouch in his breast pocket. We still have the pouch and the squashed German bullet.

Ralph served in the Ypres area as a Royal Engineer and was awarded the MC in 1915 for conspicuous gallantry and initiative. He had been exploring an enemy mine gallery and despite being attacked and wounded by two Germans, fought them off, lit his fuse and then managed to crawl out. His brother Evelyn served with the 1/1st Norfolk Yeomanry at Gallipoli and then in Egypt with the Western Frontier Force which ultimately landed in Marseilles in 1918.

I highly commend Jim for the skilful way in which he has used the correspondence between Harold and Dertha to portray their very different daily lives while at the same time revealing the strength and depth of their close feelings for each other during the tumult of a war the likes of which had never been experienced.

Jim's explanation of the correspondence within the context of the military aspects of Harold's life when on active service makes for an easy and illuminating read. The comradeship and hardships of soldiering are vividly described as is his frustration at times with the High Command! Harold clearly had little hesitation in making his views known and it is a measure of the respect in which he was held by his peers and seniors that he was listened to.

Given that it has taken quite a number of years to complete this biography, no thanks can ever be adequate to express my gratitude and that of my family to Jim, his wife Joy and daughter Sarah for their dedication, determination, and perseverance in piecing everything together. The task of transcribing all the personal handwritten correspondence was in itself a major achievement and made even more so by Harold's writing, much of which was in pencil and extremely hard to decipher.

I would also like also to express my gratitude to all from the wider family who have contributed to "Serving their Country" and especially to General The Lord Dannatt whose wife is my second cousin and a great, great niece of Harold for agreeing to write the Foreword.

Tim Ruggles-Brise
July 2023

Preface

I remember the moment as if it were yesterday. My wife Joy and I were enjoying a lovely dinner (one of many) in the magnificent setting of Spains Hall, the Finchingfield home of the Ruggles-Brise family since 1760. The late Edith Freeman described its setting in her *A Family Story – The Ruggles of Spain Hall* (1993):

> ... here is stretched the Tudor frontage of the great house, corseted by a sequence of orderly brick bays, its brickwork mellowed by centuries of later afternoon sunshine; its walls finely ornamented by crested silver-leaded down pipes; its handsome stacks of chimneys rising from a jungle of old roofs. Impressive, and yet homely, the house is set in a park of equal dignity. Across the mown grass, trees famed for their age and stature cast long shadows; oldest of all is a giant cedar planted in 1670. The drive curves to a welcoming porch, crowned by a sundial. The moat is now dry but at the rear the flower gardens descend to a chain of ponds, the largest extended to form a gleaming lake. On the horizon the bell-tower of Finchingfield church fixes the eye. The scene encapsulates the essence of England.

This glorious setting was matched only by the company in which we found ourselves. During dinner my eyes fell upon a superb portrait of a General. Most striking of all were the eyes and the setting of the jaw. His face conveyed a congeniality, a warmth and a kindness not always found in portraits of very senior military figures. This was clearly a man of bearing but also a man I immediately wanted to know more about.

At that stage I had no idea of the journey on which Joy and I would embark and the extraordinary story that would unfold. My interest in the Great War and military history germinated in the early 1980s with the death of my grandfather who served in India and Mesopotamia ('Mespot') during that mighty conflict. He was a prolific letter writer and I inherited the many wartime letters he sent to his parents. He wrote not just of combat but of people, customs, humour, friendships, history, geography and concert parties in the desert.

This stimulated my interest in the people who fought as well as the fighting – who they were, where they came from, what motivated them and their personal stories. I have walked the battlefields of both World Wars on many occasions and invariably concluded that without a thorough appreciation of topography it is impossible to comprehend the multitude of difficulties our soldiers had to overcome and thus the true extent of their achievements.

As a good friend and fellow battlefield explorer observed, history cannot be understood without geography, so what a privilege it was to visit the battlefields of Ypres with Tim and Rose and walk in Sir Harold's footsteps including Herenthage Wood where he sustained near fatal wounds during an intense German bombardment.

It is 'Tommy Atkins' who rightly emerges as the great British character and hero in the Great War. To stand under the solemn arches of the Menin Gate at Ypres as the buglers sound the Last Post, surrounded by some 53,000 names of the missing, is a deeply moving and emotional experience. Amongst those names are many of Sir Harold's men who lost their lives in the fighting of 1914 and have no known grave. Men from his old regiment, the Grenadier Guards, are also commemorated – both battalions were decimated during this time.

As entertaining as the *Blackadder Goes Forth* television series may be, it is entirely wrong to think that generals were always safe in luxurious chateaux far beyond the range of enemy bombardment. It is self-evident that the exercise of command and control at the highest rank (with necessary supporting staff) necessitated, whenever and wherever possible, locations and facilities that afforded security. The same remains true today for having senior commanders and their staffs blown to pieces is hardly conducive to effective operations.

However, at the next level down, Brigadiers and Colonels accompanied their brigades and battalions to the front line for it was only there that they could assess what was happening in in real time and make instant decisions. In doing so, they exposed themselves to the same dangers as their men. In the 1970s the historian John Terraine initiated a debate for a more balanced understanding military leadership during the Great War. In 1995, Frank Davies and Graham Maddocks[1] produced a comprehensive reference work of general officers who were killed or wounded during 1914-18. Of a total of 224 names, 78 were killed. Amongst the wounded we find Harold who suffered near fatal injuries at Herenthage Chateau whilst commanding 20th Brigade during the First Battle of Ypres.

---

1   See Davies, Frank & Maddocks, Graham, *Bloody Red Tabs: General Officer Casualties of the Great War 1914-1918* (London: Leo Cooper, 1995), passim.

When Joy and I started our research, I imagined the end product would be a book focussing on Sir Harold's service during and after the Great War. However, two visits to the archives at Blair Castle revealed a considerable number of letters between Sir Harold and Lady Dorothea including many written during his service in South Africa. Taken together, the correspondence held at Spains Hall and that at Blair Castle provide an extraordinary insight into Sir Harold and Lady Dorothea's family life, not just Sir Harold's military service. Indeed the letters written by Lady Dorothea provide accounts of life at the home front during the Great War including an eyewitness account of an air raid on Hythe.

I have wrestled with how best to include as many letters as possible without duplication or repetition. A more conventional history might have focussed on events and introduced elements of the letters to support the overall storyline, however this would have left much material on the 'cutting room floor'. Some of the letters, especially from South Africa, are so detailed that they provide a highly readable account of operations in their own right.

My inexperience as an author has worried me from the start of this project. Would I be able to do full and proper justice to Sir Harold and Lady Dorothea? Would I fail to repay the trust that Sir Timothy and Lady Ruggles-Brise had placed in me? Fortunately for us all, Alan Ogden was to hand. It is his skills and knowledge as both author and historian that have more than made up for my shortcomings.

Jim Barker-McCardle, Maidstone

July 2023

1

Early Years

Harold was born on 17 March 1864, the son of Sir Samuel Brise Ruggles-Brise and Marianne Weyland Bowyer-Smyth, the daughter of Sir Edward Bowyer-Smyth, 10th Baronet, of Hill Hall, Essex[1] who was Chaplain to King George IV. The Bowyer-Smyth Baronetcy can be traced back to Thomas Smith who was Provost of Eton, Elizabeth I's Ambassador to Paris and High Sheriff of Essex in 1563.

The Ruggles-Brise family tree is, to say the least, extensive and can be traced back to Thomas Rogyll in 1547. Amongst the possible origins of the 'Ruggles' that are explored by Edith Freeman is one William de Ruggele of Staffordshire who was rewarded for his services by Edward I. We also know that in 1337 one Simon de Rugeley commissioned the construction of Hawkesyard Hall in Staffordshire and the basic Arms of Simon de Rugeley (argent tincture with chevron gule and roses) are the same as those used by the Ruggles and Ruggles-Brise families.

It is believed that younger sons travelled from the Midlands to seek fame and fortune in Suffolk. With its burgeoning cloth trade, it was the most affluent county in England at that time. By the middle of the sixteenth century, one branch was flourishing at Sudbury and another at Lavenham where in 1568 Roger Ruggle ranked as the richest man on the tax list. The 'Brise' surname was adopted by John Ruggles (John Ruggles-Brise) in 1827. His grandfather, Thomas Ruggles, had married Ann who was daughter of one Joshua Brise. 'Brise' also appears as a first or middle name – John's son Samuel appears as Samuel Brise Ruggles-Brise on the family tree and his daughters are styled Georgiana Brise, Matilda Brise and Cecilia Susanna Brise.

Born in 1825, Harold's father, Samuel, was educated at Eton and Magdalen College and then served for three years as a Cornet in the 1st Dragoon Guards,

---

1   Hill Hall, an Elizabethan mansion near Epping, Essex, was damaged extensively by fire in 1969. It is now owned by English Heritage.

one of the oldest regiments in the British Army, originally raised on Hampstead Heath in June 1685 to help suppress Monmouth's rebellion against his uncle King James II.[2] After leaving the regular army, at the age of 28, Samuel was appointed Colonel Commandant of the West Essex Militia, a volunteer unit comparable with today's Territorial Army.

When, as a result of the Childers Reforms, the Essex Regiment was formed in 1881 by the union of the 44th (East Essex) and 56th (West Essex) Regiments of Foot, which became the 1st and 2nd battalions of the new regiment, the East and West Essex Regiments of Militia also joined it as its 3rd and 4th battalions and so Samuel became Lieutenant Colonel of the 4th Battalion the Essex Regiment.

These military commitments tended to be seasonal, revolving around summer camps and mess nights in local hotels, so Samuel was able to pursue an active political career as well. In 1868, he was elected Member of Parliament for East Essex and held the seat at two further elections before resigning from the House of Commons on 14 August 1883 by becoming Crown Steward and Bailiff of the Manor of Northstead.[3] During his fourteen years in the house, he spoke on 104 occasions about agricultural matters affecting his constituency, an impressive record by the standards of the day. He was also a magistrate and Deputy Lieutenant for both Essex and Suffolk. Made CB in 1889 and KCB in 1897, he died on 28th May 1899 and his wife, Marianne, a little over a year later on 12th December 1900.

Harold had eleven siblings (Adela, Edith, Constance, Archibald, Alice, Rosalind, Evelyn, Cecil, Reginald, Florence and Beatrice). Unlike his two elder brothers who were educated at Eton, Harold went to Winchester College. Founded by William of Wykeham (1324-1404) who later became Bishop of Winchester and Chancellor of England, the school's website today explains that Wykeham's personal motto – 'Manners Makyth Man' - proposes that 'we should be measured not by our birth right but by our own personal qualities and achievements'. How fitting this would be for Harold, a man of significant ancestry but also a man who would display marvellous qualities and achieve great things.

Harold was in Reverend J.T. Bramston's House, one of ten commoner houses, originally known as 'Culvers Close' and today as 'Trants'. Among the youngest of 61 boys who went to Winchester in September 1876, one of whom was Edward Grey, later 1st Viscount Grey of Fallodon, Secretary of State for Foreign Affairs when war broke out in 1914, Harold thrived at the school, becoming head of his house and Captain of the 1st XI, known as 'Lords', in 1882. He also enjoyed success at Winchester College football, playing in both Commoner XV and

2   Lanier's or the 2nd Regiment of Horse.
3   A procedural device that allows MPs to resign.

Commoner VI (fifteen and six-a-side teams), and in racquets where he won the Wigram Cup, an inter-house racquets competition. Taking a leaf from his father, he was a keen member of the debating society and spoke on topics as varied as the withdrawal of Government from Kandahar and women's suffrage.

From Winchester, Harold went up to Balliol College, Oxford, George Ridding having written a testimonial to the Master on 23 April 1882.

> My Dear Master,
> H. Ruggles-Brise has always been a thoroughly well conducted, gentlemanly boy during his five to six years of school life. He has excellent abilities and his father seems anxious to send him up to you, younger than we had expected. It seems necessary for his future that he should pass early through Oxford and I hope you will enable him to at Balliol. He will be an excellent member of the college.
> Yours most truly,
> George Ridding

With origins dating back to 1263, Balliol College had nurtured the English upper classes over the centuries with a preponderance of Old Etonian students. Awarded a respectable Second in Classical Moderations (an Honour Moderations in Classics long regarded as one of the hardest examinations in the world), Harold had again demonstrated his sporting prowess and as an all-rounder won a Blue for cricket in 1883. He went on to play for the MCC in 1884 and twice for Essex in non-first class matches.

With strong family military connections, Harold had long aspired to a military career and, after passing the entrance exam to the Royal Military Academy Sandhurst, was commissioned as a lieutenant in the Grenadier Guards in 1885. The regiment has an extraordinary history that dates back to 1656 when Charles II, in exile in Bruges, raised a Regiment from his followers called the Royal Regiment of Guards and appointed Lord Wentworth as its first Colonel. In 1665, the Royal Regiment of Guards and another regiment raised for the King's personal protection were incorporated into the King's Regiment of Foot Guards, later to become The First Regiment of Foot Guards and then in 1815 The First or Grenadier Regiment of Foot Guards. The Grenadiers have been awarded seventy-eight Honorary Distinctions (Battle Honours) of which 45 appear on the Colours of the Regiment and have taken part in nearly every major campaign since 1680.

In the War of the Spanish Succession, the Regiment served under a commander who had joined the King's Company of the Regiment as a young Ensign in 1667. His name was John Churchill, 1st Duke of Marlborough who, with his brilliant victories of Blenheim (1704), Ramillies (1706), Oudenarde (1708) and Malplaquet (1709), established his reputation as one of the greatest soldiers of all time. The First

Guards took part in his famous march from the Low Countries to the Danube in 1704, and, when the British stormed the fortified heights of the Schellenberg before Blenheim, the Regiment led the assault.

During the Revolutionary and Napoleonic Wars, the First Guards, crossing to Holland in 1793, were among the first British troops to land in Europe. Driven from the Continent two years later, they returned in 1799 when another British Army attempted, though in vain, to liberate Holland. In the autumn and winter of 1808 they took part in Sir John Moore's classic march and counter march against Napoleon in Northern Spain and subsequently in the battle of Corunna. When Sir John Moore fell mortally wounded in the hour of victory, it was men of the First Foot Guards who bore him, dying, from the field. Next year, they fought again in Spain under another of the great Captains of history, an officer also destined to become Colonel of the Regiment, Arthur Wellesley, 1st Duke of Wellington. Under Wellesley, they took part in the desperate engagements of the Peninsular War.

When, after the victorious peace that followed, Napoleon escaped from Elba and re-entered Paris, the Regiment returned to the Low Countries. In the middle of June 1815, the Emperor struck at the British and Prussian forces north of the Meuse. After a fierce encounter at Quatre Bras on 16 June, Wellington's Army withdrew to Waterloo, where on the evening of Sunday 18 June, Napoleon directed the Grenadiers of the Imperial Guard, which he had hitherto kept in reserve, to make a final assault against the British lines. That assault was utterly defeated by the First Guards and in recognition of their contribution to the victorious outcome of the battel they were made a Regiment of Grenadiers and given the title of First or Grenadier Regiment of Foot Guards. The Grenade was adopted as a badge and the Bearskin Cap was worn after Waterloo.

During the Crimean War, the 3rd Battalion formed part of Lord Raglan's Army, which stormed the heights above the River Alma and besieged the Russian fortress of Sebastopol. During the early part of that grim siege, the battle of Inkerman was fought in November 1854. The defence of Sandbag Battery in the thick fog against overwhelming odds is one of the epics of British military history. On that day the Brigade of Guards, of which the 3rd Battalion of the Grenadier Guards formed part, lost half its officers and men, but not a single prisoner was captured by the Russians or an inch of ground given.

Commissioned in May 1885, Harold was posted to 2nd Battalion at Chelsea Barracks. He was the only new officer but in September he was joined by Rudolph Cavan who later went on to become the CIGS (Chief of the Imperial General Staff) and a Field Marshal. In October of the following year, the battalion moved to Richmond Barracks in Dublin on a routine unaccompanied tour. During the Napoleonic Wars, some 68 garrisons had been built throughout Ireland, one of which was Richmond Barracks in Dublin in 1810. Once the threat of French invasion had gone away, the main purpose of the British Army being in Ireland was for training. Due to widespread poverty and unemployment, its presence also attracted a steady stream of recruits.

Away from their families, the Guardsmen needed a life outside barracks and frequented music halls, pubs and inevitably brothels. Dublin found itself in the dubious position of being in second place to London as far as the British Army was concerned for the contraction of venereal diseases. Not surprisingly, the ward in the Richmond Hospital was given the name of 'the cockpit'.[4] For young officers, there were the traditional country pursuits on offer such as steeplechases, fox hunting, fishing and shooting.

In August, the battalion decamped to the Curragh, a 5,000-acre training area in County Kildare that had been established on the outbreak of the Crimean War in 1854 when a requirement for additional training areas for the British Army became an urgent necessity. When the war ended, the War Office decided that training camps should be established at which the three arms—infantry, cavalry and artillery—would train together. The Curragh was so designated, and from then on it was the seasonal training ground for the army in Ireland. Each year thousands of men, both regular and militia regiments, met there on the squares and on the sward of the plain, and the major exercises became important events in the social calendar of the surrounding area, including Dublin.

For the Grenadiers, the drill period of 1861 was to have a particular notoriety. Edward, the 20-year-old Prince of Wales, had been entrusted by the Queen to the 1st Battalion with strict instructions how he was to occupy each evening of the week: on two, he was to entertain senior officers to dinner; on three, he was to dine with the regiments in strict rotation; and on the remaining two he was to dine privately in his quarters, after which he might read or write. As far as his military progress was concerned, his superior officers had 'abandoned all hope that he might be fit to command a battalion by the end of the month' when his parents were due to arrive on a visit. However, paying no attention whatsoever to his mother's instructions, his social life prospered and with the help of his fellow Grenadier officers who brought his lover, the actress Nellie Clifden, over from London, the prince thoroughly enjoyed life. This dalliance was to cause his mother great distress and she went as far as to conclude that the death of Prince Albert later that year was hastened by the prince's indiscretion as he had worried that Edward's matrimonial prospects had been damaged by the scandal. Grenadiers, it seemed, made poor chaperons.

---

4   Fairbrother, Henry, 'The British Army Presence in Dublin', *Dublin Historical Record*, Vol. 70, No. 1, 2017, pp.70-80.

The battalion returned to Chelsea in October 1887 and then moved to Victoria Barracks in December 1888[6] and to Wellington Barracks next to Buckingham Palace in October the following year. Three changes of station in three years must have been disruptive to say the least and would have undoubtedly impacted on the married families. This may have been a contributing factor to the refusal of the 2nd Battalion to attend a parade at Wellington Barracks in July 1890. This extraordinary event had much to do with the new and somewhat inexperienced commander, Lieutenant Colonel Makgill-Crichton Maitland, whom *The Times* described as 'an able and zealous officer' who has been 'rather energetic in the matter of drills and inspections.'[5]

To say he was unpopular with his men would be something of an understatement. He had ordered his men to parade in marching order in Wellington Barracks for a tunic inspection prior to proceeding to Pirbright in a fortnight's time to give a demonstration to militia and volunteers. Instead of being issued on the Saturday, the orders were not given out until Sunday afternoon which meant that some men had just dismounted from Guard and others had weekend passes. When the Commanding Officer appeared on the square on Monday morning, only a handful were present such was the level of dissatisfaction in the battalion. Company officers were ordered to their lines and eventually the battalion mustered for parade, the majority improperly dressed.

The press soon got hold of the story which meant the War Office stepped in and confined the entire battalion to barracks. That order was rescinded the next day as, according to the Press Association, an examination of the 'order' books showed that drill and guard duty had been 'excessive'. The East Yorkshire Regiment was despatched from Southampton take turns on guard duty. Two weeks later, a District Court martial was convened in Wellington Barracks and the six 'ringleaders' tried on a charge of 'failing to appear at the place of parade or rendezvous appointed by their commanding officer'. The charges against one were dismissed but the sentences handed down to the others were severe; two years imprisonment with hard labour for four men, one of whom was to be dismissed with ignominy, and eighteen months imprisonment with hard labour for another.

Meanwhile confusion reigned about the future of Colonel Maitland. Some reports stated that he had chivalrously resigned on condition that the offenders were treated leniently; others said that he had been replaced by Major the Hon. J. Eaton from the 3rd Battalion. What was indisputable was that the 2nd Battalion was 'to proceed by special train to Chatham early in the morning of 22 July and embark for foreign service'.[6] It soon transpired that Colonel Maitland who had

5   *The Times*, 8 July 1890, p.9.
6   *The Times*, 21 July 1890, p.6.

refused to resign had been suspended and the rumour circulated that he had asked for a court-martial. The day before the battalion left, the Colonel of the Regiment, HRH The Duke of Cambridge, addressed them on the parade ground. For ten minutes, he berated them and told them that he could no longer speak of them as Guards. He then singled out the Non-Commissioned Officers and the officers for inattention and complacency. *The Times* reported that 'the men effect to like the idea of foreign service but well-informed persons say they are depressed and they certainly looked so'. For a young officer like Harold, the whole affair must have been utterly disheartening and brought into question the very authenticity of the regiment he had so proudly joined.

On 23 July, the 608-strong battalion along with 46 wives and 76 children sailed from Chatham on the 4,000 ton troopship SS *Tamar*. On board were the following officers: Colonels Eaton (commanding), Lord Arthur Wellesley and Mackinnon; Captains Lloyd (adjutant), Ellice, Thistlethwayte, Crawley, Warrender; Lieutenants Bradford-Atkinson, Cooper, Sandford, Halford, Vernon-Wentworth, Bagot, Sir Augustus Webster, Ruggles-Brise, Viscount Kilcoursie (Cavan), Loftus and the Hon Richard Somerset; Second Lieutenants Corry, Heneage, the Hon Grosvenor Hood, Lord Ardee, and Derriman. That same day, the *London Gazette* carried a notice that Colonel Maitland had been put on half-pay and left the Army. His adjutant, Captain Murray resigned his position but remained a serving officer.

Public opinion had taken a dim view of the Court-martial verdicts and by 6 August several MPs presented the Secretary of War with a petition signed by about 50,000 inhabitants of London praying that favourable consideration might be given to the case of the imprisoned Guardsmen. Far from being ringleaders, it had transpired that the six men had been selected solely on the grounds that they were the eldest soldiers and ought to have remonstrated with the mutinous elements. Furthermore, four of them were married. It demonstrated the strength of popular feeling, and may have been why the jailed men, although sentenced to between 18 months and two years' imprisonment, were released on the 23 November 1890 after only four months servitude. Of the six men, only one was discharged with ignominy, the others returning to the battalion to complete periods of engagement.

Life on Bermuda turned out to be rather pleasant if undemanding. In October scurrilous rumours about the health of the battalion surfaced in New York and London. Far from being overwhelmed by enteric fever, the Governor informed London that the battalion, based at the St. Georges Garrison, had 'stood the hot weather very well' and the men had entered into all the usual Bermuda pursuits such as cricket and boating and been in excellent spirits. 'The battalion is perfectly contented and everyone seems to enjoy life here'. In January 1891, there was more mischievous reporting, this time that men from the Leicester Regiment had rioted and 'had it not been for the presence of the Grenadier Guards…the riotous troops would have taken possession of the islands.' Furious correspondence from the Leicester Regiment to the Editor of *The Times* followed and, much to its relief, Dalziells New Agency was excoriated and the Leicesters exonerated.

It was during his time in Bermuda that Harold first met Prince George of Wales. George was a second son and at the time was a 25-year-old Naval Lieutenant in command of a gunboat, HMS *Thrush*. He had sailed from England in July 1890 and joined the British North American Squadron at Halifax, Nova Scotia. *Thrush* left for Bermuda on 17 November where she remained on station until 7 January 1891 when she sailed to Jamaica to join the British West Indian Squadron. On each island he stayed at Government House where he was entertained with tennis and dances. Unlike his libidinous father, George limited his amorous activities to writing to his very pretty 14-year-old cousin, Marie of Edinburgh.

The Governor of Bermuda between 1888-91 was Lieutenant-General Sir Edward Newdigate, a distinguished soldier who had fought with the Rifle Brigade in the Crimean War where he almost certainly would have come across the 3rd Battalion of the Grenadiers. The grandson of 3rd Earl of Dartmouth and married to the granddaughter of 4th Earl of Albemarle, Newdigate must have been delighted to have a Guards battalion on the island as it certainly gave a boost to its social life; the main social event of that winter was a ball in the Hamilton Princess Hotel attended by the Prince George and all the officers of the 2nd Battalion. Prince George was also reported as enjoying 'cricket, sailing and picnicking at St. George's' where the 2nd Battalion was stationed. Harold and Kilcoursie (Cavan) were later to become firm favourites of the King

After embarking on the troop ship S.S. *Orontes* on 13 July, the battalion departed for England to an accolade of compliments. The Mayor and Corporation of St. George's 'expressed admiration at the general deportment, civility, kindness, and exemplary conduct of the Grenadiers, which had not been surpassed, if equalled, by any regiment ever stationed in Bermuda'.[7] Six Grenadiers remained behind and their graves can be found at St.George's and Boaz; one died by choking on a cherry stone and another by diving into two feet of water.[8] When they landed at Dover on 28 July, there was a neap tide which necessitated disembarkation by tugs and small boats, a process that took four hours. Harold does not appear on the list of officers published by *The Times* on 29 July, so the logical deduction is that he either went to Canada or had returned home earlier. Neither is the case: *The Times* had simply omitted his name!

In April 1893, Harold became the Adjutant of the 3rd Battalion in Wellington Barracks. In effect the personal staff officer to the Commanding Officer, the role

7   *The Times*, 13 July 1891, p.6.
8   Hanning, Henry, *The British Grenadiers* (Barnsley: Pen & Sword, 2006), p.116.

of Adjutant remains much coveted and is given to those young officers deemed to be the best of their generation. Traditionally a Grenadier Adjutant sat in the same office as the Commanding Officer and the Second-in-Command, known as the Senior Major. His duties were multifarious, ranging from the discipline of officers junior to him to publishing daily Part One orders. In the summer months, the battalion moved to the Pirbright encampment and one of the more onerous tasks of the Adjutant and Quartermaster was to keep on top of the wear and tear of tunics and bearskin caps for, unlike today, this order of dress was worn on field exercises, rifle ranges and route marches. Whenever he had a chance, Harold played for the battalion 1st XI and in a match against the 2nd Battalion Coldstream Guards, scored 160 not out. He regularly played for the Guards Brigade 1st XI as well.

Harold's first Commanding Officer was Lieutenant Colonel Laurence Oliphant who had served with the 3rd Battalion during the trying expedition to Suakin in the Sudan in 1885. The only variance in dress was that pith helmets had replaced bearskins; in tactics, nothing had changed since Waterloo as the battalion took its place in the Guards' square. He handed over to Lieutenant-Colonel Edmund Antrobus , also a veteran of Suakin. Owners of Stonehenge, the Antrobus family lived in the magnificent neo-classical Amesbury Abbey in Wiltshire. Colonel Edmund's son, also called Edmund, would have been seven when Harold took over as Adjutant. It must have been a sad blow indeed for Harold to learn that he had been killed in action with the 1st Battalion, part of Harold's 20th Brigade, during the desperate fighting around Kruiseke in October 1914.

After twenty months in London, on 1 January 1895 Harold became Adjutant of the Guards Depot in Caterham Barracks where the three Guards regiments pooled their recruits for training. This was yet another feather in his cap for the position was open to his age group across the Brigade of Guards. Built on land purchased by the War Department in 1875, the Guards Depot had opened its doors in 1877 and soon became the largest Army depot in the Victorian era. By the standards of the day, the barrack blocks and facilities were a vast improvement when measured against existing military accommodation and remained in service until well into the 1970s. The Commandant, Lieutenant-Colonel the Hon Arthur Henniker-Major, had been Adjutant of the 2nd Battalion Coldstream Guards in the Egyptian War of 1882 and would command the battalion in South Africa in 1899.[9]

Leaving Caterham in October 1896, Harold went on to study at the Staff College Camberley for the next two years. Camberley had its origins in the Royal Military College, High Wycombe which was founded in 1799. In 1802 it became the Senior Department of the new Royal Military College and in 1858

---

9   Henniker-Major became Major-General commanding the London Division but sadly
     died in post in 1912, aged 57.

was renamed the Staff College. The Commandant during Harold's studies was Colonel Henry Hildyard (later General Sir John Hildyard) who had seen active service in the Anglo-Egyptian War of 1882 and been present at the Battle of Tel-el-Kebir where the 1st Battalion Grenadier Guards as part of the Guards Brigade charged the Egyptian trenches with fixed bayonets.

Today, a p.*s.c.* (passed staff college) is mandatory for promotion beyond major's rank. Not so in 1899, when none of the three Grenadier Lieutenant Colonels had been to Staff College, only one of the twelve majors, and of the nineteen captains, only two including Harold. Both Harold and his fellow p.*s.c.*, Francis Davies[10], were the exceptions and both went on to became generals but his 2nd Battalion contemporary Rudolph Cavan, who had retired in 1912 after commanding the 2nd Battalion to become Master of Fox Hounds of the Hertfordshire hunt, proved to be the joker in the pack. After commanding the Guards Division in France and then a Corps on the Western Front and in Italy, much to his surprise he became CIGS in 1922. Another charismatic Grenadier, George Pereira, who had joined the Regiment on the same day as Harold, was given a brigade on the Western Front, having previously resigned his commission to explore the hinterlands of China and Tibet.

Harold completed his Staff College studies in December 1898. Out of the class of thirty-two officers, the outstanding candidate was Willie Robertson (3rd Dragoon Guards), the son of a Lincolnshire postmaster and the only soldier in the history of the British Army to have risen from an enlisted man to the rank of field marshal when he became CIGS in 1916. Guy Wyndham (16th Lancers) became a Colonel and was to lose his son George at the Second Battle of Ypres. Nearly all of them went to South Africa; the only casualty of the class there was James Cumming-Bruce (Royal Highlanders) who died of wounds received in action at Magersfontein in December 1899. Several achieved the rank of general in the First World War; fellow Wykehamist Reggie Oxley commanded the 8th Division and Oliver Nugent (King's Royal Rifle Corps) the 36th (Ulster) Division at the Battle of the Somme, Colin Mackenzie (Seaforth Highlanders) the Highland Division in 1914 and Lionel Banon an infantry brigade. The other Wykehamist in the class, Theodore Fox-Strangeways (Irish Rifles), retired in 1905. Poor Henry King-Salter (Rifle Brigade), an outstanding student, died in Calcutta in 1910 when commanding the 2nd Battalion of the Rifle Brigade before he had a chance to be selected for higher command. In between these demanding positions and onerous studies, Harold had fallen in love.

---

10   Later General Sir Francis John Davies, KCB KCMG KCVO (1864 – 1948) who commanded the 8th Division during the First World War

2

Courtship & Marriage

History does not recount how Harold met Lady Dorothea Stewart-Murray, the eldest daughter of the Duke and Duchess of Atholl, one of the most famous aristocratic families in Scotland. The guidebook to Blair Castle, the ancestral home of the Clan Murray, has this to say: 'Over nineteen generations the Stewarts and Murrays of Atholl have backed winners and losers, been in and out of political favour, won battles and lost them. They have been adventurers and politicians, Jacobites and Royalists, entrepreneurs and agriculturists, soldiers and scholars ...'

The first of the present line was Sir John Stewart of Balvenie, the half-brother of King James II of Scotland who rewarded him with the Earldom of Atholl in 1457. During the English Civil War, John Murray and his son were Royalists and Charles II was returned to the throne, he was made a marquis for his loyalty. His son continued to support Queen Anne and was rewarded with a dukedom in 1703. The Murrays were divided in their loyalties during the Jacobite uprisings of 1715 and 1745 with William being exiled to France, returning in 1745 with Bonnie Prince Charlie and staying at Blair Castle on their journey. Lord Glenlyon, the 6th Duke, lent Blair Castle to Queen Victoria for a three-week holiday. During her stay, the Athollmen stood guard and in appreciation she granted the Duke and his men her colours and the right to bear arms. Thus the Atholl Highlanders became a private army, the only one remaining in Europe.

Dertha's father, John Stewart-Murray, 7th Duke of Atholl, had served as a Captain in the Scots Fusilier Guards but resigned in 1863 a year after marrying Louisa Moncreiffe the eldest of the 16 children of former Grenadier officer Sir Thomas Moncreiff, the 7th Baronet of that Ilk, and Lady Louisa Hay-Drummond, the daughter of the Earl of Kinnoul. Not surprisingly, Dertha had 20 cousins on her mother's side of the family; on her father's side, there were none. Known as the Children of the Mist, according to Scottish Clans and Family Names, the name Moncreiffe is taken from the lands of which were gifted by Alexander II in 1248 to Sir Matthew Moncreiffe, who also held lands in Strathearn, Fife, and Atholl.

In 1568, William of that Ilk, 11th Chief, entered into a treaty with 'the haill Name of Murray' for their mutual defence which led to the two families intermarrying at least twice a century and sometimes more often. Like the Murrays, they had a long history of service to the Scottish and English crown: Sir Thomas Moncreiffe was Clerk of the Scottish Exchequer and Treasury during the reigns of Charles II, James II and William and Mary.

The eldest of seven siblings – one died in infancy – Dertha was born in London on 25 March 1866 at her father's London house at 84 Eaton Place, Belgravia. Her sisters Helen and Evelyn followed in quick succession, and then her brothers, John, George and James, the latter when she was thirteen. They grew up at Blair Castle in Perthshire, the ancestral home of the Murray family since the Thirteenth Century. Surrounded by hills, with a nine-acre walled garden, the castle provided an idyllic Highland setting for the Stewart-Murray children to grow up in. James could speak Gaelic before he uttered a word of English! They immersed themselves in the history and traditions of the Clan. Dertha became an expert on traditional Scottish music, amassing a significant collection including early bagpipe music from the British Isles and Border pipe music from the 18th century.[1] Her sister Evelyn collected over 240 Gaelic folk tales and songs subsequently published as *Tales from Highland Perthshire* (1891).

In 1869, 'a faint whisper of a great scandal, implicating some of the highest and noblest in the land, ran through society…but rumour, like mist upon a glass, is fleeting ; and the case faded away from all those but who were personally concerned, until the morning of Wednesday 16 February, when a crowded court listened eagerly to the opening details of the story destined to run like wildfire throughout the length and breadth of the land'.[2] It reached the Blair Atholl glen when the news broke that Dertha's aunt Harriet, a notable beauty, was being sued for divorce by her husband Sir Charles Mordaunt MP. A wealthy Warwickshire landowner, every summer Mordaunt went fishing in Norway. One year Harriet opted to not to go and when she gave birth to a daughter Violet, she was left with no option other than to confess the name the father to her husband as he had been out of the country at the time of conception. It subsequently transpired that she had entertained numerous lovers, including the Prince of Wales and several of his friends. Feeling betrayed, Mordaunt sued for divorce and threatened to name the Prince. This prompted Dertha's grandfather Sir Thomas Moncreiffe, who had

---

1   Now housed in the National Library of Scotland and the A. K. Bell Library, Perth.

2   Mordaunt, Charles, *The Lady Mordaunt Divorce Case. Full Report of the Proceedings. Letters from the Prince of Wales. His Royal Highness in the Witness-box: Evidence of the Nurse and the Doctors* (London: Temple Publishing, 1870), passim.

several other daughters to marry off, to declare she was mad in order to prevent a divorce trial and save the family reputation.

Nevertheless, the case came to court and the names of four of her lovers including the Prince of Wales and Lord Cole (later 4th Earl of Enniskillen) were revealed.[3] It was a sensation. The prince, it was alleged, had been intimate with her before her marriage and had continued their affair in her London and country homes when her husband was absent. The prince's testimony before the defence lasted just seven minutes. Despite letters and his handkerchief being offered as evidence, he denied anything improper had happened between them, although he did admit to spending time with Harriet alone when Sir Charles was not at home. In the absence of Harriet who had been deemed unfit to attend court, the case was postponed until she was better. In 1875, Mordaunt sued again. This time Lord Cole, the alleged father of Harriet's child, did not contest the action and the jury found Harriet guilty of adultery; Mordaunt got his divorce and poor Harriet spent the next 37 years of her life in a number of private asylums in and around London. Violet, only three years younger than Dertha, was sent to live with her grandparents at moncrieffe House near the Bridge of Earn and the two cousins would have known each other well.

Presented at Court by her grandmother the Dowager Duchess of Atholl in the Drawing Room of Buckingham Palace on 13 May 1885, along with the other 500 young ladies who had been presented that day, 19-year-old Dertha was now officially in the marriage market. There is a social footprint of sorts provided by *The Times* Court Circular notices. The Marchioness of Salisbury's lunch at the Foreign Office to celebrate the Queen's birthday was attended by Dertha and her father; in June 1890, she was a bridesmaid at the wedding of Lady Henrietta Hay to Count Alexander Munster and somewhat mysteriously was reported to be 'still at Homburg' in August that year after her parents had returned home; a wedding at Scone Place of her cousin Margery Murray to Lieutenant Mackenzie of the Rifle Brigade in April the following year was followed in July by an invitation for Dertha and her mother to a dinner given by the Duke and Duchess of Westminster for the Duke and Duchess of Connaught. Then in December 1891, *The Times* dryly recorded that Dertha had 'sailed to the East with Lord and Lady Brassey in the *Sunbeam*'.

The *Sunbeam* was already a legend, after the first round-the-world voyage by a private yacht in 1876-77. A three-masted topsail-yard schooner, iron framed and with teak skin, *Sunbeam* measured a length of 159 ft and a beam 27.5 ft, weighting 532 tons. The sail area was 9,000 square yards. With an auxiliary compound steam engine of 70 hp that developed a top speed of just over 10 knots, her bunkers could hold 80 tons of coal and although primarily a sailing vessel, she could steam for

---

3   Sir Frederick Johnstone and Captain Arthur Farquhar were also named as co-respondents.

approximately 20 days without refuelling. When not in steam, the funnel would be lowered and the propeller feathered to reduce drag.

Lord Brassey was the eldest son of railway magnate Thomas Brassey, who by the time of his death in 1870 had built one in every twenty miles of railway in the world. With money no object, Brassey decided on a political career and served as an MP and Minster with various governments. Like his father who had been a shareholder in Brunel's *Great Eastern*, he was fascinating by maritime engineering and had commissioned the *Sunbeam* in 1873. His first wife Anna had written a book about their circumnavigation which was published as *A Voyage in the Sunbeam: Our Home on the Ocean for Eleven Months* (1886). It became a best seller, later translated for sales overseas with equal success. Anna died in 1887 aged 47 of malaria on a voyage back from India and was buried at sea off Mauritius.

By now remarried, Brassey set sail for Melbourne via Cape Horn to take up his new appointment as Governor of the State of Victoria. In March 1892, Dertha was spotted in Jamaica on *Sunbeam* in the company of the Duke and Duchess of St. Albans, Admiral Sir William Houston Stewart, a veteran of the Crimean War, 46-year-old the Hon Spencer Lyttleton, one of Gladstone's Principal Private Secretaries, 48-year-old Major Seymour Wynne-Finch, a man about town, and 32-year-old Henry Hannen, the barrister son of the High Court judge Lord Hannen who was a neighbour of Brassey in Kent. The Duchess of Atholl had chosen not to accompany her daughter.

By May 1893, Dertha was back in Belgravia for the season, attending the wedding of the heiress Flora Sassoon and the next year at a dance given by the Earl and Countess of Dudley (her aunt Georgina Moncreiffe) at Dudley House in Park Lane, this time once again under the watchful eye of her mother. In July 1894, they both went to the wedding of Leonard Brassey and Lady Violet Gordon-Lennox, daughter of the Earl of March; six months later, they attended the wedding of Lord Wolverton and Lady Edith Ward, the Duchess's niece. Marriageable daughters were in high demand.

It must have been around this time that she met Harold. One commentator suggests that he may have been invited to a house party by Charles Corkran, a fellow Grenadier officer, at his brother-in-law's family home, the resplendent Polesden Lacey house which had been totally rebuilt in the early 1820s by Thomas Cubitt who went on design most of Belgravia and indeed Osborne House. A signed photograph of Dertha dated 1894 is in the National Trust Collection on display there today. There would have been many similar house parties and balls where eligible young Guards officers were eagerly enlisted by mothers to dance with marriageable daughters.

Little is known about Harold and Dertha's courtship but three letters touch upon their wedding plans. Dertha did not (unlike her father) want a Presbyterian service:

7 December 1894
Central Hotel, Edinburgh

Dearest Father,

As I couldn't see you before I left, I want to write to you about what I was talking to you about. I have been thinking over it a good deal and I am afraid you will be disappointed when I tell you that the more I think of it, the less I like the idea of being married in the Presbyterian service. There is nothing else I wouldn't have done to please you, as you have been very kind to me – but if it is possible I had much rather be married in the way I have always seen it done. It is not a fancy only – I hate not doing what you want.

Your affectionate daughter Dertha

Her preference clearly prevailed as the Reverend Albert Baillie, later Anglican Dean of Windsor, officiated.

24 December 1894
84, Eaton Place, SW

Dearest Father,

Mamma says she was going to write to you, but she hadn't time. I asked her if she would put in the Morning Post about my being married on the 5th and she says as she doesn't suppose you have any objection she has done so. I found the Spains Hall people nice kind old fashioned sort of people and it is a lovely old house, but hideous country. The eldest brother and his wife are very nice and I have asked their daughter – a girl of 17, to be bridesmaid (1). I think the brother and his wife will have to be asked to Blair and they don't want to come before the Monday. Then there is one of Harry's sisters and his other brothers who will have to be asked too and I think that is all. He is very anxious to have Mr Heywood-Lonsdale as best man and he could come on Monday. I am going to see the house at Caterham on Wednesday.

Bardie has a nasty face. The knock he got started an abscess under his teeth and he had two pulled out and his cheek is still sore and swollen and looks pretty bad.

I won't wish you a Merry Christmas as I know you despise it.

Your affectionate daughter,
Dertha

Note

1.   The bridesmaid, one of six, was Marjorie Ruggles-Brise, the eldest daughter of Harold's brother Archibald and his wife Mabel.

13 January 1895
84, Eaton Place

Dearest Father,
Just a line to tell you from Harry that he says he will certainly wear uniform at the wedding if you would rather, only he will have to ask Colonel Oliphant as a form if he may.

I have no time for more just now, and I can't see in this horrid fog.
Your affectionate daughter,
Dertha

Her late maternal grandfather, Sir Thomas Moncreiff, would have been delighted: he had joined the Grenadier Guards in 1840 and served with them for three years.

On a bright and frosty day in early February 1895, Harold and Dertha were married at Blair Castle where the ceremony was performed in the Great Hall, adorned with stags' heads - all shot on the Atholl estate – and 'tastefully decorated with palms and choice exotics'.[4] Forty Atholl Highlanders formed a Guard of Honour along the aisle. To the left of the bride stood the 14 pipers of the Clan, playing *Lady Dorothea Stewart-Murray's Wedding March*, a pipe tune specially composed for the occasion by Aeneas Rose, the Pipe Major. The groom and best man, Henry Heywood Lonsdale, both wore the full dress uniforms of the Grenadier Guards, and the six bridesmaids – Lady Helen Stewart-Murray, Miss Ruggles Brise, the Hon Ciceley Drummond, Miss Lilian Murray, Miss Drummond Forbes, and Miss Maryel MacGregor (all of them save Marjorie were Dertha's cousins)[5] – attired in white crepon wore small bows of pink velvet in their hair and carried bouquets of orchids and maidenhair fern. They all wore Harold's brooches of a blue cornelian heart with a pearl star.

The Hall was crowded to its full extent long before the hour of the ceremony and some hymns were sung by a choir of children placed in the gallery. As Dertha descended the stairs in the Great Hall, one of her bridesmaids to pointed out that she was still wearing her slippers. Hurrying back for her shoes, her return confirmed there had been no last-minute change of mind! Given away by her father, Dertha wore an ivory duchess satin wedding dress with a full court train and zouave of antique Mechlin lace, the skirt being draped with family Brussels lace and edged with orange flowers. On her head she wore a coronet of real orange-blooms, covered by a fine tulle veil and carried a large shower-bouquet of 'choice hot-house flowers'. Her only decoration was a diamond heart brooch, a gift from Harold. After the

---

4   *The Brigade of Guards' Magazine*, February 1895. Other accounts note the Banqueting Hall was the venue.
5   *The Penny Illustrated Paper*, 9 February 1895.

signing of the register, the pipers formed up and played the bride and groom back into the front hall of the castle where the reception was held.

That afternoon, the bride wearing a *costume de voyage* of a dark green skirt and green corduroy jacket under a long travelling-cloak lined with sable and on her head a black and green velvet hat trimmed with violets and marten, and the groom left in a Landau drawn by four horses for Dunkeld House, lent to them by the Dowager Duchess of Atholl to begin their honeymoon. 'They started amidst showers of rice and a volley of slippers, the pipers playing and the Atholl Highlanders under the Duke huzzaing wildly with bonnets raised. It was a sight not likely to be forgotten by all who saw it, the vast pile of the historic castle lying deep down amid the snow-clad mountains, adding a strange romance to the scene'.[6]

Some two and a half months later Harold and Dertha found themselves living at the Guards Depot, Caterham where Harold was Adjutant. In her letters to her father, Dertha paints a picture of peacetime soldiering in Surrey.

25 April 1895
Guards Depot, Caterham

Dearest Father,

I have got a wet day at last and have plenty time to write. Usually I spend half the morning worrying the servants, then play the piano till luncheon time at one o'clock. Then Harry comes in and bolts his lunch and is off at 1.30 and that is all I see of him till 3 o'clock. Then we go out, and then we turn ourselves into painter and carpenter – I am very pleased with the house now.

Thank you for the plovers eggs: they were most acceptable. They were finally demolished by Fat Bill who came here to luncheon one day. Stray bicyclists come here sometimes as it is a good road from London. The other day Colonel Sawle (1) suddenly appeared with three young Coldstream, all on bicycles. I thought it was most undignified of him! We gave ourselves two days holiday to go to Hawthorne Hill races (2). Bardie (3) rode someone else's horse and came in a good last, but he rode well. He didn't look his best in a pink silk cap. Reggie Ward (4) jumped over a fence without his horse which stopped short. Did you see in the papers that a Grenadier shot himself in the barracks here? There was a great commotion about it.

I hear your solitude is soon coming to an end. Poor Mamma seems to get well very slowly.
Your affectionate daughter,
Dertha

6 *Essex Examiner.*

Notes
1. Sir Francis Graves-Sawle, Bt, (1849–1903), a colonel in the Coldstream Guards.
2. Popular with Guards officers and first raced in 1888, Hawthorn Hill race-course was situated between Maidenhead and Windsor, close to the village of Hawthorn Hill.
3. Bardie (short for Tullibardine) was the family nickname for Dertha's brother John.
4. The Hon Reginald Ward was Dertha's cousin, son of the Earl and Countess of Dudley

5 January 1896

Dearest Father,

If it isn't too late, and I don't see why it should be, I will wish you a happy New Year now. I am not having a very lively time of it as Harry is always working all day and half the night. He bicycles two or three times a week to a mathematical crammer and yesterday he got what might have been a very nasty fall though he wasn't hurt. He was getting out of the way of a cart when his wheel caught in a tram line and over he went, and he was as near as possible run over by another cart only the horse wouldn't go over him.

Everybody is in a tremendous state of excitement about Dr Jameson as there are a lot of people one knows supposed to be with him (1). I went to London the other day and saw Aunt Georgie (2); she is in a great state and I really am very sorry for her. She has just been paying up some of Reggie's debts. He is the one in the Blues and has already run through most of his money. Amongst some of his little purchases he has just paid £2000 for a horse. She says she is perfectly sick of them all and they have never been anything but worry and trouble – and then she began to cry and said she wished they had all died when they were babies! Everybody who is 'broke' in London is rushing off to South Africa under the vague impression that they will make money when things have quieted down – as if the Jews and old hands wouldn't take good care to be there first! Ronald Moncreiffe (3) has gone and Lord Roslyn (4) and lots more of that type.

We have had very mild weather on the whole, though a good many white fogs but we have the whole of January and February to go through first, so it doesn't do to boast. They are having a court martial here over a sergeant who had charge of the drink for the sergeants' mess. They commented that the whisky tasted uncommonly like water and when it was examined it was found to be 69 per cent below proof!

Goodbye – I didn't know I had material enough to write such a long letter.

Your affectionate daughter,

Dertha

Notes

1. The reference to 'Dr Jameson' is to Leander Starr Jameson who played a key role in the collapse of British-Boer relations in South Africa. An outspoken imperialist, he led a raid in Matabeleland. One of his commanders was Raleigh Grey, the great grandson of 1st Earl Grey and went up to Brasenose College, Oxford. He was four years older than Harold; another was Sir John Willoughby, Bt. Both had dormant commissions in the British Army and it is little wonder that Dertha talks of 'the excitement of Dr Jameson as there are a lot of people one knows supposed to be with him'.
2. Countess of Dudley.
3. A Captain in the Worcestershire Imperial Yeomanry, her uncle Ronald fought in the Matabeleland Campaign and took part in the Jameson Raid.
4. James St. Clair-Erskine, 5th Earl of Rosslyn, a Captain in Thornycroft's Mounted Infantry and later a *Daily Mail* war correspondent in South Africa in 1900.

Dertha enjoyed visiting friends and, when duties permitted, Harold joined her. She wrote to her father from Cloverley Hall, the country house of the banker John Pemberton in Shropshire where she and Harold had enjoyed an excellent pheasant shoot.

10 December 1896
Cloverley, Whitchurch
Salop

Dearest Father,

If you have not had enough of us already, we propose coming to Eaton Place on Saturday next and ought to arrive about half past five at the house. We are having a big shoot here, over 1100 pheasants yesterday and they expect as many pheasants today and a lot of rabbits as well, only the rain and wind must have spoilt things. I am sure that you must have heard with such pleasure that we didn't leave many birds for you at Sheriffton(1)! We spent Saturday and Sunday with the Gordon Gilmours (2) – such a nice old place and full of lovely old furniture. Unless I hear to the contrary from you I shall see you on Saturday.

Your affectionate daughter,

Dertha

Notes

1. 'Sheriffton' is in the parish of Scone in Perthshire.
2. Sir Robert and Lady Susan Gordon Gilmour. He was a fellow officer of Harold in the Grenadier Guards.

In January 1897, they moved to a house in Blackwater near to the Staff College at Camberley.

26 February 1897
Blackwater House
Blackwater
Hants

Dearest Father,

I should have liked to have seen you before you left but I am afraid it is too late now. I expect you will like Russia when you get there and it will make a nice change (1). I have hardly been in London at all as it is rather tiring coming up for the day. Harry has just got through his riding course. Things are rather mixed here as they turn the cavalry men into infantry and vice versa. Also next week Harry goes to Shoeburyness to study guns. It is all rather dull for me as the military ladies here are not at all to my taste. Mrs Dick Cunningham (2) occasionally swoops down on me as her husband has settled down at Aldershot in command of the 92nd (3). Hamish came here yesterday for the day. He seems to have quite got over his bad cold and looks very well.

Goodbye – 'bon voyage'

Yours affectionately

Dertha

Notes
1.   The Duke left for St Petersburg on 26 February 1897.
2.   Wife of Lieutenant Colonel William Dick-Cunyngham VC, 2nd Bn Gordon Highlanders (1851-1900).
3.   The Gordon Highlanders.

10 April 1897
South Cavalry Barracks
Aldershot

My darling little woman,

I am very anxious to hear how you and your mother got over the journey; and you are not to think that I did not want to come and see you on Sunday morning, only I was afraid I should be in the way. I try and amuse myself as best I can over here. It is a dreadful place, so on Sunday my bike came into requisition. Yesterday I went and lunched at Pirbright with young Charlie Corkran (1) and then went and saw the Baileys (2) at Chobham and rode back here after tea.

The work we do in the morning is quite interesting. This morning we went out on to the Hogg's Back (sic) and did reconnaissance and outposts for almost 5 hours. Nellie so far is first rate, and quite takes to all the horses, but does not like the men at all when they begin to fire.

This afternoon I have been playing racquets and have just had all my hair cut off. The whole place is full of rumours of war – 3 Batteries of Artillery are going to South Africa and they say they are going to send a lot of men from India. Now I have told you everything I have done, so you must do the same – with all my love,
Ever your most loving Harry

Notes
1. Later Major General Sir Charles Edward Corkran, KCVO, CB, CMG (1872-1939), he was commissioned in the Grenadier Guards in 1893.
2. Captain Joseph Bailey, 2nd Baron Glanusk, Grenadier Guards (1864-1928)

11 May 1897
Blackwater House
Blackwater

Dearest Father,
Your books arrived here yesterday and I am really quite delighted with them. I sat up half the night reading them and I am still at them. They are a great deal better even than I thought they would be and most interesting. You have done something really to be proud of and you know I wouldn't say so if I didn't think it. The engravings are particularly good. I wish you had had a few more of them.

I am going to London this week for a little while, having asked myself as usual to stay in your house. Harry is still at Aldershot and only gets here from Saturday to Monday. He is attached to the 15th Hussars. He said he can teach Bardie a good deal about cavalry that he doesn't know! I suppose I shall see you soon. Thank you again for the book,
Your affectionate daughter,
Dertha

In May, Dertha's grandmother Anne née Home-Drummond (Glenlyon) died aged 84. Her death, preceding that of the Queen by three years, marked the end of an era for the two had been firm friends throughout their lives. Anne had held the office of Mistress of the Robes between February 1852 and December 1852 and again in 1892; she was also a Lady of the Bedchamber between 1854 and 1897.

18 June 1897
Blackwater House
Blackwater

Dearest Father,
What a bother the review people are (1). I am sure it will be alright. The Commandant here wrote to Harry formally asking him if he wished for a pair, which I suppose he will get. I am sure as soon as anything is done officially in London you will hear. People are buying some at Martin and Wells, Aldershot (those that are not required officially). I don't know what price they are asking. Harry was asked whether he wanted them for £1 or 15/- and he said the first. I suppose with everything else they haven't had time to finish arranging them officially, but it sounds as if they were beginning.

I sent back your paper duly signed to Jamieson. I tried to understand it and couldn't! But I don't suppose that much matters as long as you give me 4%! The only thing I have been wondering is should I be able to lay hold of the capital to buy a house with after next year? That being the height of my ambition as it would be so much cheaper in the end than instead of always paying rent in London. However that doesn't matter now.
Your affectionate Dertha

Notes
1. Dertha is discussing tickets for the Diamond Jubilee Review of the Fleet at Spithead on 26th June 1897.

15 July 1897
Blair Castle,
Blair Atholl

My dearest Mums,
Very many thanks for your letter. I am not sure whether you have gone home again, so I think it is best if I send my letter there. We came here on Monday via Edinburgh and the Forth Bridge. Our train rocked so coming into Edinburgh that Dertha and a Miss Laming who came with us from Hartrigge (1) were nearly sick and Dertha's maid was sick on arrival here. We have had the most awful weather and I have been wet to the skin three out of the four days I have been here. I went out shooting for half a day on Friday in the pouring rain and got 12 ½ brace on a small piece of ground. There is nobody here except the family. The Duke has gone off with his second son to a shooting lodge. He is rather grumpy as

he has got the rheumatism. The Duchess is alright again. I hope they have not had the rain at home to spoil all their barley.

No more to say with best wishes to Pa and all,

Your most affectionate Harold

Notes

1. The home of Hallyburton Campbell, 3rd Baron Stratheden of Cupar and Campbell of St. Andrews.

In late December 1897, Dertha's brother Geordie embarked for India with his regiment, the 1st Battalion Royal Highlanders (Black Watch).

> 29 December 1897
> Blackwater House
> Blackwater

Dearest Father,

I went to Southampton yesterday as it is only about an hour from here and saw Geordie off. It was blowing a perfect hurricane and is still doing so. It was all very well for Geordie who was sharing a cabin with Lavington (1), or whatever his name is, but I was sorry for the wretched men, 1200 of them who were packed like herrings. Though overcrowded with men they were rather short of officers, which seems rather want of management as so many would give anything to be able to go. There was one Captain Crealock, Somerset 1st Inf (2), who I thought looked particularly nice, but all the others were the mangiest lot I ever saw. Geordie's little flock of Borderers (3) looked well; they are one of the best regiments in Aldershot, but two of them arrived handcuffed. They also had with them two of the darlingest little drummers I ever saw.

We had a really nice week at West Dean (4); they certainly know how to do one well there and the inside of the house is beautiful. There was good shooting – both partridges and pheasants, though it was not supposed to be a big week. Harry has bought a horse about the size of an elephant and went out hunting on it for the first time today – it seems an excellent purchase in every way and ought to sell well when we leave.

Wishing you a happy New Year

Your affectionate daughter

Dertha

Notes

1. Most likely Captain Charles Lavington Yate, 2nd Battalion King's Yorkshire Light Infantry.
2. Captain Stradling Crealock, Somerset Light Infantry

3. King's Own Scottish Borderers. It is not clear what Geordie's connection to them is.
4. Formerly the home of the Selsey family, the West Dean Estate had been bought in 1891 by William James (1854-1912), the son of Liverpool-based self-made American millionaire who owned 18 percent of Phelps, Dodge & Co., considered to be the largest mercantile house in the world dealing in metals. William was also an 18 percent shareholder. He and his brother Frank (1851-1890) were well-travelled explorers, photographers and sportsmen. His wife, Evelyn James (née Forbes) (1867 - 1929), was the daughter of a Scottish baronet whose estate bordered Balmoral. She became a great society hostess and was a friend of Dertha.

In August 1898, the Battle of Omdurman in the Sudan dominated the news with the defeat of Mahdist forces by Kitchener's Army in which the 1st Battalion of the Grenadier Guards had played a major role. Far from the drums of war, Harold found himself umpiring a military exercise in Wiltshire.

30 August 1898
Umpire's Camp
Fovant,
Wiltshire

My darling little one,
Thanks very much for your nice letter. We have had very little to do so far as the armies are too far apart. Tomorrow hostilities begin and the cavalry only are going to fight as the infantry are about 30 miles off one another. So I shall have another day without doing very much, except looking on.

I went over to see (?) yesterday. He had just got home after a very long day and was very much done up and rather frightened about his feet. I waited until he had put them into some salt and cold water. They were a bit swollen and there were several blisters but I have seen worse.

I saw Rollo (1) and Alistair Murray – I think the latter was rather knocked up after an 11 hour field day. Old Henderson (2) has just turned up to lunch and is full of talk. The 1st Division (Jimmy's) come into camp next door to us tomorrow so I will go over and see how he is getting on. His lot have an easy day today. No more to tell you darling, and it is not very long now.
Ever your most loving Harry

Notes
1. William Wordsworth (Rollo), 11th Lord Rollo, 3rd Battalion Royal Highlanders (Black Watch) (1860-1946).
2. Colonel George Henderson had been one of Harold's instructors at Staff College. He served with distinction on the staff of the Commander-in-Chief, Lord Roberts, as Director of Intelligence

1 September 1898
Umpires camp
Fovant, Wiltshire

My darling little woman,

I got your nice letter last night. I am very sorry for Miss Ramsay (1). She has a most anxious time and I am afraid Bardie (2) was rather selfish in leaving her. I hope we shall hear soon as the general opinion here is that the fight will come off on the 2nd. I have had a very long ride today. There was a chance of the cavalry of the two armies meeting up so I rode about 10 miles to see it, but unfortunately the enemy didn't turn up. Tomorrow the two armies come closer and I think there will be a small infantry fight. I hope your mother is not too anxious about Bardie. I think this time it will be a purely infantry and artillery fight and the cavalry won't have so much to do…I hope my old horses will stand the long days and their old legs won't go wrong . We move on Sunday to Umpires Camp, Wishford near Salisbury. So, darling mums, only 1 more week.

Ever your loving Harry

Notes

1. Katharine ('Kitty') Ramsay was born on 6 November 1874. She was the daughter of Sir James Henry Ramsay, 10th Bt. Bardie married her in July 1899 at St Margarets, Westminster.

2. The 21st Lancers found itself short of officers when ordered to the Sudan as the sole cavalry regiment. This caused a rush of cavalry officers, from across the army, to obtain attachments to it: Bardie was one of six officers from other cavalry regiments who joined

Dertha's brother Bardie had returned from service in the Sudan, somewhat the worse for wear.

12 October 1898
84 Eaton Place

Dearest Father,

Mamma wants me to write to you all about Bardie. He seems so much better than when the specialist came yesterday and made a long examination, I was very much disappointed when he said it would be a long job yet, and though he is not very ill, he will still want the most careful nursing for some time. Apparently he had a slight attack of dysentery before leaving Omdurman; he took the very strongest remedies possible for it, with the result that though he stopped it at the time the poison has been in him ever since. The doctor says he finds elements of dysentery, malaria and typhoid, none of them acute, but necessarily slow. He said the last disease

had better not be mentioned as there was only a symptom of it and the word always alarmed people, in this case unnecessarily and mamma is particularly anxious that should not get into people's heads. Also that the best name to give it was Egyptian fever. He will have to have a second nurse to relieve the others and then he will have to be left absolutely quiet. The fever is not high nor likely to be so, though it always rises in the evening. We don't quite know yet whether Kitty had better see him seldom or often, but it irritates him intensely if he thinks she is being kept away, so I expect they will have to let her be, but that remains to be seen. He gets dreadfully annoyed if he thinks anyone wants to 'manage' him and his head is quite clear and he knows exactly what he wants, though of course he is very tired and weak. I have copied out for you exactly what I heard the specialist say and I cannot think of anything else to tell you. Mamma has been very well so far, though she has now started a slight cold. I go to Blackwater this evening but come back on Saturday.
Your affectionate daughter,
Dertha

Doctor's report
The disease is a mixture of dysentery, malaria and typhoid – none of them acute, but necessarily slow. Must have been accumulating in the system for some time. Great care is necessary. He is not to be allowed any worry or talking and visits must be particularly forbidden. It is no use thinking of doing anything different for about a month, but no time can be defined.

Dr told him he might see only one person per diem, that he has had malaria and dysentery and is not yet out of the woods and must keep very quiet and not talk or read.

In February 1899, the 2nd Battalion Grenadier Guards was dispatched to Gibraltar as part of the East Mediterranean garrison. Much to their chagrin, they were refused permission to take their Bearskin caps. Harold set sail for Gibraltar accompanied by Dertha and two maids.

5 February 1899
Blackwater House,
Blackwater,
Hants.

My dearest Papa,
I was very glad to find you so much better and I hope you will gradually get alright again, but you must not try and do too much all at once, as you must be weak from not being able to eat.

I have at last got final instruction from the War Office. Dertha and I and two maids start from the Albert docks London on Thursday and my soldier servant goes in the trooper *Verona* on Saturday. We are as you can imagine very busy packing up, as everything has to go off tomorrow. The War Office would not give Dertha a passage, so the tickets are rather expensive. I am sorry the East wind and the frost have gone as it would have ensured a smooth passage. Luckily we start in the Thames, so we get smooth water to start with. The ship we are going on is the India. I think it is a good boat and is large enough – 8,000 tons – not to roll except in a bad sea. I wish you could have come to see us off as you said, but you must not think of it. Besides, it would not be worthwhile, as the ship is in the middle of the Thames and sails directly we get on board, and no-one from shore is allowed on.

Give my best love to Mums, and I shall soon be back again.
Ever your affectionate Harold

The battalion's destination was the Buena Vista Barracks located with a nearby battery at the southern end of the British Overseas Territory of Gibraltar. Originally a lookout post and guard room, the fortification was further strengthened in 1834, 1872 and 1896. Dertha described their new postings to her father.

26 February 1899
Buena Vista Barracks
Gibraltar

Dearest Father,
I meant to have written before but the time has gone by so fast. We were given a horrid little cabin where one person could hardly turn around, but just as we were unpacking an order came for it to be changed and then we got a splendid three birth one; so you were a great deal of use. There were two Wilbraham girls on board and besides Lord Rowton (1) and a brother of Lord Hillingdon's (2), nobody else I knew. We caught a gale coming through the Bay; we had here very nasty days, then we got into smooth waters, arriving nearly a day late. I was pretty well the first two and worst days, then I knocked-up and had to spend my first three days here in bed. I ended by staying a week with the Lloyd's (3) as I couldn't get any furniture. These barracks are high up the hill looking over a nice view. We have a house at the end of the mess, opposite the barrack gates. The rooms are all very large; in fact I have too much instead of too little room, so I can't furnish it properly and it looks very bare. Captain Nugent (4) has got me up a Burlesque this week, so everybody has gone mad. I have seen it three times, so I have had enough of the jokes. Captain Nugent,

not being gifted with much tact, sung a topical song on the first night about Spain and America and what a good thing it was we were friends of the latter! Can you imagine the insult among the natives. Frankie Lloyd nearly had a fit. The other great excitement here is that Mrs Scott-Kerr (5) got a fall out riding the other day and broke her skull. She was all alone and was picked up some time afterwards and taken to the hospital. I am going to try her horse tomorrow; he slipped on a flat stone so it wasn't his fault. Tell Helen she needn't bring a saddle out as there are plenty to borrow.

We have got the rooms nice and clean but when we first came we found a lot of bugs! I had the whole place washed out with some chemical. How disgusting one would think that in England but people don't seem to mind here. Nothing more to tell. Will write to Mamma later.

Your affectionate daughter, Dertha

Notes
1. Montagu William Lowry-Corry, 1st and last Baron Rowton (1838-1903).
2. Hon. Geoffrey Edward Mills.
3. Francis ('Frankie') and Mary Lloyd. He was the commanding officer of the 2nd Battalion.
4. Captain George Nugent, Grenadier Guards.
5. Wife of Major Robert Scot-Kerr, Grenadier Guards.

Although he had sailed with the 2nd Battalion of the Grenadier Guards, Harold was now with the General Staff and not the regiment. His job was that of the Brigade Major of the Gibraltar Brigade comprising the 3rd Battalion Grenadier Guards, the 1st Battalion Coldstream Guards and the 3rd Battalion (7th) Royal Fusiliers. It so happened that the Major General commanding the brigade was another Grenadier, Henry Colvile. Twelve years older than Harold, Colvile had been commissioned into the 1st Battalion in 1870. After nine years of regimental duty, he was made ADC to Major-General the Hon. Leicester Smyth,[7] the GOC of Cape Colony, and then served as an Intelligence Officer with the Suakin Expedition of 1884 (Battles of El Teb and Tamai). Employed on special service in the Sudan prior to the Nile Expedition of 1884-1885, he served on the Expedition staff as a DAAG. At the close he was Chief of the Intelligence Department of the Frontier Force and present at the Battle of Ginnis. Attached to the Intelligence Department, he wrote the official history of the Sudan Campaign. In November 1893, as Acting Commissioner for Uganda, he commanded the Bunyoro Expedition, a massive Anglo-Buganda force of 13,000 (with some 3,000 riflemen,

---

[7] Lieutenant General Hon. Sir Leicester Smyth KCB KCMG, born Curzon-Howe, (1821-1891).

several maxims and cannon), and after defeating Kabalega, one of the claimants to the Kingdom of Bunyoro, at Mparo in August 1894, he presided over Uganda becoming a Crown Protectorate. For this he received a KCMG.

Count Gleischen paints an eloquent pen picture of Colvile, first and foremost, an excellent professional soldier, with plenty of experience.[8] He was a many-sided person, too: an aeronaut, a writer, an acrobat, a yachtsman, a bit of an artist, an actor and a first-rate carpenter and mechanic; he was, besides, gifted with daredevil pluck, such as walking on impossibly narrow ledges on high buildings, snap-shotting charging bulls from the front and at very close quarters in Spanish arenas, riding through fanatical Moorish country in disguise, honeymooning by balloon and doing various other risky things just for the pleasure of danger in them. He was absolutely fearless under fire ... He also had a keen sense of satiric humour and unfortunately a bitter tongue when he chose, and he could not stand stupid people.'

However, there was a downside to Colvile as a commander 'for he seemed to care little or nothing for the comfort or well-being of his officers and men – except they must have enough rations to fight on. He showed himself but rarely, and never inspected his troops. In fact he seemed to look upon war as a series of problems which had to be coldly solved by intellect alone, and upon his troops as so many pawns to do it with; and he troubled himself but rarely about the human side. A man of this type was not likely to be popular'.

Dertha soon decided to return to England, a decision which Harold was somewhat philosophical about.

21 May 1899
Buena Vista Barracks,
Gibraltar

My dearest Mums,
Very many thanks for your letter. I hope you are getting back again into your wanted good health and spirits now that you are able to get out again. I am very sorry to hear that Papa is not yet quite recovered from his attack – but I hope the fine weather will do him good. Here I simply long to feel a good biting East wind to put a little energy into one. We have nothing but a deep blue sky and a blazing sun. I am now a lone bachelor and very dull. I had a wire from Dertha to say she had arrived alright at Plymouth after a good journey. All the other wives of officers are at present staying out here but I think she was right to go home as this place did not suit her and she never could sleep properly. I forgot whether I told

---

8   Gleichen, Major-General Lord Edward: *A Guardsman's Memories* (Edinburgh: Willian Blackwood & Sons, 1932), pp.210-12.

you that my servant would not stay out here. He got his father to buy his discharge and I sent him home to look after Dertha during the voyage. I had my first game of cricket yesterday for the Battalion and officers of the Royal Engineers. I made 52 not out, at which I was satisfied as I had not touched a bat before, and here we are having to play on coconut matting as there is no grass.

We have a grand parade here on the Queen's Birthday - the whole garrison turns out- but as the ceremony takes place at midday it will be a bit hot. No more to tell you. With best love to Pa and all,
Your most affectionate Harold

25th June 1899
Gibraltar

My dearest Mums,
Very many thanks for your letter. I have been very busy all this week and have not had a quiet time to write to you, so I take advantage of the peace of a Sunday morning.

I see by your letter you will be home again now and I hope are much the better for your visit to the seaside. I do not quite know when I will be able to get away, but I am looking forward very much to a change from this place. Dertha has not yet made up her plans for what she is going to do. I see the brother is to be married on the 20th of July which will probably keep all her family in London this August. She is now at Blackwater but went up to London to be escorted to Lords by old Algy which was very kind of him.

We have been very lucky here so far, we have not been boiled nearly so much as we expected, though the sun is very hot in the middle of the day, but I do not think it is nearly such a nasty moist heat as it was in Bermuda. The only people who seem to get ill are the young boys, both officers and men who are not hardened by age. I myself keep extraordinarily well, but I lead a very active life – out of bed at six and am quite ready to turn in again at 10.30 p.m. after a good day's work. People out here have been excited over a chance of a war in Transvaal, but I do not think there is the slightest possibility of any war at present, but I think – as Mr Chamberlain said – old Kruger will be given sufficient rope to hang himself with. With best love to all,
Your most affectionate Harold

It is during Harold's Gibraltar posting that he learned of the death of his father, Samuel, on 28 May 1899, aged 73 years. The next surviving letter from Harold to his mother is dated the following month.

28 June 1899
Buena Vista Barracks
Gibraltar

My dearest Mums,

Just a line to thank you very much for your letter. I hope by this time you have settled down in your old home and the many little interests you have in your daily life help to divert you from the great loss we have all sustained.

It is getting very hot out here, and what makes it worse we have got a bug which makes one feel terribly slack. I find I cannot take my daily hard exercise as it takes too much out of me. Everyone is trying to get away off the rock and I grudge their going. The old Governor (1) is going away on leave. He is a very old fashioned customer of 64 but he is very active. His chief of the staff has got a game leg so it is rather amusing to see him hobbling along after his superior. I have nothing more to say today. I wish I could send you some of the blue sky and dark blue sea.
Your most affectionate Harold

Note

1. General Sir Robert Biddulph, GCB, GCMG (1835-1918) was a senior British Army officer. He served as Quartermaster-General to the Forces in 1893 and was then Governor of Gibraltar until 1900.

2 July 1899
Gibraltar

My dearest Mums,

I must write you my usual Sunday letter, though I have not much to tell you. We have been having the usual scorching sun and dark blue sky but luckily there has been a good breeze so we are not panting with the heat.

I heard the good news from Dertha that she has succeeded in letting our Blackwater home for the autumn, so I hope she will come out here again this autumn. She tells me she is going to stay with Edith in July and continue her flirtation with old Algy – and I think she is going to see the other sisters.

I dare say you saw that Heywood-Lonsdale was going to be married at last, much to his mother's joy. I believe his future wife (1) is very nice indeed. There is a brother of his in the Battalion of Coldstream out here (2). I am going to have a quick supper tonight with Raymond the military chaplain. I did not wish to refuse their invitation as she wrote a very nice sympathetic letter, and she would probably think me a stuck up guardsman if I did not go, but I wish I wasn't.

I have thought of you a great deal, dearest Mums, since you have got back to Spain's hall, and I know that everyone will do all for you that loving affection can possibly do.

Your most affectionate Harold

Notes
1. Hon. Helena Mabel Hamilton, daughter of Lord and Lady Dalzell
2. There is no record of a Heywood Lonsdale serving with the Coldstream Guards at this time.

9 July 1899
Gibraltar

My dearest Mums,

Very many thanks for your letter. I have been spending a very quiet week apart from my military worries. The proud position I occupy has the disadvantage of being a go-between. The people who want to change everything, and those above won't move their little fingers to put anything right. I consequently get my share of blame from both, but my shoulders are broad and I give way to neither side. Jesser Coope's yacht was in the harbour this week (1). I wrote and asked him to come up and dine, but he didn't. I believe Mrs Jesser was on board but more or less in bed with a chill. We have not been quite so boiled this week. We have had a dark cloud over the rock which hides the sun.

I hope to leave here on the 18th July but I can't tell for certain yet as if anything important turns up I shall have to wait. So I hope to be able to run down to SH before the end of the month. I am counting the days till I get away as I want a change badly. My supper with the Raymonds went off very well. She had her sister staying there. I do not quite understand what relation he is to Sammy of Bolchamp. I have nothing more to tell you.

With best love to all,

Your affectionate Harold

Note
1. E. Jesser Coope of the Ind Coope brewing family was a keen yachtsman and the owner of the magnificent 345 ton auxiliary steam yacht *Sunrise*. In 1899, at the outbreak of the South African War, he sailed *Sunrise* to Durban and placed her at the disposal of the authorities for use as a hospital ship. The offer was gratefully accepted, and the Sunrise was used as a tender to the hospital ships *Lismore Castle* and *Trojan*, as well as a hospital ship for officers. Harold was clearly looking forward to his leave and he docked in Plymouth on 22 July 1899 and headed straight to London. He and Dertha were able to spend some time together at Blair Castle from where he wrote to his mother.

27 August 1899
Blair Castle,
Blair Atholl

My dearest Mums,

Very many thanks for the little locket with a piece of my dear father's hair. [9]I do not think you could have sent me a nicer memento of him whom I shall always associate with the very many happy days spent in our old home. I do not think I have so much news to tell you in my letters as you have to tell me. We really live quite quietly here and Dertha and I keep very much together as it is an enormous place and plenty of room. The Duke is not nearly so grumpy as usual and takes quite an interest in my career, always offering to do things for me so as to help me on. The Duchess one does not see so much of as she is busy arranging for the gathering party. At present there is no-one else here, Tullibardine having taken his Marchioness to her own home. I leave here Wednesday night and sleep in Eaton Place Thursday and start for my boat early Friday. With best love to all and I hope soon to be back again.

Your most affectionate Harold.

In late August 1899 Harold made his way back to Gibraltar. Talk of war in South Africa was gathering pace.

31 August 1899
84, Eaton Place

My own darling,

I do miss you frightfully and I don't like leaving you. I got here alright this morning and have been very busy all day. Everyone is talking of the Transvaal. If there is war they are going to send an enormous force – so they say – of 60,000 men, of whom 48,000 from England. But it is by no means certain that I should go and it would take three months to get them all out there. However I am glad they are going to do the job well if necessary, but this morning's papers are much more peaceful again. I had a long talk with Joe Maude (1) and we are the most peaceful candidates for Brigade Major of the Guard's Brigade. You will see they have stopped the 3rd Battalion going out for a bit and I think the crisis will come about the 19 Sept. I met your Uncle Ronald (2) who says he is going. I also met

---

9   In Victorian times it was common for bereaved family members to keep locks of hair from deceased children or family members.

the commissioner who is coming out by the same boat and I am going to dine with him tonight.

I have nothing more to tell you, darling one, and I can't bear leaving you.
Ever your most loving Harry

Notes
1.   Major Joseph Maude, Coldstream Guards
2.   Ronald Moncreiff, who had been on the Jamieson raid, returned to join Baden Powell's Staff in Mafeking.

7 September 1899
Buena Vista barracks
Gibraltar

My dearest Mums,
I am writing to tell you of my safe arrival on the rock. I had an extraordinary smooth passage on the Orient ship *Ophir* and never felt the least bit 'dicky'. It is not so hot as I expected, the sun is very powerful but there is a nice breeze. But the worst time is at night when the wind goes down and it is horribly stuffy. I found everyone here very well, but all very much excited about the Transvaal. I still do not think there will be any fighting, but an expedition may have to go out. The great Admiral Dewey (1) is staying in Gibraltar, but he is so seedy that he does not show himself at all. The rock is not so burnt up as I expected to find it, there are several green trees yet, but the whole of Spain is very brown and parched up. There are two or three of the battalion ladies who have stopped out all the time and they seem none the worse. We have got a fresh regiment here, the Royal Fusiliers. I met the Colonel this morning, a Colonel Briggs (2), he was quartered at Colchester some time ago and knows most of the family. His Sergeant Major is an old Grenadier who was a drill Sergeant in the 3rd Battalion when I was adjutant. I have nothing more to tell you,
With best love to all
Your most affectionate Harold

Note
1.   Unless Harold is referring to the United States Admiral George Dewey, there is no trace in Royal Navy records.
2.   Colonel G. E. Briggs commanded the 3rd Battalion from 1899-1903.

16 September 1899
Buena Vista Barracks,
Gibraltar

My dearest Mums,
Very many thanks for your long letter which told me all the little bits of news I like to hear. I am afraid I have very little to tell you. We are leading a monotonous life but thank goodness it is getting cooler again. Everyone here is very much excited about the Transvaal, and no doubt if there is a big expedition they will send a Guards Brigade, but I think today things look more peaceful and the Boers will climb down.

This Battalion of Grenadiers is going home on the 28 September and I only wish I was going too. The 3rd Battalion comes out to relieve them. Several of the younger officers have had a touch of fever but my old bones have as yet defied attacks. Plenty of exercise is my recipe. If things settle down I hope Dorothea will come out. I have an official house in the town but it has only three bedrooms for ourselves and for female servants. But I think I can make a dressing room in a cupboard sort of place as otherwise it is impossible to get our three female servants in. Give my best wishes to all,
Your most affectionate Harold

17 Sept 1899
Gibraltar

My own darling one,
I got your nice letter this morning and the news about Geordie. He is very lucky, I think, to have got out, even if there is no war, as I should think the Cape is a better place than India.

You have not told me very much about your gathering party and I know very little of what my little has been doing.

I did a wonderful brave act yesterday. I went and left cards on a lot of people – among them an old friend the chief staff officer Col Dundas. A very dirty soldier opened the door and told us that the lazy old brute was in bed and this at 4 p.m. The 2nd Battalion are off home for certain about the 20th. I shall be very sorry when they go as I have not nearly so many pals in the other Battalions. I think things much more peaceful this morning and the Boers are going to climb down. I wish things would settle down one way or the other, don't you darling mums, as I should like to be thinking of you coming out again but it is better to wait a bit before making plans.

Codrington (1) dined with me last night and he says Mrs C (2) will come out directly things are settled. Do you think you could come out with her? Has Bardie heard anything of going out to the Cape? I have no more to tell you, darling one. I spend most of my Sunday thinking of you and how happy I should be if you were here.

Ever your most loving Harry

Notes

1. Alfred Codrington (1854-1945) commanded 1st Battalion Coldstream Guards in the Second Boer War and later became a general.
2. Adela Portal, a niece of the Earl of Minto.

The increasing agitation and uncertainty in England is clear in Dertha's letter to her father.

27 September 1899
Shaw's Hotel

Dearest Father,

I have a wire from Harry telling me not to start on 5th but to wait till we learn more, so I will not go to London on Saturday. I suppose you have heard they have suddenly told the 2nd Grenadiers they are not to go, but the two Coldstreams instead. It is rather a shame after they had told them to get ready for it. Frankie Lloyd is furious. The 3rd Grenadiers of course go. Major Maude is reported to have said that he knows he is going as Brigade Major, but one doesn't know that officially.

I have just seen Major Henniker on the train and he is in a great state of excitement. He says he supposes they will all know on Saturday after the Cabinet meeting. Nothing more to tell you. This is a vile hole.

Your affectionate Dertha

1 October 1899

My dearest Mums,

Very many thanks for your letter. We have had a week full of excitements and war scares but nothing has come of it yet. The 3rd Battalion Grenadier Guards arrived and the 2nd Battalion had just embarked when a telegram arrived from London to detain them. Of course everyone thought they were off to South Africa but another telegram arrived in the night ordering them home. I have changed my address with their departure. I now live in my official house in the town. I had it well cleaned out and I am fairly comfortable. But I am a long way from the Guard's mess and I do not care about feeding anywhere else. However I shall have to make up my mind to do it soon directly the rainy weather comes on. I have now left a lot of ponies to look after, three dogs and a wild boar and several cats so my back yard is like a zoo. The weather is still hot but I hope we shall have some rain soon as my tank is dry and I only get five gallons of water carted to me daily. Luckily there is plenty of salt water which does to wash in. No more to tell you.

Best love to all,

Your most affectionate Harold

6 October 1899
South Barracks
Gibraltar

My dearest Mums,

Very many thanks for your letter. I do not think I shall be selected to go to South Africa. I have now nothing to do with the Regiment but am on the General Staff of the Army, and if I go out I shall go out as a staff officer. I can't think that the Boers will fight really. After they have been a week in camp they will want to go back to their farms, and even if they do fight, they will soon get tired of it, as it will be at least three months before the campaigns will really open. Everyone is very unsettled here and all are longing to get out of the place. Dertha is leaving London today to come out here so I shall not be so lonely but our household will be rather a scratch one. I will write again shortly. With best love to all,

Your most affectionate Harold

On 8 October Harold learned that he was to go to South Africa as Brigade Major of the Guards Brigade. Dertha was on the high seas bound for Gibraltar and destined to have a few days with Harold before he sailed for the Cape on 25 October with 3rd Battalion Grenadier Guards. Harold was to be proved terribly wrong in his belief that 'the fighting will have fizzled out before we get there …'

8 October 1899
Gibraltar

My dearest Mums,

I got my orders this morning that I am to go to South Africa as Brigade Major of the Guards Brigade. It is a much coveted post and I am very proud of having got it, but of course the little wife comes a good deal into one's thoughts. She is now on the sea and I expect her here next Tuesday or Wednesday. I don't know when we shall start but I expect not for a

fortnight. You must not think there is any danger as I have got the safest post in the army, and I don't believe now that the Boers will fight when they see all the troops we have sent out. Anyhow fighting won't begin for us for 3 months. I will write again shortly,
Your most affectionate Harold

The day after he wrote this letter, Paul Kruger, President of the South African Republic, issued an ultimatum, giving the British government forty-eight hours to withdraw all its troops from the borders of the Transvaal and the Orange Free State, failing which they would go to war with Britain. The British government rejected the ultimatum and war was duly declared.

The Second Anglo-Boer War (1899-1902), as it became known, was the termination of the struggle left unresolved in the ten-week dispute of 1880-81 between Great Britain and the descendants of the original Dutch settlers who had landed in the Cape in 1652 to establish a depot to provision ships on route to the East Indies. Farming communities developed and French Huguenots arrived having fled Louis XIV and his persecutions. From this mix of settler and Huguenot emerged the Boers, hardy, independent, religious and proud people. Staunchly biblical, they believed the land was theirs by the grace of God. After Britain annexed the Cape in 1815, tensions began to appear and in 1835 some 15,000 Boer *Voortrekkers* began to migrate inland, seeking land beyond British administration. They established two Boer republics - the Transvaal Republic and the Orange Free State. To this frictional mix of imperialism and republicanism were added diamonds and gold for in 1866 diamonds were discovered at Kimberley on the borders of the Orange Free State. Twenty years later gold was discovered in the Witwatersrand area of the Transvaal.. Britain initially recognized the two Boer republics but sought to annexe the Transvaal in 1877, a policy that led to the First Anglo-Boer War (1880-81). Britain suffered some notable defeats and independence was restored. Tensions, however, remained.

Motivated by trying to constrain European empire-building competition in Africa and, as always, with an eye on the bottom line as the profits from the diamond and gold fields gushed like inexhaustible fountains, the British government egged on by Cecil Rhodes embarked on the first modern media war with Fleet Street as the hub of the Imperial spin machine.

The *causus belli* revolved around the refusal of the Boers to grant Burgership to the thousands of *uitlanders* or British foreign workers who had flocked to the area to work in the mining industry in the frenzied search for more and more precious metals and stones. This was construed by the British as a barefaced attempt to treat them as second-class citizens with no political rights. This time round hostilities were preceded by a barrage of propaganda. London newspapers painted a dire picture of the flight of the uitlanders, inciting their readers to clamour for war.

The Times led the charge, describing how 'refugees … tell stories on all hands of outrage and insult...by the Boers, who are behaving like semi-savages' . An eyewitness reported in the *East London Standard* how 50 Boers thrashed British train passengers with 'leathern sjamboks'. Portrayed as vicious, inhuman and backward, the Boers were demonized to such an extent that a collective moral outrage gripped Britain. As the principal cheerleader, *The Times* opined gleefully in September 1900 that 'the war, more than any other in modern times, was and is a popular war'.

18,000 Boers crossed the frontier of Natal at daybreak on 12 October 1899.

15 October 1899
Gibraltar

My dearest Mums,
I have not very much to tell you. My little wife arrived out here quite safely and is very well. We have got together a splendid establishment, Lady Colville (1) having lent us a cook and we have got a housemaid. I start from here on the 25th with the 3rd Battalion Grenadier Guards for our voyage of about 3 weeks. Everyone here thinks that the fighting will have fizzled out before we get there, and I think so too, as the old Boers will not stop for long away from their farms and they don't appreciate being short of food and shelter.

I have been very busy as you may imagine – with no more to tell you at present,
Your most affectionate Harry

Note
1. Lady Colvile nee Zélie Richaud de Préville was the wife of Brigadier-General Sir Henry Edward Colvile, commander of the Infantry Brigade at Gibraltar.

3

With the Guards Brigade in South Africa
17 November 1899–10 February 1900

The Second South African War was Harold's first 'hands-on' experience of the battlefield and command in wartime. His time there would shape his development as a soldier, and ultimately forge him into the caring and courageous leader of men in the Great War. It also tested his marriage for, with her husband being far from home on campaign, Dertha had the challenge of managing affairs at home, the worry of her three brothers and two of her cousins all fighting in South Africa, and her mother's poor health (the Duchess was to die on 8th July 1902, a little over a month after the Boer surrender). Moreover, it often fell to Dertha to copy and circulate Harold's letters to family.

The conflict was to last three long years, by the end of which time Britain had fielded some 450,000 men against an enemy no larger than 60,000 at any one time. It was not the Crimea or a typical Victorian colonial war. The scarlet tunic would be replaced by khaki and there would be no more forming squares or advancing in line with bayonets for Britain faced an enemy unlike any faced before. The Boers had modern smokeless magazine rifles and employed guerrilla tactics, fighting, vanishing, reappearing and fighting again. Like the Crimean War, deaths from disease continued to way outnumber deaths in action. The war also saw the construction of defensive blockhouses, the extensive use of barbed wire, the field telephone, search lights and the heliograph. Soldiers in trenches had both rifle and machine gun. A new breed of war correspondent and cameramen allowed people at home to read of events, often resulting in soldiers' families knowing more of what was happening than the soldiers on the ground.

On 29 October, Harold arrived at Tenerife on board the freight ship *Ghoorka*, a Union Company vessel.

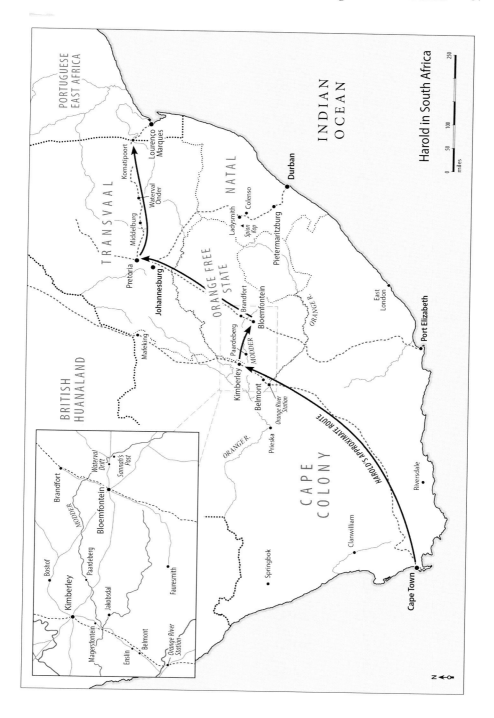

Harold in South Africa

My own darling one,
I am still thinking of my little wee and how brave she was and of all her months in getting things home without anyone to help her. We got into Tenerife about 7am this morning, so we made an expedition in land. We were to have driven to Laguna or some such place but we could not find a cab. Kinlock (1), Fryer (2) and myself went for a good walk while the ship was cooling. It looks nicer from the distance than it does when you are on shore and the view of the peak above the clouds as you go away is imposing. There was a ship from the Cape in the harbour which was full of Johannesburg refugees . They were more or less in a state of mutiny and the provisions had run short. They cheered us tremendously as they left and so did another ship from New Zealand. We had the drums up and played Rule Britannia. We sailed again with the sea like a mill pond and nothing exciting has happened except that Crabbe's horse will try and jump out of its box. I went to see what was happening. I stood on one of our men who was fast asleep. When he felt my 13 stone on his stomach he jumped up and said 'Oh Jesus'. I apologised and fled and went to bed.

Note
1. Major David Kinloch, Grenadier Guards. Later retired as Commanding Officer of the 1st Battalion, having failed to prevent his subalterns from 'ragging' three young officers.
2. Lieutenant Francis Fryer, Grenadier Guards. Son of Sir Frederic William Richards Fryer, first Lieutenant-Governor of Burma, he joined the King's Own Scottish Borderers in November 1892 and then transferred to the Grenadier Guards the next year. He was Adjutant of the 3rd Battalion and later killed at Belmont.

Dertha, safely back from Gibraltar, was already becoming concerned about her brothers.

4 November 1899
84 Eaton Place, SW

Dearest Father,
I came back yesterday after a very troublesome time and want to stop here a few days before going off visiting. I hear from Hamish that you had been under the impression that Geordie was at Elandslaagte (1), but I have verified today what I had supposed all along from what I had heard, that the only two uninjured officers of that half battalion were Baird and Streatfield (2) and of course Geordie was at Ladysmith – though according to the papers Geordie's lot have been fighting since then. People now say in London that the Boers have lost so heavily that

unless they have another real success there is still a strong possibility of things being patched up before the Army Column arrives – but I suppose nobody really knows. I think somebody might have taken the trouble to telegraph to me that Bardie was going.
Your affectionate Dertha

Notes
1. The Battle of Elandslaagte (21 October 1899) was one of the few clear-cut tactical victories won by the British during the conflict.
2. Both were serving with 2nd Battalion Gordon Highlanders. The Commanding Officer, Dick-Cunyngham was severely wounded.

Whilst at sea, as Brigade Major Harold had drafted Tactical Instructions for 'Infantry on the Offensive' and circulated them within in the Guards Brigade. He first noted that 'the principals laid down in the Drill Book fully suffice. The chief difficulty is to apply them at the right time and the right place.' How prescient this observation was to be. He went on to remind the brigade that 'many officers are apt to pay too much attention to their men and too little to the enemy'. This was to prove an universal military truism throughout the campaign.

After a long voyage, Harold landed at Cape Town and immediately went up to the Orange River. The opening phase of the war had begun. Boer commandos invaded northern Natal and besieged the town of Ladysmith, and then laid siege to the British garrisons in Kimberley and Mafeking in the Cape Colony. While the British did achieve some tactical victories at Talana and Elandslaagte, there were serious defeats for the British at Stormberg, Magersfontein and Colenso which became known as 'Black Week' (10-15 December 1899).

19 November1899
Orange River

My own darling wee,
I got your letters from Gib. I have not been able to keep a diary as I promised as I have simply not had one minute to myself. We came from Cape Town directly we landed up to the Orange River – about 40 hours journey, fairly comfortable and well-arranged but slow. We started at 9pm at night, Wednesday, after dining with Morrison (1) and Glyn (2) (2nd Battalion); breakfasted next morning at Magersfontein and had all our meals at various places on the way up. Eventually we arrived at The Aar junction at 12 midnight Thursday and Orange River station at 12 noon on Friday. We were then chucked out of the train just north of the bridge of the Orange River where after a walk of about half a mile I found the camp of the Coldstream and Scots Guards. It is a very nice camp,

but very rough ground within half a mile of the river. The Orange River, which I have always thought to be an enormous one, is not nearly so big as the Tay at Perth, with very muddy waters which we have to drink and in which we have to wash when we can get it. I have been up to my eyes in work since I got out of the train; everybody wanting everything at the same time. I was supposed to provide everything. I was literally at it from 4am till midnight and then went to my little bed on the ground. It was so hard that I could not get to sleep. This has been my programme up to to-day, where after a route march though it is Sunday, I have just time to sit down.

I believe we are off in a day or two towards Kimberley and must leave off now as I can't spare any more time. I will write to my mother and say I am extraordinarily well in my camp on the Orange River and I honestly have not a moment to spare.

With all my love darling wee,

ever your most loving Harry

Notes

1. Lieutenant James Morrison, Grenadier Guards.
2. Lieutenant Arthur St. Leger Glyn, Grenadier Guards.

The 3rd Battalion Grenadier Guards had sailed with Harold on the *Ghoorka* and together with 1st and 2nd Battalions of the Coldstreams and 1st Battalion Scots Guards comprised the Guards Brigade under Sir Henry Edward Colvile who had commanded the Infantry Brigade at Gibraltar. The Guards Brigade with a strength of 4,344 All Ranks and the 9th Brigade were the infantry of Lieutenant-General Lord Methuen's 1st Division, which also included the 9th Lancers, two companies of mounted infantry plus the 18th and 75th Batteries Royal Field Artillery. Incredible as it might seem today, there were only two staff officers of a brigade – the ADC and the Brigade Major. Methuen's 1st Division had eleven.

The Orange River is 1,400 miles long, rising in the Drakensburg Mountains and flowing westwards to the Atlantic Ocean. Orange River Station was the site of Methuen's headquarters prior to his march north along the railway line to relieve Kimberley, some 70 miles away. Methuen had the 8,000 men of the Guards and 9th Brigades with him and the Highland Brigade guarding lines of communication back to Cape Town some 600 miles away. Methuen, however, was short of intelligence, mounted troops and transport whilst stiff opposition in the shape of up to 8,000 Boers under of the command of Piet Cronje lay ahead.

On 26 November, Harold wrote to Dertha. This correspondence included the first mention of casualties and his first experience of warfare. With the letter is a diary covering the period of 20-25 November 1899.

26 November 1899

My own darling wee one,

I have neglected you, but you have no idea what an awful lot I have had to do, and even the General says he would not be a Brigade Major on active service for anything. I am going to write my daily history down on a different sheet so that you can pass it to my mother in case I have not time to write. I am sorry Tullibardine has come out, on account of your mother, and I hope I shall see him as after we have relieved Kimberley we shall move forward with the Army Corps. I am afraid your neat paper of the Army Corps is upset by events – we have got various bits of it marching with us. It is very often country covered with thin scrub and tufts of grass and small hills, and very hot in the daytime – in fact the backs of my hands are so sore from sunburn that I hardly dare go out, but it is nice and cool at night. At present we are without our tents, so I sleep under a wagon. The ground is very hard, but I am generally so dead beat that I fall asleep at once. Our mess is getting on alright; the Frencher (1) does very well and the General (2) devotes a good deal of his spare time to supervising him. We have hardly had any news at all and I had not heard about Blackburn.

It is dreadful all the officers we have had wounded, but they did their work splendidly. I am extraordinary well and I like the life outdoors – but I shall never get used to seeing people shot.

Ever your most loving Harry

Notes
1. Major-General John French, later Field Marshal Lord French, 1st Earl of Ypres.
2. General Sir George White, formerly Gordon Highlanders.

Monday 20th
Orders were given to leave our tents behind and start at 1a.m. to Witteputs Station. Had to pack up all our things and sleep with only a greatcoat on which was beastly cold. Was woke up in my first sleep and told the start had been put off three hours and then had to rush around battalions to let them know. When we did get off we had a pleasant enough march parallel to the railway and encamped on a great plain where we soon had everything comfortable with plenty of good water from a reservoir.

Wednesday 22nd
Started at 4 p.m. and marched to Belmont. Saw very little owing to the dust and nothing exciting occurred. Got into our camping ground in the dark and the usual confusion resulted of getting 10,000 men and

transport into their places in the dark. When I had just got square, word came about 9 p.m. that the 1st Battalion Coldstream were coming in, so I had to go and meet them. When I got back I had to go and reconnoitre the ground as I was to lead the advance at 2 a.m. the next morning. Did not get any sleep at all that night.

Thursday 23rd

Started at 2 p.m. with the Grenadiers and Scots Guards to advance on a position I had only seen on a map and over ground which I had not reconnoitred. I got Freddy Bathurst (1), Russell (2) (Grenadiers), Larking (3) (Scots) to help me and with the greatest good luck went the right way. The Battalions got quite close up to the Boers without their firing at all, and all the loss occurred climbing up the kopje. When the General came up with the Coldstream battalions, I joined him and rode about with him over the ground. My horse got dead tired and I was dead beat myself by this time. When I got back into camp no power on earth could have kept me awake after I had had something to eat. Everyone got a lot of loot; I was too busy to pick up much but Ryan (my groom) collared two saddles; however they are rather too small for my liking.

Friday 24th

Started at 4 a.m. to march to Swinkpan (4). Got in again in the dark and confusion worse than ever…My bed under the wagon was rather harder than usual, as it was on the rocks. I was half the night looking for the bits of my brigade to tell them to start at 4am next morning.

Saturday 25th

Started at 4 a.m. on porridge and a cup of cocoa to convoy the baggage of the whole force to Enslin (5). It took two hours to get in and out of camp and then only with a deal of beating of the mules. The other brigade was going to attack a small force of Boers, and it was thought it would be unnecessary for us to help. But in the middle they wanted 'the Guards', so we had to step it, but the battle (6) was over before we got there and we arrived on our camping ground at 12 noon but had to wait till five for our baggage. I nearly died of hunger , but a friendly doctor gave me some arrowroot and brandy out of his medicine chest which pulled me together. The Boers had about 1,500 men and 6 guns – a much larger force than we supposed, so we were well out of it. It was a very long day indeed and officers and men were absolutely dead beat when they came in. Also of course it was very hot and there was uncommonly little water. The only amusing incident was in my brigade staff. My 3 letter sorters were sorting letters in the train when a shell passed just over their heads. They immediately lay flat in the truck and the engine drivers got scared and ran away so fast with the train that they collided with another, and very nearly had a bad accident.

My horse was pretty tired. My Spanish one, 'Fashoda', cut its foot against the rocks and is lame so I have got a local one to go on with. It is capital ground for galloping about, but there are huge holes. So far however, I have not had a toss.

Notes
1.   Lieutenant Freddy Harvey-Bathurst, Grenadier Guards.
2.   Lieutenant the Hon Alexander Russell, Grenadier Guards.
3.   Lieutenant Reggie Larkin, Grenadier Guards.
4.   Swink's Pan.
5.   Enslin Siding.
6.   Battle of Graspan, 25 November 1899.

Up to 1,500 Boers held a strong position near Belmont some 20 miles distant. Methuen's orders were that in the early hours the Guards Brigade were to take the hills on which the Boers were established, the Scots and Grenadiers attacking Gun Kopje in the early morning, followed by the Coldstreams assaulting Middle Hill (or Grenadier Hill as it came to be known). The approach and advance went smoothly and by 3.50 a.m. it seemed that the Boers had left their position. Not so; the ridge suddenly burst into flames and the attackers came under modern rifle fire for the fire time.

Gun Hill was speedily taken by the Scots and half a company of Grenadiers, but the objective turned out to be very much smaller that the sketch map had indicated and seriously enfiladed from Middle Hill. This feature, a steep kopje of iron-stone boulders, had to be cleared at all speed. In only 15 minutes the Grenadiers did so but at a cost for 36 killed and 114 wounded. Most of the casualties were incurred in doubling forward into the protection of dead ground. The Boers called it a day, mounting their ponies and trotting off the battlefield, leaving behind 50 prisoners, 100 horses, 64 wagons and quantities of ammunition.

News was to travel fast and in due course Harold received a letter from a Guards colleague congratulating him for the Guards Brigade's achievement at Belmont:

24 November 1899
Guards Club

My dear old Ruggles,

I cannot tell you how eagerly I read the papers through this morning and how pleased I was as I realised that most of my old pals were safe.

It does seem so sad that poor little Leslie (1) should have been taken. He was such a first rate little sportsman and so keen. And poor old

Blundell (2) too. It seems to me only a day or two ago since I was chaffing him and saying that the 2nd Bn were sure to go and that he had no chance! He was a good chap.

Poor old North (3). He is the most unlucky man I ever saw, but I do hope that his wound is not a bad one. Do give all the wounded my best love, if they are still with you, and say how much we are thinking of them in England.

The first news we heard that led us to believe there had been a fight was a telegram from Lord Methuen. Of course this did not go through the press and reached us within six hours of the time of the despatch. The official telegram did not come in for six hours afterwards.

The list of names of rank and file killed and wounded has not reached us yet. I have just been to the War Office (10 p.m.) but can ascertain nothing. Of course it must take a long time to get all the names and Regt numbers, but it is a very anxious time for some of the poor women. I am pleased to hear that old Polly Carew (4) has got Douglas's brigade (5). It is a piece of luck for him but he deserves it. Please give him my best love.

It must have been a great fight, splendidly planned and bravely carried through and I would have given a good deal to have been there even as a private soldier.

Things look a bit risky in Natal and the situation there at the present moment is the most extraordinary that war has ever produced. I don't think half the people in this country have grasped the great power of mobility that the Boers possess and how little they suffer from their defeats. Many appear simple to retire when they have had enough of a fight and wait for another day.

Ruggles, mind you let me know if I can do anything for you or anyone else over here. I shall be only too delighted. I hope your mobilization equipment turned up alright and that everything that came from England was fairly right.

One bit of news. The Mil. Secretary (6) wrote a few days ago to ask the General (7) privately whom he would like to succeed me and I am glad to say that he has sent your name in.

Goodbye, old Ruggles. Give my very best love to old pals, especially Putty (8), whom I must congratulate on his new rank which no-one deserves better. I only hope he will come back a brevet Colonel.

Take care of yourselves and give the Boers beans!

Yours ever,

Joe (9)

Notes

1.   21-year-old Second Lieutenant Theodore Leslie, Grenadier Guards, later died of his wounds

2.   Lieutenant Wilfrid Blundell-Hollinshead-Blundell, Grenadier Guards
3.   2nd Lieutenant E. North.
4.   Old Polly Carew is Reginald Pole-Carew, formerly Coldstream Guards who took command of 9th Brigade on 27 November 1899. Later Lieutenant General Sir Reginald Pole-Carew, KCB, CVO.
5.   Brigadier General Charles Douglas, later General Sir Charles Douglas, GCB, ADC (1850-1914). He was CIGS during the first three months of the First World War but died from strain and overwork.
6.   Major-General Sir Coleridge Grove KCB (1839-1920).
7.   Major General Sir Henry Trotter, GCVO, DL (1844-1905), Major General commanding the Brigade of Guards and General Officer Commanding the Home District from 1897 to 1903, formerly Grenadier Guards.
8.   Major William Pulteney Pulteney served with 1st Scots Guards with the brevet appointment of Lieutenant Colonel from 11 November 1899.
9.   Captain Joseph Bailey, Grenadier Guards, ADC to the Major-General commanding Home District.

Methuen's advance on Kimberley continued including the reconnoitre of the Modder River for he believed the Boers to be some ten miles further on, about halfway between the Modder and Kimberley. The actual position was somewhat different for a substantial force of some 3,000 Boers were dug in on the banks of the Riet River and the Modder. At 4.15 a.m. on 28 November, the Guards Brigade which now had the Naval Brigade attached to it, left its bivouac at Kolkfontein with orders to attack the Modder River from the East. The Grenadiers and Scots left the start line at 7.5 a.m. but within an hour were checked by a murderous fire from machine guns and rifles. All attempts to approach the enemy by the banks of the river were frustrated and consequently the situation remained the same throughout the day with the Guardsmen lying on open ground under artillery and rifle fire, stricken with thirst and sunburn in temperatures of over 100°F. At nightfall, the brigade regrouped and by dawn the next day it transpired that the Boers had evacuated their position during the night. The battle of the Modder River was another costly engagement for the brigade; one officer and 28 ORs had been killed, seven officers and 153 ORs wounded. One man was missing.

Cronje's men eventually withdrew from the Riet and across the Modder. The Boer General, Koos De la Rey, was wounded and his son Adriaan killed; Lord Methuen was slightly wounded and amongst the 1st Division's 470 casualties was Methuen's chief of staff, Colonel Northcote and Lieutenant-Colonel Horace Stopford, shot while leading the 2nd Battalion Coldstream Guards into action. Boer casualties totalled 80.

Harold's letter to Dertha is a reminder that domestic affairs had still to be managed from the battlefield.

5 December 1899
Modder River

My own darling wee,

Very many thanks for your letter. I am so sorry and very much annoyed that you should have been bothered so much about the insurance money. What I thought I had arranged and what I intended was that Hunter should look after my interests and pay what was due. He ought to have about £2000 of my money bringing in interest so he could borrow the amount and then wait till I came home to settle it. Instead of that he has paid more than he need and given you a lot of worry and I am very angry with him indeed.

However darling one, this is not the time to worry your dear self about this. If you have paid it out of your investments, I will put by every penny I can to make it good, and will you promise not to worry about it until I come home, as we must share our little worries and it is not fair that you should have all the bother.

I will try and tell you something about ourselves. Up to the 28th we had a real hard time, marching and fighting every day – 3 battles and two nights I never lay down for a moment. One morning I had to start with only a cup of cocoa and had no food for 24 hours except a tot of rum which warmed up my inside. We have had real hard work and plenty of bullets flying around. I have always looked upon war as a business and as my ambition is to get one I was glad to get the opportunity, though I could hardly stand leaving you; and darling it was only that we might benefit in the future that I ever wanted to go. I am so afraid that you will think I am not fond of you as I more or less volunteered.

We are now encamped in a bend of the Modder and are very comfortable. All the wounded are doing well. Colonel Crabbe (1) is coming back today – not a bad performance as he had two bullets through him, but these small bullet wounds soon heal up. Dalrymple was badly hit but is going on all right. All the fellows who went through the battle of the 28th say it is the worst day they ever went through and you will know Lord Methuen was wounded in the leg and Colvile is commanding the Division, so we are temporarily separated and Arthur Paget is commanding the brigade. I live in a tent alone in my glory trying to keep people up to the mark but it is hard work. Freddy Bathurst is in fine form and one sees who are the good ones at this game.

We are going to advance again in a couple of days. The Boers have collected between Jacobsdal and Spitfontein, but we have got a Field Battery and Howitzer Battery coming up and we hope to give them what for.

After that I expect we will join in the main advance up the Orange Free State.

I woke up this morning dreaming about you and I could not realise for a moment why I felt so hap.

God bless you darling one,

Ever your most loving Harry

Note

1.   Lieutenant-Colonel Eyre Crabbe, commanding 3rd Battalion Grenadier Guards.

Methuen brought up Major-General Andrew Wauchope's 3rd Highland Brigade comprising of 2nd Battalion Royal Highlanders (Black Watch), 1st Battalion Argylls & Sutherland Highlanders, 2nd Battalion Seaforth Highlanders and 1st Battalion Highland Light Infantry. Bridges over the Modder had to be repaired and Kimberley was thought to have 40 days' worth of supplies. The next objective was the Magersfontain Ridge on the borders of Cape Colony and the Orange Free State, heavily entrenched and defended.

8 December 1899
Modder River

My dearest Mums,

I feel very much ashamed of myself for not having written to you more, but really all I have been able to do is send a sort of diary to Dertha who I hope has sent it on to you. We have had a very hard time so far, but we have now had a week's rest since our last battle and have all quite recovered. We are in a standing camp on the Modder with plenty of water so that we can wash ourselves. I have been extraordinarily well all the time. The open air life suits me down to the ground and the only horrible part is to see the poor dead and wounded in the battles. So far I have been mercifully preserved. But my duties do not take me so much in front as the regimental officers. The Boers are fighting very much better than I expected, but so far the Guards Brigade has carried everything before it. We have so far had very little cavalry or artillery but we have been reinforced with both and we are expecting to get orders to advance towards Kimberley. There are a lot of Boers between us and that town but we are expecting that they will soon run away when they have got a few shells among them. When we have relieved Kimberley we are going south by train and to be part in the advance up the Orange Free State. So we have got a good deal of campaigning to do yet. The rascals of the Boers have cut the railway line behind so often the letters are delayed coming

up to us, but I hear the cavalry have chased them away. The Boers never come out into the open and are most difficult to get at. One never sees one except when he is galloping away on his pony. I think the lot in front of us are getting a little bit funky as they don't wait till we come up to them, but try and do as much damage as possible before running away. We have already repaired the railway bridge over the Modder and trains are now running into our camp, so we have plenty of food though it is rather tough and the biscuits very hard. The General, ADC and self, have a little mess of our own. The first named is very particular as to what he eats, so we do well. We are now in luxury with fresh milk and vegetables. I have not quite got used to sleeping on the ground, but I find I often go to sleep at odd moments which makes up for it. The country is very bare and dry and we have awful dust storms and thunderstorms. The sun is beastly hot and my hands are so blistered with it that I have to wear gloves. With very best love to all,
Your most affectionate Harold

8 December 1899
Modder River

My own darling wee,
I must write you a line though I have nothing very much to tell you. We have been sitting here very quiet since our last battle of the 28th and are fairly comfortable as we have got our tents and a little baggage. I have not kept a diary for you since we started, every day is very much alike. All the men are employed on fatigue but I still find plenty to do. The Boers are all around us, but I do not think we are very frightened of them. They never dare to attack us in the open and the skulking brutes only shoot at us from behind rocks and then get on their ponies and bolt. However we are getting up a little treat for them in the shape of some lyddite shells which I hope will scare them. I am very sorry for your mother having her two sons out in the war and I hope that by the time Bardie joins we shall have such an overwhelming force that the beggars will give in. The Boers certainly fight much better than I expected, but we really have not got at them yet. All that I have to tell you is such stale news by the time you get this. A wire has come to say that the 2nd Bn Gren Gds is coming out but I think they must have muddled this with the Life Guards.

The country here is very desolate and bare, but the climate is delightful – rather too hot in the day and nice and cool at night. I eat enormously and get very hot and very thirsty owing to the dust. The General and Nugent are in a sort of villa on the Modder, while I live in camp. We are going to have a dinner party tonight. We have bought some lager beer, a bit of ration beef and some tinned fruit. Some of the rations dealt out are very good, especially the rum and the lime juice. The former is capital stuff to keep the inside warm.

I must now leave off darling one and I am always thinking of you. With all my love,
Ever your most loving Harry

At 4.45 p.m. on 10 December Methuen's artillery opened fire on the Boer positions on the Magersfontein ridge; the attack was to go in at dawn the next day. The Highlanders[1] were to attack along with the King's Yorkshire Light Infantry and two battalion of the Guards Brigade protecting their right and rear. The Boers occupied a low ridge that blocked Methuen's advance. In front of the Kopjes were the Boer trenches, skilfully camouflaged with grass and branches. Methuen's forces numbered some 15,000 men plus artillery against 8,000 Boers and artillery.

The night started oppressively hot, but during the march a storm broke with lightning, thunder and heavy rain, bringing intense cold. As the sun rose on 11 December, news reached the Guards Brigade which had set off at 1 a.m. that 'Highland attack has been checked; may fail. Keep your brigade in hand so as to protect Highland right and their retirement, if necessary. Perhaps retirement of whole force'. During the day, the brigade remained in support of the Highlanders covering their flanks. After nine hours exposed to constant fire from the Boer trenches, having lost their commander Major-General Andrew Wauchope who had been killed in the first few minutes of the battle, the Highlanders finally broke up and withdrew, suffering substantial losses as they rose from whatever cover they had found and made for the rear. The soldiers were halted, rallied by their remaining officers and NCOs and brought back into support of the rest of the line.

The Highland Brigade's casualties were horrendous; it had lost 64 officers and 650 soldiers, including three commanding officers, Lieutenant-Colonel John Coode of the Black Watch, Lieutenant-Colonel Gerald Goff of the Argylls and Lieutenant-Colonel Downman of the Gordons. Never had Scotland a more grievous day than that at Magersfontein. For Dertha and her family, the loss of friends like James Cumming-Bruce must have brought the realities of the war home.

The Guards Brigade had emerged comparatively lightly: it had lost one officer[2] and 10 ORs killed with five officers and 78 ORs wounded. One was missing. Boer casualties were 236.

---

1   The 3rd Highland Brigade consisted of 2nd Black Watch, 1st Highland Light Infantry, 2nd Seaforth Highlanders and 1st Argyll & Sutherland Highlanders.
2   Major The Lord Winchester, Coldstream Guards.

This was the end of Methuen's attempt to reach Kimberley. He was relieved of his command and Field Marshal Lord Roberts of Kandahar VC, the greatest solider of his time, was despatched to South Africa with Lord Kitchener as his chief of staff to sort out the mess.

Harold's version of events reached Dertha in early January:

Sunday 10 January

We had a quiet morning in camp when suddenly the order was received to move off. Some of the force was to start in the afternoon and the Guards Brigade was to move at 1am on Monday morning. I had to go with the other brigade to find out where we had to go and started at 3 p.m. When we had marched about 5 miles we began to shell an enormous hill and this went on until dark when I was sent back to bring up the Guards Brigade. We first had to cross a river which we did at dusk; the transport mules were very troublesome and it took a long time. Eventually I got my lot in order, about 12 midnight.

Monday 11th

We started off at 1 a.m. and marched along a line of telegraph wire. It soon began to rain and became so dark that we could only get on by feeling along the wire with a long stick and it also began to rain heavily. After many mishaps we arrived at our rendezvous and almost at once a tremendous fusillade came from the attack on the trenches by the Highland Brigade who were driven back. The Guards Brigade got into position on their right and the battle lasted till late in the afternoon when both sides were too exhausted to go on. Meanwhile we had given the Boers a tremendous shelling with some Howitzers firing Lyddite, but we could not get on at all as the Highland Brigade were quite done for and our brigade on the right could only just hold its own – we relieved the whole of the Highland Brigade about 5 p.m. and remained all that night lying down quite close to the Boers. It was bitterly cold and someone had bagged my blanket, so I could not get to sleep and was only too glad when the sun rose and warmed us.

Tuesday 12th

The Boers seemed to have had enough shooting for the present as they did not open fire and we remained facing one another till 12. When our force retired covered by the Guards Brigade, Lord Methuen was very pleased with the way we covered the retirement and I am glad to say we got out of the place without any more losses and returned to camp on the Modder about 2 p.m.

I was absolutely done when I got back – two nights without lying down and very little food except a biscuit which I carried in my haversack, and I slept a real good sleep that night. We are all terribly disappointed at not getting on better, but there were too many Boers for us. The hill they occupied was practically impregnable and the Highland Brigade, as you will know, lost terribly and I am afraid are rather demoralized. I must say some of them fought magnificently – especially the Gordons and the Black Watch. Personally I think it was the old story of 'someone has blundered' and to have a fine brigade like that cut up is a terrible loss to the army. The Boers hid themselves completely. They were in a trenches about 5 ft deep and directly anyone appeared they loosed off as hard as they could, but they must have got a real dressing from our artillery as they did not dare to fire at us the next day. I think they must have been pretty well hammered. But we have had to go back again instead of forward which is very serious.

Wednesday – Friday
We have been having a quiet time to recuperate. So far whenever we have had a battle we have had no sleep and nothing to eat and one relishes anything in the shape of food.

15 December
Modder River

We have had a bad doing, but luckily for the Guards Brigade we were not told to do what the Highland Brigade were. I think perhaps we might have done it, but there would have been no more Guards Brigade. The losses in officers were terrible. I have been so busy that I have not had time to get over and see if young Ramsay is alright. I only pray he is, but I am afraid there were few uninjured. You know far more about the battles than we who are fighting them, so I don't speak much of them. It is more than enough to have seen them and then I try and forget all about them. So far, I think our brigade has been extraordinarily lucky, and I the luckiest of all. I have plenty of work and keep extraordinarily well.

I don't quite know what we shall do now. We have fought four battles already and we do not seem to get any forwarder.

We have the experience of a dust storm this afternoon, a hot burning wind and tons of filthy dust, and my face is quite black. The sun is very hot by day but the nights are deliciously cool if one has enough on. I have three blankets on my bed on the hard ground and I sleep wonderfully. A lot of people are suffering from dysentery, among them Colonel Paget who has gone down to Cape Town to recruit. Colonel Crabbe has turned up after his wound and is full of energy and go and is quite well. Many who were wounded at Belmont have come back, some of them apparently none the worse. Colonel Codrington was slightly wounded in the fleshy part of the thigh but went on looking after his battalion all day in spite of it. When he was shot he exclaimed 'Hello, an outer low right!'

I have not much peace or time to myself. I am continuously being interrupted by various fussy people, and the flies and the dust make life a burden.

Meanwhile Dertha had compiled her own version.

12 January 1900
84, Eaton Place SW

Dearest Father,
I asked Neil Menzies (1) to sit and watch the tape, and he telegraphed to you as soon as the news came out. Three days ago I heard that the war office knew there were fourteen officers killed, but wouldn't publish it till they knew more, and I followed their example. It is too dreadful about Colonel Dick Cunyngham. COs seem to carry their lives in their hands, and hardly any have escaped. It is still an anxious time for Ladysmith. Lord Methuen is to be recalled. I think it will either kill him or drive him into a lunatic asylum. I see they are trying to let him down easy by putting an inspired telegraph in today's papers about his health being bad from a fall from his horse, but he is not chronically mad in the least, only impossible to work with. I am dreadfully sorry for him, only of course it is right he should be removed.

The Guards Brigade was ordered to do what the Highland one did; the Grenadiers to lead. The order was cancelled at the last moment – nobody quite knows why – and the Highlanders sent instead. Sir Henry Colvile and General Wauchope expostulated with Lord Methuen and were told to hold their tongues. Wauchope was thoroughly shaken and unnerved at having to do what he knew to be impossible. He quite forgot they were marching in quarter column. When the Boers opened fire he told his men to charge with bayonets, having forgotten to tell them to have any. Then he called halt and some contradictory order and the end came. That seems to be the true story. He had had a tremendous fight with Methuen about it.

Nothing more to tell you. You might show this to Hamish.
Your affectionate Dertha

Note
1. Sir Neil James Menzies 8th Bt, formerly Scots Guards.

By this stage, the scale of the challenge and duration of the war had certainly dawned on Harold.

15 December 1899
Modder River

My dearest Mums,

I have not got your normal welcome letter by the last mail but I heard all about you from Dertha who was at Spains Hall. We advanced again last Sunday and had a tremendous battle at Magersfontein on Monday. The Highland Brigade lost a tremendous number of men but I am very glad to say the Guards Brigade came off very well. The Boers in front of us are too numerous and too well posted so I expect we shall have to stop and not relieve Kimberley after all. We have had a very hard time for two days but I keep wonderfully well and sleeping on the ground seems to agree with me. I have no time to do anything but soldier so you must excuse a rotten letter. We have been having a very bad dust storm and the sun is very hot but the nights are nice and cool and I am always ready to eat and drink whatever I can get. The climate seems to be a very healthy one, very dry and sandy, and enormous plains with here and there little hills out of them. These Kopjes as the Boers call them are very rocky and our enemy is a wonderful hand at concealing himself as we never see him. The Doctors who have been over in the Boer camp say that there are people of all nationalities fighting against us – French, Scandinavians, Germans and a lot of English speaking people. They do not give us much of a chance as they never come out of their trenches and I believe the only way to fight them would be to starve them out, but we are generally ordered to go straight at them, so the brutes shoot a lot of us. I expect the war is a much bigger job than they expected at home and they will have to go on sending more troops for some time to come. I must leave off now as I have to go to Headquarters to get my orders. Hoping you are flourishing and are able to get out of doors and enjoy a little toddle.
With best love to all,
Your most affectionate Harold

There now followed Colvile's 'six dreary weeks: how we trenched and demonstrated, how we had scares and slept in our boots, and read the telegrams from Natal and did not understand them'.[3] The brigade retired to the Modder River which they reached at 2 p.m. on 12 December. Apart from an epidemic of diarrhoea, life

---

3   Colvile, Major-General Sir Henry, *The Work of the Ninth Division* (London: Edward Arnold, 1901), p.17.

was uneventful and the brigade received replacement of 17 officers including 14 Grenadier officers and 373 ORs. Not wishing to alarm Dertha, Harold made light of conditions in camp which were far from safe. 22-year-old Lieutenant Lord O'Hagan of the 3rd Battalion Grenadier Guards died from enteric fever on 13 December; in August the following year, another young Grenadier officer, Second Lieutenant Guy Tryon died from the same fever. Harold reflected further on the reality of fighting the Boers in his letter of 20 December.

Modder

My own darling little wee,
I have not kept a regular diary since I last wrote as we have been stationary at this place. We met with what is called a check and we have been doing nothing since but dig forts and redoubts. I am awfully sorry for the Highland Brigade and you must have known so many people who never came back. I liked your telling me to take care of myself, and I do, and you must feel as confident as I do that I shall come back to you all right.

We are having a very quiet time of it; the only excitement is afforded by the sailors who have got a big gun up in the outpost line and directly the Boers show their heads they fire at them with lyddite. I wonder what all the people at home think of the reverses? That old windbag Gatacre (1) made an awful mess of his first battle and now Buller (2) has gone and done the same. Certainly these Boers are a difficult people to tackle; they hide themselves up completely and if you attack one part of their position they all flock there on their ponies and the country is just made to suit their tactics. In front of us we have about 10 miles of ridge and whenever we go at it they get there in thousands. Cronje sent his ADC in yesterday with a note to Methuen. He was practically an Englishman and told us that they were all very sick of the war and wanted to go to their homes, and that they did not like the lyddite at all, the force of the explosion making everyone near quite insensible for hours, even if they were not blown up. I suppose we shall wear them out in time, but we are doing it very slowly. Colonel Douglas (3) came as chief staff officer of this division and really makes himself most pleasant, and Drummond is now also on the staff and Jones RE of Gibraltar is the balloonist. We have got the 9th and 12th Lancers, 2 batteries field artillery, 1 battery horse artillery, 1 howitzer battery, the Guards Brigade, the Highland Brigade. Col Codrington is all right again and is expected today and nearly all those who were wounded at Belmont have come back again. I met young Douglas the other day, he is in the Argyll and Sutherland Highlanders and was very lucky to have got out of the battle. Lewis Dawnay (4) (late of the Coldstreams) has attached himself to the brigade and seems quite happy doing nothing. Gregson (5) did his best to come up this way. We have got back to quite decent food and unless they pack us off again I shall soon be as fat as a pig. I have had all my hair cut off, and the flies keep worrying by settling on my head. My breeches and boots are all wearing out and my khaki is not fit to be seen. I do not like this sitting still; we might go and annoy the Boers even if we do not fight them.

I am not going to write any more now as I am expecting to get a dear letter from you. I am thinking of yourself asleep in your wee beddy as it is only just 6am.

Darling I have now had time to finish this letter. I have been busy the whole day but I got your dear letter and I must now leave off as the mail is closing. God bless you darling one,
Ever your most loving Harry

Notes
1. Lieutenant General Sir William Gatacre KCB DSO (1843-1906) commanded the Imperial forces at the Battle of Stormberg during 'Black Week' in which 135 men were killed and 696 captured during a Boer ambush. He was sent back to England.
2. General Sir Redvers Buller, VC, GCB, GCMG (1839-1908), once rated 'an admirable captain, an adequate major, a barely satisfactory colonel and a disastrous general', had presided over the defeat at Colenso on 15 December when the British lost 143 killed, 756 wounded, and 220 captured. He was relieved of his command but remained on in South Africa.
3. Later General Sir Charles Douglas, GCB, ADC (1850-1914)
4. Lieutenant Colonel Hon Lewis Payn Dawnay MP
5. This could be the war correspondent Francis Gregson who had made his reputation in the Mahdist War of 1898.

On 22 December Harold found time to write to his friend, Frankie Lloyd, with a very candid assessment of shortcomings in the command and preparation of British forces in South Africa. These included the disregard of theory, lack of sleep and food before battle, the failure to attempt to mislead the enemy, the failure to reconnoitre and the lack of artillery preparation.

22 December 1899
Modder River

My Dear Frankie,
I am sure you must think me very forgetful and ungrateful not having written to you before, but the fact is that I have been so busy and I had not a moment before, also we were convinced that you and your Battalion were coming out, and we are not now certain that you are on the way (1).

Dertha has told me how kind you have been to her in every way and I cannot ever thank you enough for all that you have done for us. I am sure you will have heard all our experiences. I never saw such a hopeless muddle as the Divisional staff were in. The DAG Mainwaring (2) was a perfect fool and a very rude one, so eventually there was a general strike amongst the brigadiers and Colonel Douglas was sent up. The DAAG was killed at Modder River and now we have Benson a gunner who does well enough. I have not learnt much tactics since I have been out here, and all our theoretical principles have been disregarded. When the brigade has gone into action it as a rule had no sleep the night before, no breakfast to start on, no idea of the enemy's position as it has never been reconnoitred, and no artillery preparation. There has never been any attempt to 'mislead and mystify' in the words of our friend Stonewall (3). The Boers do not have to come out into the open but they fight magnificently in their trenches, but I must say that generally they are so placed that it is much more dangerous for them to come out than remain.

I think the brigade have done very well on the whole, we have had some very long days fighting in the blazing sun, and water and ammunition has failed, simply because anyone who tried to take it up was shot. Between you and me, there was a good deal of skulking, one reason of it being I think that the adjutants thought their proper place was in the firing line, and there was no-one to whip the brutes on. On another occasion a sergeant major was found behind a bush a long way out of the zone of fire. But in our last battle at Magersfontein I think things were better. As usual we could not locate them (Boers). We advance with a large extension – 5 paces – and the result is companies lose their sections and whole companies are lost to the Bn Commander. But we should lose very heavily if we advanced in any less extension, and I hope when the Bns get used to it we shall do good work. The Boers occupy such extended positions that it is most difficult to get round their flanks but if we only took advantage of the fact that they don't dare to come into the open, we could march round them.

You will have seen all about the destruction of the Highland Brigade. They made a night attack on the filthiest night you can imagine, came upon a fence unexpectedly and were fired into in mass of columns. I don't think they would ever have got anywhere near, if they had advanced in proper formation as it was such a foul dark night with heavy rain and the ground had never been reconnoitred, and no-one had any idea where the trenches were. I was directing the brigade in a night march and was helped by long strides with a stick – and though we marched the whole way, it took us a long time to get over about four miles.

Coddy (4) has just come back completely cured of his wound and the Brigade on the whole is very well. Fisher (5) and Powell (6) have had to go to the base for dysentery and Arthur Paget (7) is at Cape Town for the same reason.

The men were a bit knocked-up after our first advance but they are fit again now. The climate is not at all a bad one, very hot in the middle of the day but cool in mornings and evenings and cold at night. I am afraid I have written you a bit of rubbish and I still hope this may find you on the way out and thanking you again very much for all the care you have taken of Dertha, and all the trouble you have taken over my affairs.

Yours ever,

Harold Ruggles-Brise

Notes

1. The 2nd Battalion sailed on the *Dunera* on 18 March 1900, and arrived at the Cape about 11 April.
2. Maj-Gen R.B. Mainwaring CMG (1850-1926) DAG is an abbreviation of Deputy Adjutant General and DAAG of Deputy Assistant Adjutant General.
3. Confederate General Stonewall Jackson's dictum: 'Always mystify, mislead, and surprise the enemy, if possible; and when you strike and overcome him, never let up in the pursuit so long as your men have strength to follow; for an army routed, if hotly pursued, becomes panic-stricken, and can then be destroyed by half their number'.
4. Lieutenant Colonel Codrington, Coldstream Guards.
5. Captain Laurence Rowe Fisher-Rowe, Grenadier Guards. Later killed in France in 1915 when commanding 1st Battalion.
6. Second Lieutenant John Powell, Grenadier Guards.
7. Lieutenant Colonel Arthur Paget, commanding 1st Battalion Scots Guards.

On Boxing Day 1899, Dertha wrote to the Duke. Particularly striking is the experience of Captain Earle.

84, Eaton Place SW

Dearest Father,

I haven't heard from Harry this mail; Lady Colvile hasn't either, so I suppose he and his General took extra trouble about posting them with the result that they didn't arrive. Everybody seems to have written home saying that Harry led the advance at Belmont splendidly. I read part of a most gruesome letter from Captain Earle (1) to Frankie Lloyd in which he says that at Modder he was in a high fever all the time. He did everything he had to do but doesn't remember how. He went twice off his head but got round again and went on. At the end of the day he was carried off senseless and put in a hut amongst the dead and the delirious wounded where he lay all night seeing ghosts. He says he did see his brother's riderless horse, but he was so mad it made no impression on him. He and a good many others had been sixteen hours without food. He is alright now only too weak to travel and is coming home when he can. Colonel Paget is to be invalided home from dysentery. The C.O.s have been rather unlucky. I suspect there will be a fearful lot of invalids from overwork.

I wish I had got Harry's letter. It would have been an interesting one. I suppose you have heard Colonel MacKinnon (2) has got the command of the volunteers. It is a bitter blow for me! I am anxiously wondering who his successor will be.

Your affectionate Dertha

Notes
1.   Lieutenant and Adjutant Maxwell Earle, Grenadier Guards.
2.   Later General Sir William Mackinnon, GCB, KCVO (1852-1929), formerly Grenadier Guards. Mackinnon was appointed Colonel commandant of the City of London Imperial Volunteers in December 1899. It proceeded to South Africa in January 1900 under his command, returned in October and was disbanded in December.

Two letters from Harold to his mother and one to Dertha throw more light on Christmas celebrations and life in camp.

29 December 1899
Modder River

My dearest Mums,
I must write you my weekly note although I have nothing much to tell you. We are sitting here very quietly with the Boer about 5 miles away and only very occasionally they send a shell into our camp. But as they don't burst, we don't pay much attention to them. I expect we shall be here a long time so we have sent down to Cape Town for footballs and games so as to make men run about. But I don't fancy the idea of playing games very much as you may as well play on 'Buck field' with a good many dust storms thrown in. I have made my tent as comfortable as I can, with a large awning in front made out of the waggon cover , but it is a tent an inch deep in dust which makes the use of ink impossible. We have a capital parson attached to our brigade. Falkner (1) by name, I had met him before as he used to be at Caterham. We have open air services and communion every Sunday and the old man preaches a capital little sermon. On Xmas day all the Grenadiers dined together and we had a most luxurious repast – soup, barbel out of the Modder River which tastes like the tench out of the pond – turkey and sausages and plum pudding so we are not starving. (2) Champagne to drink followed by brandy and

the latter completely cured for me what is generally called 'Modders' out here i.e. diarrhoea.

We have had several tremendous thunderstorms and I never saw such lightening. We are now beginning the rainy season – so far I prefer it as the dust is not so bad. My general lives in a house about a quarter of a mile off and I go and have my meals there. I find I take a ton of sugar in everything I eat or drink. One seems to want it out here. I am sorry to say I am wearing out my clothes and what are not rags are very dirty. So I think I shall have to order some more in case we are kept a long time out here. With best love to all,
Your most affectionate Harold

Notes
1. The Reverend Thomas Falker. Awarded DSO for services with Lord Methuen's Division and the Brigade of Guards. He was the first Church of England Chaplain to receive this distinction.
2. Eddie Lygon described it in his diary as 'a very cheery party, considering - drums playing - but after all it don't seem a bit like Xmas'. He listed the Grenadier staff officers as follows: Colvile, Nugent, Ruggles-Brise, Loch, Sheldrake and Magill - and those from the 3rd Battalion, Crabbe, David, May, Profeit, Trotter, Heneage, Travers, Glyn, Duberley, Corry, Lygon, Morrison, Bouche (attached), Poley, Clive, Bathurst, Russell, Roberts, Kerry and Taylor.

29 December 1899
Modder River

My own darling wee,
I have just got your letter of December 8th and as the mail arrived late I have not much time to write to you. We are still doing nothing here with the old Boers sitting on a hill looking at us. All the men are employed as fatigue. The outposts are about 6,000 yards from the Boers and they amuse themselves with throwing shells towards us but as they never burst, no one has been hit except an unlucky dog which formerly belonged to a Boer and was captured at Belmont. A lot of the 2nd Battalion has come out to reinforce the 3rd Battalion Grenadier Guards. Monson and Glyn (1) both disguised by awful looking beards. Maxwell Earle has gone home again. We had a great dinner with the Grenadiers on Christmas night. I thought of my darling little as I sat down. We were all Grenadiers and they did us right well. I drank their health in neat brandy which cured what you call 'a running about of the inside'. The first person I met in the campaign was Delaware (2) who had the impertinence to report that at Magersfontein the Guards were running away and if he dares to turn up in camp again I am going to have his blood. Another correspondent is Whigham's (3) brother who seems quite a decent fellow. Lord Methuen

wants us to get up cricket and football matches but I do not somehow feel inclined. The Boers are getting very funky at night. They blazed away for 20 minutes the night before last at absolutely nothing.

I suppose people in England are very much down at all our disasters. I think it is very lucky that they have not been worse as we have been blundered into a campaign without even a map of the country and with very false ideas as to the numbers opposed to us. I believe however that if we can give them a good licking in Natal, a great many of them will come over.

Good-bye my darling one with all my love, and your letter is the one thing in the week I look forward to.

Ever your most loving Harry

Notes
1. Captain Arthur St Leger Glyn, Grenadier Guards
2. Major Gilbert Sackville, 8th Earl De La Warr JP, DL (1869 –1915) 2nd Cinque Ports Volunteers.
3. Later General Sir Robert Whigham, GCB, KCMG, DSO (1865 – 1950). He was Major-General Macdonald's ADC. His brother was Second Lieutenant Julian Whigham in the Royal Scots Fusiliers.

As the New Year opened, the Guards Brigade was still in camp at the Modder River. Harold had his work cut out organizing a Brigade Gymkhana, which included a Driving Competition, an Obstacle Race and the strange sounding Oolta Poolta Race. Inactivity had fostered some bad habits such as gambling for large sums of money which had come to the attention of the GOC. He not only desired NCOs to check the practice but appealed to the men 'to bear in mind the liberal manner in which all classes in England, including the very poorest, are giving their money to aid their wives and families left at home.' A torrent of administrative instructions cascaded down from division, everything from the ration for forage for mules to the distribution of HM The Queen's Gift of Chocolate and a ban on bugling in camp.

Lord Roberts arrived in Cape Town on 10 January and told Buller to have another crack at relieving Ladysmith. At home it was increasingly thought that leadership in the field, at the highest level, was faulty. Buller, Gatacre and Methuen had all flung troops at camouflaged and entrenched Boer positions and failed to gather intelligence. Buller was anxious to jettison his newly founded title 'Sir Reverse' as opposed to 'Sir Redvers'.

Life in camp provided no end of duties for Harold coupled with frustration at the inaction. Clean drinking water was hard to come by and disease was a constant worry. Enteric fever or typhoid, characterised by a high temperature and abdominal pain, was becoming as great a threat, if not greater, than the Boers.[4] Add to this, dysentery and intestinal infections, and a number of 12,000 deaths can be arrived at.

23 January 1900
Modder

My dearest Mums,

I never answered your nice letter, but I have been kept very busy as we had a sense that the Boers were going to attack us, which of course was all humbug. But it made us scamper about a good deal. We really are comfortable here, plenty to eat and nice muddy water to drink which upsets most of the gents' tummies but so far I have not had a bad attack. It is a frightfully thirsty country owing to the heat and the sand and it is very difficult to keep off drinking. We are getting tired of being in the same place so long. This is supposed to be the maiden-head of Kimberley but I am afraid we have rather spoiled its appearance as we have had to chop down all the trees along the river to cook our victuals. The whole country is churned up into sand and when the wind blows one can hardly see 100 yards. The old Boers sit on a hill about 5 miles off, but luckily we have got some better guns than they have so they don't dare to show themselves too much. You can imagine we long to go on and finish up the job and our only consolation is they must be far more tired of sitting still than we are. Old Col Hall (1) whom you used to know at Colchester is in command of the artillery. He is a nice old gentleman but not enough of a dasher. We hear that nearly everyone one knows is coming out either with the yeomanry or with the corps of gentlemen but I suspect a great many of them will soon knock up. I am getting a regular old campaigner, sleep on the ground with my clothes on and a waterproof sheet and two blankets to keep me warm. It was a bit hard at first, but I sleep like a top now and I go to bed at 9pm and get up at 5am. Luckily my General is very particular as to what he eats, so I get good grub and consequently think I have got fatter than when I started.

Nothing more to tell you,

Your most affectionate Harold

4   Ancestry.com.au, *UK Casualties of the Boer War 1899–1902* <*https://www.ancestry.co.uk/search/collections/1912/*>

Note
1.   Lieutenant Colonel Francis Hall, Commanding Officer III Brigade, Royal Artillery (18, 62 and 75 Batteries) and staff, South Africa November 1899 to late 1901.

26 January 1900
Modder River

My dearest Mums,
Very many thanks for your letter of Jan 4th and all your home news interests me very much. I also heard all about you all from Dertha and she enjoyed the quiet of being with you immensely. I have got very little to tell you as we are still sitting looking at the Boers, without doing one another any harm. I believe we shall have to wait here for some time. The new regime of Roberts and Kitchener do not mean to make any mistakes but to concentrate on overwhelming force and advance up the Free State. We have had some torrential showers of rain and thunderstorms but the country is so dry that the day afterwards we have dust storms just the same. Thank you very much for sending me the meat lozenges. I will carry them with me. I have got a good big water bottle so I ought to get on first rate. Perhaps I shall meet Tatia's young man but there is already such a crowd of us that it is difficult to find anybody. We rather thought Roberts would come up here and have a look at us and at the Boer's hills but so far he has kept very quiet. We got a fresh draft of men from England today. They are all reserves now and looked very fat and well, many having been policemen. We are all very anxious about Ladysmith and we just fear that if Buller fails things will be serious. I think people in England thought things worse than they were, after all we only met with small disasters and nothing big. I think the Free Staters are getting very sick of the job and will soon want to be home to their farms. We all got our box of the Queen's chocolate. All the men are taking the chocolates out and sending the boxes home to their 'gals'.

Will you thank Alice (1) very much for her nice letter and tell her I hope to write to her soon.

I am still most flourishing, very thirsty at times and not wanting in appetite. Unless they move us soon I shall be as fat as poor old Digby (2) was. With best to all,
Your most affectionate Harold

Notes
1.   Harold's sister Alice Catherine.
2.   One of the Digby family who worked on the Spains Hall estate.

A series of letters from Harold in February continues the story.

2 February 1900
Modder River

My dearest Mums,
Very many thanks for your letter of January 17 and I am afraid I have very little to tell you except that I am still most flourishing.

The weather here has been cooler and we have had no scares of being attacked so we have had a peaceful time but I get plenty to do. I am out in the air really all day, cantering about on my ponies and there has been a certain amount of excitement as a lot of fresh troops have begun to pour in and we think Kitchener means to do something with us. Some of the younger ones have bought an old gun and shot pigeons and plover which they duly present to the General and so we have had some good eating. We are all very anxious about Ladysmith but we hope everything will go right. I am sorry to say my servant has gone in with the rheumatism I'm afraid but hope he will soon be alright again.

Much to my surprise young Thompson turned up today, he is Brigade Major of one of the newly formed brigades so has done very well for himself. I see from the papers that everyone is very angry with Lord Methuen because he made a blunder. Everyone has been very kind to the men, sending all sorts of presents, tobacco and knitted caps but what they appreciated most was the Queen's chocolate. They have eaten the chocolate and sent the boxes home to their young ladies. Days pass very quickly here and the weeks slip by and we are only reminded it is the end of the week by the much looked forward to amount of letters. I hope you are now getting better weather and able to get out of doors.
With best love to all,
Your most affectionate Harold.
We are all very anxious about Ladysmith and pray it may turn out alright

13 February 1900
Modder River

My dearest Mums,
I have been so busy the last few days that I have not had a moment to spare. Lord Roberts and all his staff have arrived here and they keep me busy night and day wanting all sorts of things. We have got a great lot of troops massed on the line and they are going to have an advance in force, but Lord Methuen and his original brigade have got to stop yet awhile

at the Modder, at which we are all very sorry, as we are very tired of this place. We had to move our camp at very short notice across the river which is what has made me so busy, as they are going to take away the Highland Brigade and put it in another division.

We are all very anxious about Ladysmith and pray it may turn out alright and I hope the big move they are making from here will be a success too and will go a long way towards polishing off the Free Staters anyhow. Lord Methuen is very down on his luck, and no wonder. If he reads the papers he must see some nice things about himself and I think that a good many people out here are much more inclined to stick up for him than they were. All sorts of odd people turn up here in various capacities. Will you send a line to my mother to say I am most flourishing. This is supposed to be the rainy season, but never a drop of rain do we get and there is nothing but dust and it is hotter than ever. All the brigade is now again in very good spirits and they turned out yesterday and cheered Lord Roberts like fun and he made them a little impromptu speech which they all liked. All our sick officers are getting on well; they have formed an officers' sanitorium 13 miles from Beaufort West. The Highland Brigade was sent out the other day to Koodosberg Drift (1) to go after some Boers, but the latter cleared off without being much damaged, and several of the poor Highlanders succumbed to a very long march and a fearfully hot day.

I am sorry I have had to hurry my letter so.

Your most affectionate Harold

Note

1. The Highland Brigade marched on 3 February to Koodosberg Drift, some distance west of the Modder River camp. After some stiff fighting, the hills commanding the Drift were seized, and the brigade was then ordered to rejoin the main body. Two Black Watch officers, Captain Eykyn and Lieutenant F G Tait, and two ORs were killed: seven ORs were wounded.

On 15 February, Dertha wrote to her father with the news of her brother Hamish (Cameron Highlanders) and his embarkation.

84 Eaton Place SW

Dearest Father,

I heard on Tuesday that the boarding was due to start at 4 o'clock, so I went there and got there about twelve. Hamish (1) and his lot, however, didn't arrive till past four instead of 9 a.m. They had got snowed up somewhere along the way. The wretched men had had nothing but a pie and coffee since 10 the morning before, and what with starvation and previous drink they looked ready to drop. The embarkation officer was cross because he couldn't make out that they had any officers at all and he kept roaring out: 'Who is in command of the Cameron Highlanders? Is there anyone?' I didn't see Hamish for very long as I had to leave at 5.30 as it was dark then and I couldn't stop the night there, so didn't see the boat actually start. Hamish looked very ruddy and cheerful.

The news today is better but I can't help thinking Cronje has slipped away somewhere north; there was one place he could get through.

The first time I went out to Gib with Harry was at the beginning of February. I came home without him at the end of May and then went back to see him off in the beginning of October. He started on the 25th on the Ghoorka and arrived at Cape Town on November 15th.

Harry's natural place just now is still his old place, but people seem to think that Sir H. Colvile will try and get him by hook or by crook on his staff, as he doesn't know how to do anything without him.
Your affectionate Dertha

Note
1.   Hamish (James), Dertha's younger brother and later 9th Duke of Atholl.
2.   This presumably was a draft sailing from England for the 1st Battalion Cameron Highlanders sailed from Egypt, where they had been stationed, on 3 March 1900, and arrived in South Africa twenty days later. They reached Bloemfontein in time to join the 21st Brigade under Major General Bruce Hamilton. The Camerons took part in many actions up to the occupation of Johannesburg. Seventy-three did not return.

Dertha was correct in her prediction that Colvile would get Harold 'by hook or by crook'. On 10 February, Colvile had been appointed to command the hastily formed 9th Division. For Harold, the handover marked the end of a demanding four months in the field on active service. Confronted by a determined and skilled enemy operating in a harsh and inhospitable terrain, Harold had excelled in his first staff appointment. New lessons from mule husbandry to improved sanitation in camp were learnt every day. Navigation based on poor maps and night marches with pack trains had proved particularly challenging; Harold had successfully resolved them. No wonder Colvile described him as 'a Staff Officer of the highest class'.

4

The 9th Division
A Commander and His Reputation, 11 February–21 March 1900

Composed of Major General Macdonald's[1] Highland Brigade (Black Watch, Argyll and Sutherlanders, Seaforths and Highland Light Infantry) and Major General Smith-Dorrien's[2] 19th Brigade (Shropshires, Gordons, Duke of Cornwall's Light Infantry, and the Canadian Regiment), Colvile began to assemble his staff for his hastily formed new division. He quickly put together a small team from those already on the spot. He chose Lieutenant Colonel Spencer Ewart of the Cameron Highlanders as his Chief of Staff[3] and Harold as one of his three Deputy Chiefs of Staff, another of whom was Major Edward the Count Gleichen,[4] a Grenadier contemporary of Harold who had been with the 3rd Battalion at Modder River. Captain George Nugent came over as his ADC.

Gleichen was a fascinating character. His father, the son of Queen Victoria's half-sister, had run away from school in Dresden and thanks to Queen Victoria had been allowed to join the Royal Navy. At one stage recommended for the VC in China, he was forced to retire on grounds of ill-health and set himself up as a sculptor in a studio in St James's Palace after losing all his money in a bank failure. He made a great success of his new profession and is perhaps best remembered for his monumental statue of Alfred the Great in Wantage. Edward had served with the 2nd Battalion in the Nile Campaign of 1884-1885 and on his return wrote a well-received memoir *With the Camel Corps up the Nile* (1888). At Modder River,

---

1   Later General Sir Hector MacDonald (1853-1903). During the Boer War he commanded the Highland Brigade and in 1902 became commander of British forces in Ceylon (modern day Sri Lanka). His celebrated career ended on 25 March 1903 when he shot himself in a Paris hotel room after homosexuality allegations in the newspapers.
2   Later General Sir Horace Smith-Dorrien, GCB, GCMG, DSO, ADC (1858-1930).
3   Later Lieutenant General Sir John Spencer Ewart KCB (1861-1930).
4   Later Major General Lord Gleichen KCVO CB CMG DSO (1863 -1937).

he had been shot in the neck and evacuated back to England to convalesce. In his Despatch of 1 December, Lord Methuen drew attention to 'the coolness shown by him throughout the engagement, especially in attending the wounded under fire' when the two Grenadiers with him Sergeant Brown and Private Martin, were both shot.

Gleichen was an apt choice for the new post of Divisional intelligence officer. Methuen had had little regard for battlefield intelligence, indeed his main intelligence asset, a large inflatable manned balloon, had not even been deployed before Magersfontein. If it had been, then the Boer trenches at the foot of the ridge would have been revealed. In the age of colonial wars against a vastly inferior enemy, intelligence may not have been a priority but in a war against a well-armed enemy of comparable profile to the British contingent it was essential to success.

On 13 February, Roberts told Colvile to take his division to Ramdam and from there to march via Waterval Drift to Jacobsdal which he was to occupy. The march got off to a bad start when it became clear that the mules were in no condition for a long trek. The decision was made to ditch the greatcoats and just keep the blankets. More problems followed when the ox transport was captured. Meanwhile Ewart and Harold turned their attention as to how to get the 4.7- inch guns, each towed by 36 oxen and 400 men on pull-ropes, across the Riet River. Fatigue parties of 200 men worked through the night. When they reached Jacobsdal, no sooner had they been ordered to proceed to Kimberly, when they were told to march to Klip Drift on the Modder and they finally set off at 10 p.m. and much to their surprise, at 4 a.m. the next day, met up with Kitchener who told them to follow him to Koedoesrand Drift that afternoon. After marching on and off for nearly thirty-six hours, the Division bivouacked at Klip Drift by the Modder River and apart from the sentries was soon fast asleep.

At 5 a.m. on 18 February, Ewart woke Colvile and told him the Boers were advancing from the east. This was the beginning of the battle of Paardeberg when Kitchener's two and a half divisions – nearly 15,000 men in all – faced off 7,000 Boers. The 11th Division found itself advancing up the Modder River; the Gordons, and Shropshires with a battery of guns crossed over onto the north bank and occupied the high ground at Gun Hill overlooking the Boer laager. Then the Canadians, the Duke of Cornwall's Light Infantry, the Seaforths and the Black Watch crossed the river and began to creep steadily through the scrub until they were within 500 yards of the enemy at which point they charged. It was an heroic effort but at a terrible cost: by nightfall, some 24 officers and 279 men were killed and 50 officers and 847 men wounded. They were the highest for any day in the war.

For the next week, the opposing forces spent their time either fortifying or, in the case of the 9th Division, extending their trenches. On 21 February, General Roberts seriously considered retiring to Klipkraal Drift west of Paardeberg. It was only when news reached him that afternoon that De Wet had abandoned the hill called Kitchener's Kopje, that he changed his mind and at 2.30 a.m. on 27 February, the 9th Division launched an all-out assault against the Boer laager. The Gordons and Canadians with a company of Royal Engineers infiltrated through the scrub to within 80 yards of the Boer trenches. After a prolonged firefight, the Boers surrendered. This time British casualties totalled 45 of which 12 only were killed. Cronjé finally surrendered with some 4,019 men and 50 women; around 10% of the Boers' entire army were now prisoners.

25 February 1900
Paardeburg

My own darling one,
We are now about 40 miles in the Free State and I don't get your letters which makes me very unhappy. I am now DAAG of the 9th Div commanded by Colvile and we had a very rapid march and a battle and we have bottled a lot of Boers in the bed of the river and are sitting round them, as we have not yet got up sufficient food for another advance. I have kept a sort of record of our movement for you, but I do not think you will be able to follow them very well, as the places won't be on the map.

I am taking advantage of a Sunday afternoon to write and think about you and long to hear what you have been doing. The hard work and the open air life agree with me and I keep wonderfully well though I have been wet through several times. Gleichen has just joined the division as intelligence officer so he and I will poke about together. We are bivouacked close to the Battlefield and the smell from dead oxen and horses is simply appalling. We have caught the Boers' convoy and our artillery fire slew their ponies and oxen in hundreds. However we have got as far away from the fighting as possible, so we are better off than some. The cavalry did very well didn't they? I think our friend Haig was the moving spirit of their march and I see they have just made him a Lt Col. Henderson (1) has already gone sick with malarial fever and it is not thought likely he will come back, so Mackenzie of the Staff College (2) is running the intelligence department. Whigham is in this division, ADC to Hector Macdonald. The Highland Brigade suffered very much the other day. Cuthbertson (3) is in command of the Black Watch and the Camerons are coming up to complete the brigade and I am wondering if Jimmy will be among them (4). We have heard no news from Ladysmith. Lord Roberts who is encamped just below us seems to think that Buller will succeed this time as we know a lot of troops have been drawn off to meet us here. We can't get on as fast as we should wish as food and ammunition cannot be brought up in good time. I must leave off darling

one, as I am sending this to Hd Qs on the chance of its being posted some time or other. Look after your precious self and God bless you.
Ever your most loving Harry

Note

1. Lieutenant Colonel GFR Henderson, Yorkshire and Lancashire Regiment, Director of Military Intelligence (1854-1903). He did not return on account of ill-health.
2. Later Major General Sir Colin Mackenzie KCB. Served as Intelligence Officer to Lord Roberts.
3. Lieutenant Colonel Archie Carthew–Yorstoun had been in command during the battle; Cuthbertson was a company commander.
4. The Camerons were to join the Highland Brigade in 9th Division meaning Hamish and Harold would be in the same division. Now all three of Dertha's brothers were fighting in South Africa.

28 February 1900
Koodo Rands Drift
Nr Paardeberg Drift

My own darling one,
I hear there is a mail going out this evening so I must send you a line. All our bothers were over yesterday as Cronje surrendered, and we had the pleasure of seeing 4,000 Boer Prisoners marched off to the Modder on route to Cape Town. We have now moved our camp closer to the river where there are some nice shady trees. We have also looted two Boer Wagons and put up awnings so we are in a land of peace and comfort for the time – but I expect we shall soon be on the go again. However we have scored our first real victory of the war and how the Boers lasted for so long I cannot imagine. The stink in their laager was something awful from the dead horses and oxen and the Boers practically lived under ground the whole time, they did not dare to show themselves. They really are the biggest cowards imaginable, all they can do is to dig a deep hole and sit in it and shoot until they are either stunk or starved out, they never dare come outside.(1) The Guards Brigade is at Klip Drift about 12 miles from here and they are attached to this division. The Cameron Highlanders are to be put into the Highland Brigade, so they will come under my eye. Darling, I have not had a letter from you for three weeks. I went to Hd Qrs about getting up our letters today, and they have promised to have them forwarded from the Modder. There is a rumour that the Free Staters won't fight much more, I think they are pretty sick of it and now that we are bagging all their cattle they don't half like it. Our great difficulty is getting up enough food for our enormous army. I must now leave off

darling one as they are shouting for me all over the place, and there is no peace or quiet to write you a nice letter.
Ever your most loving Harry

Note
1.   Colvile had a somewhat different view: 'Cooped day and night in their deep narrow trenches, out of which they can rarely have stirred, in the midst of that appalling smell [decaying animals], it struck me that, grand as is the devotion that makes our men stand up to the heaviest fire, there was something very admirable in the dogged determination that held these men at their posts during those ten weary days and nights, and that perhaps we are too apt to look upon our own particular brand of courage as the only genuine sort'.

Harold next wrote from Osfontein, five miles up the Modder River where the division had moved after Paaderberg.

5 March 1900
Osfontein Farm

My own darling wee,
I am more than hap I have got three letters from you all at once and the last is Jan 27. So I am now hoping to get another one directly. We are still close to the place where we fought the battle, but a little higher up the Modder River and well away from all the stink of dead horses and cattle. I should think a tremendous feeling of relief must have gone through the country when the people heard of Ladysmith, and according to Reuter the peops in London went quite mad. We have now pitched our bivouac on the river bank and everything is very nice except the most awful thunderstorms with sheets of rain which wet you through to the skin in a minute, and your poor man has to sleep in a pool of water, but it is an extraordinary climate. The next morning you are none the worse. We have now got into a much more open country with nice rolling grassy downs and very few kopjes. There are still some Boers in front of us – said to be about 5,000 but no one knows if they will stop to fight. We ought to have at least 3 divisions by the time we have concentrated about 21,000 men, so if there are only 5,000 we ought to catch them like we did old Cronje. We have to stop here as we cannot get enough food up, Kitchener who was called Lord K. in Egypt is dubbed Lord Chaos now, and Lord Methuen has now been christened Lord Let-you-in. It was very nice of Colville putting my name in his despatches wasn't it?
Did you ever read such rot as Methuen wrote? I am delighted Frankie is at last coming out, but I am more than horrified to hear that Campbell is coming as brigadier – I think it is perfectly monstrous that 4,000 men

should be entrusted to him to be murdered. I have been very anxious about Bardie and Geordie but I hope it is alright with them as I have heard nothing. And now, darling, I hope all your anxieties are over – at least for a time. They seem to think that the Free Staters won't fight much more, but I don't believe anything I hear, as the Free Staters so far have fought just as well as the Transvaalers. We rather expect to move tomorrow to Marau's Drift about 5 miles on but we don't know for certain. Darling one, I do not like your being by yourself in London, do get someone to keep you company. I did not get the deed of sale for Sanders Farm (1) – will you write and ask Archie for it. I am very glad I have got back my 300£ so I shall not have to rob my wee of so much.

With all my love, ever your most loving Harry

Note

1. Staceys Farm at Broomfield is also known as Saunders Farm. There is another Saunders Farm at Eye in Suffolk.

On 7 March, the division moved towards Poplar Grove Drift in pursuit of De Wet and his commando. When the British infantry came into view about 8 a.m. the next day, the 1,500 Boers immediately began to withdraw to Driefontein. It was here that the 9th Division arrived on the evening of 10 March and witnessed the aftermath of the Boers' final attempt at preventing Lord Roberts from capturing Bloemfontein, the capital of the Orange Free State. Elements of the Cavalry Division encountered the Driefontein defences early on 10 March and alerted the 6th Infantry Division. The British had not fallen into the trap of frontally assaulting the position, and finding the cavalry working around his flank, de Wet was forced to hurriedly redeploy his force to counter this threat. At about midday the 18th Brigade launched their attack, taking their objectives with ease as the Boers had fallen back. At 2 p.m., the infantry assaulted the main republican positions, with the men of the Essex Regiment driving the burghers before them at bayonet point.

Total British casualties at Driefontein were 438, including 87 killed. A war correspondent who had been there throughout the battle recorded 'the Boer loss was heavier than either side had (so far as was known) suffered up to that date. We buried 170 Boers on the two ridges, and 42 were later found and buried on the nek where our guns had caught them in retirement.'[5]

---

5   *On This Day in 1900* <https://www.chrisash.co.za/2019/03/10/on-this-day-in-1900-battle-of-driefontein/#_edn12> (accessed 3 February 2023).

With de Wet's force thus shattered, the way to Bloemfontein was open and Roberts made his formal entry into the capital of the Orange Free State on 13 March

By 16 March Harold had arrived at Bloemfontein. By this stage in the war London had been forced to recognise the need for substantial reinforcements to be sent to South Africa. The Boer was a brave and wily fighter. The landscape was often unforgiving, the Boer was hard to pin down, disease was a real threat and British losses significant. There was however a sense of profound relief that Kimberley and Ladysmith had been relieved. The latter siege had lasted 118 days and many felt it should have been relieved earlier. Nearly 400 civilians and soldiers had died from disease, mainly typhoid fever. There was a growing sense that fortunes had changed – the Boers had been pushed back and the British had advanced into Orange Free State.

However, trouble still lay ahead and not far from where Harold was to write to his mother.

16 March 1900
Bloemfontein

My dearest Mums,
Very many thanks for your two letters which I got this morning. Well, we have arrived here all safe and sound after some very hard marches and with very little fighting. The only time we thought we should have a tussle was at Poplar Grove when the Boers all bolted in full view of our guns, and our cavalry and artillery horses were so tired and done that they could not catch them. However the 9th Division caught one of their guns which was left by itself on the top of a hill. We have got into a much nicer country, grass nice and green and with nice farmhouses surrounded by trees, but very far apart. After leaving Poplar Grove we marched to Dreifontein , Aswogol Kop , Vonters Vlai (1) and a little railway at Fererra's Spruit from where we had a nice easy march into our present bivouac just south of Bloemfontein. The town is quite English, all the shopkeepers have English names and notices and you hear nothing but English spoken. It lies right in a hole and I much prefer to bivouac on the veldt to stopping in any of the houses. There are a few things in the shops, but all at ruinous prices, 10 shillings for a bottle of very bad whisky, but one can buy bread – a great luxury after biscuit – and some fresh butter. I have got a bit thinner after my march but shall soon get fat again as we shall wait here for 3 weeks or so as the Guards Brigade is resting which means that I shall be invited to share their good cheer. I don't think the Boers have much more fight in them, a great many never wanted the war at all and are only too glad to go back to their farms, but I think the more

ignorant of them will probably want to fight again. But if they will only stop and not run away we may be able to catch a lot more of them.

Will you thank Flo very much for her little parcel of most useful articles and also for her two letters. I will try and answer them now we have a little rest.

I have no more to say. With best wishes to all and I shall keep most flourishing.

Your most affectionate Harold

Note
1.   Ventersvlei.

On the same day Dertha wrote to the Duke:

16 March 1900
29, Devonshire Street

Dearest Father,

Thank you for your letter. I really feel alright now, but they won't let me walk about for fear of my throat bleeding, or catching cold, or something equally unpleasant. I really hope things will settle down in Africa now – but every day they keep sending more troops out. I am glad Geordie will be with Harry's lot, though I don't quite like the idea of General Macdonald. I saw in a letter of Sir H. Colville's that if he (Macdonald) was allowed to carry out his plans, he would have uncommonly little brigade left. I missed hearing from Harry last week. I dare say I shall have two this time. I will send you them on as soon as they get interesting.

I am to stay in this house another week and then a week in London with Lady Colville and then country. Kitty I see is still hanging about. I shall believe she is going to Blair when she actually gets there – not before!

Your affectionate Dertha

16 March 1900
Bloemfontein

My own darling wee one,

I have not got another letter from you but I am hoping one will arrive daily, and I am quite ashamed to say I forgot where I wrote to you last from. After we had polished off old Cronje the Boers entrenched themselves about 8 miles off at Poplar Grove on the Modder, so we went for them the 9th Division on the N bank, the 6th and 7th Divs with

Guards Brigade on S bank. The result was that they literally bolted as hard as they could, in spite of old Kruger who had come down to urge them on. We then halted for a day and they decided to make a dash for the railway. So we had 4 long weary marches. The 6th Div was engaged on our left at Driefontein, but we did not come under fire. Yesterday we marched the remaining 6 miles and bivouacked on a slope just south of Bloemfontein, which was captured without a shot being fired. Nearly all the inhabitants are English people, the few Dutchmen that are in the town have mostly been drunk since our arrival. I have hardly been into the town yet but there are some nice houses and trees, the General and Nugent have gone to live in one but I am glad to say he thought I had better stay with the division so I sleep on a nice grassy site overlooking the town. The General has broken up our mess and, Mummie, I am very glad. It is the incarnation of selfishness and always cursing his servants, that at last I really quite dreaded a meal. I was only too glad to get away though I shan't get nearly as good food. At the same time he has been very nice to me always, but I didn't like him at meal times. I find everyone gets very selfish on active service and I expect you will find I have too, and you will have to scold me out of it.

I dare say you will have heard that Geordie has applied to come to the Black Watch, so I hope he will. Our division in future is to consist of the Guards Brigade and the Highland Brigade, the same as we were at Magersfontein.

The Guards Brigade are encamped next door to us, they had some very long marching and say they had to do 40 miles in 24 hours. And Roberts had intended they should march into Bloemfontein with him, but somehow or other through some mistake they were left outside. I wish we could get Frankie into our division. But I don't think we could do much with old Campbell [6](1). It was a perfect disgrace giving him a brigade, and Wolsey[7] ought to be hung. We have seen no newspapers later than 2 February so we are a bit short of news. But the Grenadiers and Scots Gds have gone down the line to clear it, so I hope we shall soon have some newspapers.

And now darling Mummy I can't help thinking that it may not be very long before I get back to you. I do not think the Free Staters will fight much more and we shall have an overwhelming force I hope – if ever they try to bar the way. But still we are a long way off Pretoria yet, and we may have to march every yard of the way. The people here seem very

---

6   Major General Barrington Bulkeley Campbell, KCB, CVO, DL (1845-1918).
7   Later Field Marshal Garnet Wolseley, 1st Viscount Wolseley, KP, GCB, OM, GCMG, VD, PC (1833 – 1913)

friendly – bringing vegetables, eggs etc and we have had some good food. I enjoyed eating some of President Steyn's own pet potatoes and carrots. Goodbye, my own darling one.
Ever your most loving Harry

23 March 1900
Bloemfontein

My own darling wee,
Thank you very much for your letter of the 23 and I can't help fussing about the operation to your throat. I tried to get a telegram through yesterday asking if you were all right, and I hope I shall get an answer from you, as I can't bear to think of   your being in pain and being by yourself in a hospital – so you must not mind my worrying, as I simply hate even a doctor hurting you. I only hope I shall get a wire from you, and not have to wait for nearly a month before I hear how you are.

You must not scold me for not telling you things as you know I am not in the least afraid of your gossiping, and I try and tell you anything that I think will interest you, but honestly I think the people at home know more about things than we do. We are now settling down here in our bivouac, the General and Nugent live in the town. It is now getting very cold at nights and I am very glad to sleep in a tent which we bagged from the Boers at Poplar Grove. I believe the army is going to be reorganised and we are much disturbed at the idea of their breaking up our division. There is some talk of a Guards Division. 6 battalions of Guards and 2 of colonials, also of the Guards and Highland brigades being in a division together, but our Sir H Colville is not very popular with the Guards Brigade or with its General – Pole Carew. I think people on active service ought to be prepared to do what they are told, and not let themselves be influenced by personal questions. I think that the best plan would be to have the Guards and Highlanders together and increase the Guards Brigade by the 2 battalions coming out. I hear that old Boer is not going to be allowed to come north of the Orange River. I have now got into a sort or restless mood – I'm not sure that it is not because I want to get done with this war and come home to my mum – I hate sitting still like we are now but I am afraid it is necessary as all the horses are completely knocked up, and there are 4000 more expected here to fill up again.

I heard your Geordie had applied to come back to the Battn of the Black Watch so I hope he will come by here. I think he must be all right again as I have heard several people say that he is none the worse.

Campbell (Camerons) (1) the new ADC to the General has just turned up. I must say I do not envy him his billet, and I pity George

Nugent tremendously. Luckily I have nothing to do with the General's comforts and I keep well out of the way and consequently he is always very nice to me, partly I think because he knows I am not a bit afraid of him. I see it does not mention our division at all in the account of the Paardeburg fight, but all the correspondents were 20 miles off (much to their disgust) with Lord Roberts. The number of casualties is due to Kitchener, who like every other general buys experience at the expense of soldiers. We ought not to have had more than 100 casualties, and we could have done all we wanted with less. Our division just came on the battlefield at Driefontein in the evening, and we only saw all the shells bursting. We picked up 103 dead Boers and we hear they looked upon it as a big defeat. I hope I shall hear you are alright darling one before long, with all my love.

Ever your most loving Harry

It was very good of Colvile mentioning me twice in despatches wasn't it? I wonder if the Magersfontein despatch will ever come out? Did you ever read such rot as Methuen's despatches, and besides they are not true. I think he is cracky and I hear he is heartbroken at having his division taken away from him.

Note

1.   Captain John Campbell, Cameron Highlanders

28 March 1900
Bloemfontein

My own darling wee,
I got your nice letter of March 2nd alright and I was very glad to get a wire to say you were quite well. I had a frightful difficulty in getting a telegram through, but I am quite repaid by knowing you are alright. Darling one you must forgive me for not telling you that I was scratched at the Modder. I did not want to frighten my wee, and I thought that only four or five people knew I had been hit. It happened in this way, the general and I were standing close to a machine gun of the 1st Bn Coldstream, when what we call the Pom Pom (1) put a shell into the middle of us, and a splinter went through the seat of my breeches and just cut the skin and bruised me a little. It was nothing at all, and I thought that if I told you, you would always be thinking that I would be hit whenever there was a fight. I expect by this time you know that I was with the 9th Divn and present at Paardeberg; all the same I can't help wishing I was back with the Guards Brigade, as I feel thoroughly at home

with them, and a Brigade Major has more work to do than a DAAG but still I suppose I am lucky really.

Geordie turned up to my surprise the other morning, he looked very pale and rather thin, as he really has not quite got over his attack of dysentery, but already his cheeks have begun to fill out, and he gets better daily. I took him out for a walk on Sunday, and he was seized with a bad stomach ache, but it leaked out that he had been eating pork for luncheon, which is enough to irritate the strongest stomach. He is living not a 100 yds from where I live, but he has got all his Indian equipment and is much more comfortable than I am, as he has a bed to sleep on. I am going to make him come out riding with me in the afternoons, so that he does not get too lazy. He has kept a capital diary of the siege of Ladysmith, which I read with the greatest interest.

One of the worst calamities of the war happened the other day and I dare say you have seen all about it in the newspapers. Crabbe, Codrington, Trotter and Lygon were out riding requisitioning cattle and food, when 4 Boers appeared on the skyline and Crabbe shouted to the others to pursue, and they went like madmen close to the kopje where of course these Boers had dismounted and shot them all down at about 300 yds. Poor Lygon killed, Crabbe with a bullet through his forearm breaking both bones, Trotter with his forearm smashed and amputated, Codrington with a bullet through his groin. Did you ever hear of anything so miserable, and another life simply thrown away. Crabbe is going on very well as is Codrington and both hope to be about again in 8 weeks. Trotter is doing as well as can be expected and is in very good spirits and most plucky. (2) We are still in camp S of Bloemfontein, waiting for the railway to be mended. At present we have got nothing up except food, and no luxuries are yet purchasable. We shall have to wait till the second week in April before we can move and then I expect our progress will be very slow as the Boers have blown up the line all the way between here and the Vaal. Old Kruger is said to be putting all the Free Staters who won't fight into prison in Pretoria, so I expect they won't fight very seriously when we do tackle them. I drank your health on your birthday, mum, I don't believe you remembered mine. Bee has been very kind in sending me out flannel shirts and socks and handkerchiefs and I don't know what I should have done without them. Some of my underclothing is rather ragged but it will have to last until I get home. I got a new pair of breeches and boots all right so outwardly I can be quite smart. With all my love,

Ever your most loving Harry

Notes
1. The 37mm one-pound Maxim Nordenfeldt fired a comparatively small shell that the British had thought too heavy for a machine gun and too light for an

artillery piece. The Boers, however, thought it a good light support weapon and with smokeless powder it was hard to detect. The weapon also had a demoralising effect as no whistling noise heralded arrival. Lieutenant Lygon, the Adjutant of the 3rd Battalion Grenadier Guards, wrote in his diary 'the Boer had an infernal machine ... which terrified us'[8]. Ammunition generally came in 25 round belts, about 125 or 150 rounds constituting first-line ammunition. Bursts were usually five rounds and ammunition was usually common shell (that is high explosive) or shrapnel. Given the sound it made with one round per second it became known as the 'pom-pom'.

2.   On 15 March, the 3rd Battalion Grenadiers and 1st Battalion Scots Guards entrained for Springfontein to join hands with Gatacre. This was done without any fighting, and the brigade was shortly afterwards stationed at Glen, north of Bloemfontein. It was here that the unfortunate affair occurred when (on 23rd March) Colonel Crabbe, Captain Trotter, and Lieutenant the Hon Robert Lygon of the Grenadiers, and Colonel Codrington, Coldstream Guards, rode eight or nine miles beyond their camp without an escort except one trooper. They were fired on: Lygon was killed, and the others all severely wounded. The Boers took care of them and sent them back to British lines the next day.

Dertha was a 'straight talking lady' and she certainly didn't hold back from sharing her opinions with the Duke.

28 March 1900
Wellington Court,
Albert Gate SW

Dearest Father,

I am sending you a copy of Harry's last two letters. I have also been allowed to copy a letter of Sir H. Colvile's which I thought would interest you. Of course it is not meant to be shown. He says in another part of his letter that Ewart the AAG is doing very well and that what he doesn't know, Harry teaches him! He complains rather about General Macdonald whose only idea is rushing at everything and doesn't understand the game. He says the Highland Brigade fought splendidly. I have since heard and seen in the papers that it was Kitchener who was responsible for their false move – wasn't that a stupid affair of Col Crabbe and Col Codrington? I heard this morning from Mrs Trotter that her son has had his arm amputated. Everybody is furious with the two Colonels and it may spoil their chance of getting a C.B.

Col Riccardo (1) and Col Currie and Col Fludyer (2) are holding sort of indignation meetings because they have been passed over for

8   Grenadier Guards Library: Hon. E.H. Lygon diary, 26 October 1899-21 March 1900, privately published, n.d.

Col Mildmay Wilson (3) as Major General. They were passed over two months ago and when they remonstrated they were told it couldn't be given to another Guardsman just now, so this is adding insult to injury! It is rather odd, but one couldn't find three stupider men to command their regiments.

I go to Spains today.

Your affectionate Dertha

Notes

1. Colonel Horace Ricardo, Grenadier Guards.
2. Colonel Henry Fludyer, Scots Guards (1847-1920). He commanded the 2nd Battalion, Scots Guards 1892-1896 and the regiment from 1 June 1898.
3. Dertha is confused. Henry Trotter was the Major General commanding the Guards Regiments and the Home District; Colonel Mildmay W. Wilson, Scots Guards, had commanded a Scots Guards Battalion in 1899.

29 March 1900
Bloemfontein

My dearest Mums,

I hear that there is a mail going out today, so I must just send you a line to say that I am most flourishing and getting fat again with only rest here. There is not much going on by way of amusement. There is a cricket ground but the weather is inclined to be unsettled with very heavy rainstorms. Luckily I have got a tent to keep dry in. We secured it from the Boer trenches at Poplar Grove and it has proved a great blessing. Our meals are taken in a shelter formed by two waggons with a cover stretched across, so we are fairly comfortable. We are also in possession of a cow and a calf which we bagged on the march and which gives us fresh milk in the morning and we can buy a limited amount of fresh butter. All the inhabitants seem to have settled down quite peaceably and we might be in England if it was not for the blacks. I went out shooting yesterday with another fellow. I gave him the gun and I rode along as beater. We secured three Koraw (1), a sort of black game, but my pal shot very close to me once, so I shall keep further off him in the future. The Guards Brigade are bivouacked alongside us, but they have been sent away, the Grenadiers and the Coldstream to the Modder about 12 miles north and the Scots Guards to Edenburg about 30 miles south. We hear that old Kruger has annexed the Orange Free State, which I think would make the Staters angry, but I believe the old rascal will fight to the end as Pretoria is full of ammunition and provisions. So we may have a long job before us yet, but I hope the fighting will soon be over. No more to say.

With best love to all,

Your most affectionate Harold

Note
1.   The southern black korhaan (*Afrotis afra*), also known as the black bustard.

30 March 1900
Bloemfontein

My own darling little wee,
It is mail day and I must send you another line though I really have nothing to say. We are still quietly sitting here, waiting for the bridges over the Orange River to be mended before we can get up sufficient food and ammunition to resume an advance. There was a small skirmish yesterday about 19 miles from here, not far from where they wounded old Crabbe. I hope they gave the Boers a good doing but I hear we lost about 100 wounded. I saw Col Mackinnon (1) the day before yesterday and he told me all about my mum, which I was very glad to hear. I am sorry to say he has gone away again, but eventually he and the CIV are to form part of a new division the 10th, and to take part in the advance. I can't make out if Frankie has started yet from London, I am so afraid that they will leave him in Cape Colony and that he won't get up to the front. I am going to try to do my best to get him out of old Bar's (2) hands, but my best is but little I am afraid. I look upon that old wretch as the personification of what Napier calls a 'military murderer' – if only he ever gets the chance – and I trust that he will not be allowed to cross the Orange River. Mum, I don't think much of Lady Dudley's daughter in law (3). Don't you think I am one of the luckiest men you know in having a little wee who gives up everything for her great lump, I does. Geordie is getting better daily, he grows more like his father every time I see him, and he has a got the ducal bend behind. I am still rather anxious to hear about your throat, and you have got to write and tell me all about it, and how the nasty docs bullied you. The General has got a new ADC Campbell in the Camerons, a brother in law of Joan's I suppose. He seems a very nice fellow but I should think he is rather bored with the job. I never see the General at all now but I work away for him all the same, and he really does appreciate it as he always mentions me in his despatches whenever he can, and if you hear people abusing him as I expect you will, you must stick up for him. I hear London is full of a horrendous quarrel which is supposed to have taken place between the Gen. and Methuen at the Modder. Of course this is all a lie, and you must contradict it. I am very sorry for Lord M. He thinks he has been badly used and is now raking up all that is past to try and find excuses. I am very disgusted with his despatches, though he did mention me, and I think he would do much better if he acknowledged he made mistakes. Old Gatacre is not allowed to come up to the front at all, a real good punishment for the old madman, and he is off to guard the

lines of communication. I do not believe there is a single Egyptian Hero who has done well so far. I hear Hilliard (4), too, is not a great success, and I am very sorry.

Goodbye my precious mum and God bless you.

Ever your most loving Harry

Note

1. Colonel Mackinnon, City Imperial Volunteers (Yeomanry), formerly Grenadier Guards.
2. Harold is referring to Major General Barrington Campbell.
3. Lady Dudley, Dertha's aunt, had two daughters-in-law at the time – Rachel née Gurney and Evelyn née Crichton, daughter of 4th Earl Erne of Crom Castle.
4. General Sir Henry Hildyard GCB (1846-1916).

On the afternoon of 30 March, Colvile was sent for by General Roberts and ordered to join General Broadwood's 2nd Cavalry Brigade which was retiring to the Modder River Waterworks.[9] After a last-minute round up of fit mules, at 5.30 a.m. the next morning the division set off towards Boesman's Kop, planning to arrive at Waterval Drift by late afternoon. Shortly before reaching Springfield, they heard the sound of artillery fire coming from the direction of Boesman's Kop about a four-hour march away. Colvile and his staff including Harold made their way forward on horseback as quickly as they could and by 11.15 a.m., they had linked up on the top of Boesman's Kop with Colonel Henry Martyr's Mounted Infantry Brigade. From this point they had a good view of the battle at Waterval Drift or Sannah's Post as it became known. Martyr told Colvile that Broadwood had got clear of the enemy and was reforming about two miles away, having lost his all baggage and seven of his 12-pdr guns. Harold was sent to inform Broadwood that the 9th Division would be at the Drift by 2 p.m. and in the meantime he was to come to Divisional HQ to be briefed along with the two brigade commanders.

It was past noon when Colvile's two brigades caught up with him at Boesman's Kop. They had been on the go since 4 a.m., so he ordered the transport to be watered and the men to fill their water bottles and eat their packed meal. In Colvile's opinion, there was no point in throwing his men on the Boer rearguard six hours after the loss of Broadwood's guns which by now were at least eight miles away. Harold arrived back with his report. Broadwood had told him that he was too tired to come, so after questioning some of the officers Harold had ridden eastwards to the unmolested outpost line facing the Waterworks. There was no sign of the retreating Boers. He told Colvile that the 2nd Cavalry Brigade was thoroughly exhausted, and would, he feared, be unfit for any further operations

9   Lieutenant General Robert Broadwood, CB (1862 – 1917)

that day. As the division prepared to march off again at 1 p.m., Colvile sent Harold back to Broadwood to bring him up to date and give him a chance of co-operating if his men were fit enough to do so.

The 9th Division marched off for Waterval Drift and soon came into contact with the Boers. Some canny outflanking movements persuaded the enemy to melt away but there was no sign of French's cavalry which Roberts had promised Colvile. They turned up the next day by which time but they were too late to interdict the Boers, who still held the Waterworks and Mamena. The division helped Major Porter's Cavalry Brigade attend to some of Broadwood's wounded and then wisely fell back on Boesman's Kop and concentrated there on the evening of 1 April. They marched to Springfield the next day and on the morning of 3 April reached their old camping ground at Bloemfontein.

At Sannah's Post, the British had suffered 159 casualties and had 373 men captured along with artillery and over 100 wagons and ammunition. It was hardly surprising that Colvile and Broadwood were not on speaking terms; the former thought Broadwood's versions of events verged on fiction for Winburg's Commando numbered more like 1,500 rather than the 5,000 claimed in his despatches and furthermore he had never given Harold a message about the best line of advance; the latter held that Colvile, although aware of the urgency of the situation, had been too cautious and arrived too late.

Some three months later, in a despatch dated 19 June, Roberts considered that Colvile 'would have done better, if on his arrival with the 9th Division at Boesman's Kop, he had at once proceeded to the scene of the engagement and ascertained personally how matters stood before deciding on the flank movement to Waterval Drift'. Broadwood was exonerated. At the time and in hindsight, this was an erroneous conclusion, fostered by the discrepancies in timings between the two generals' reports and by Broadwood's account of his conversations with 'a staff officer' i.e. Harold. Broadwood had written in his report that 'About noon a staff officer arrived from GOC 9th Division to say he had reached Boesman's Kop. I suggested that a direct advance on the spruit offered the best chance of assisting. About 2 p.m. I was informed that the 9th Division had moved towards Waterval Drift so seeing any hope of recapturing the guns at an end, I began sending the units to their camps as owing to the loss of the baggage train it was inadvisable to bivouac where we were'.

Harold chose to differ from Broadwood and submitted his own report.

'On arrival at Boesman's Kop I was sent forward by the GOC to Brigadier General Broadwood. I rode forward for about two to three miles and found Broadwood and delivered my message which was to the effect that the GOC wished to see him at once. The latter at once replied that he and his horse were so done up that he could not come. Finding that I was unable to obtain any information from him, I went to a squadron of Life Guards and found out what had happened, and also to a squadron of mounted infantry who were on higher ground to the right. I could then see a large force of Boers some two miles ahead the numbers were estimated by the Mounted Infantry at 2,000 to 3,000. I then rode back to the GOC and reported what Birdwood[10] had said, and also that as far as I could see the only way of driving out the Boers was either to cross the river and turn to their right or to make a turning movement round their left. I believe that the GOC had – by the time I got back there – already issued orders that the Division was to march on Waterval Drift and cross the river, and I heard subsequently that he had received a telegram from the Chief of Staff that he was to cross the river and cut off the Boer retreat to the north.

'I was then sent back to Broadwood to tell him of the GOC's intentions, and the former told me to inform the latter that he wished to retire and bivouac at Springfield. After the 9th Division had secured the drifts, I was sent back with a written order to Broadwood to bivouac at Boesman's Kop, but I met him on his way to the GOC who promptly gave him his orders. I should like to add that on the arrival of the 9th Division the Boer right extended along the Modder north of Waterval Drift and that there was a gun in position close to the Drift. This is written purely from my recollections of what had occurred'. H. Ruggles-Brise, Kroonstadt, 20 May 1900.

Roberts appears either to have been hoodwinked or had chosen to turn a blind eye or, more likely, had not been shown Harold's statement.

The 9th Division was then charged with planning the defence of Bloemfontein but no sooner had Colvile and his staff started, the order came through to march to Rietfontein with Porter's 1st Cavalry Brigade and two Horse Artillery batteries and from there to push on to Leeuwkop where a large meeting of Boers was said to be taking place. With their boots by now in shreds, the division wearily set off to rendezvous with Porter at his bivouac. Although it was only 11 miles as the crow flies, there was no sign of Porter's brigade when they got there and it was entirely by luck that in the pitch black of the Veld night Gleichen had come across it in a hollow off the main road. By midnight the rearguard and baggage train finally stumbled in. The next day the division found no sign of the Boer gathering and set off back to Rietfontein and then Bloemfontein.

10   Brigade Major of Porter's Cavalry Brigade, later Field Marshal Lord Birdwood, GCB, GCSI, GCMG, GCVO, CIE, DSO (1865 – 1951)

More bad news awaited them. On 2 April, 600 men of the Royal Irish Rifles and a mounted company of the Royal Fusiliers had left Dewetsdorp for Reddersburg[11], a town 40 miles south of Bloemfontein, to 'proclaim the Queen's Peace' and encourage the Boer farmers to surrender their arms. Much to their surprise they found themselves up against de Wet and his 4,000-strong Commando. Called to surrender, Captain McWhinnie[12] declined. After a very uncomfortable night with little food and water, at dawn on 4 April, de Wet and his Boers closed in and overran part of the fusiliers' position. So close were the Boer riflemen that when Bugler Longhurst attempted to dash five yards from an exposed position to a safer one he fell dead into his chosen spot with nine bullets in his body. Later when the infiltrating Boers split what was left of the defensive position, McWhinnie surrendered. The Rifles' losses totalled nine killed, 26 wounded and 388 taken prisoner, with the Fusiliers' casualties numbering some 14.[13]

Whilst Reddersburg and Watevall Drift might be regarded as minor setbacks when framed in the wider context of British progress, they reflected major mistakes which Harold addressed when next writing to Dertha.

6 April 1900
Bloemfontein

My own darling wee,
I was horrified to hear that you had to undergo such a severe operation, but Kitty and Frankie Lloyd wrote to me and told me that you were going on very well. So I hope, darling one, by this time you will be almost right again and I am looking forward to getting a letter from you tomorrow to tell me all about it, and I doesn't like to think of my precious one suffering.

We have been having a very busy time. You will have heard of our disaster near the Bloemfontein Watervaal. Another Egyptian hero has blundered (1) and though a great deal of blame should be thrown on to the HQ staff, convoys and guns should not be sent through a drift without an escort. Our division was sent out to support Broadwood, we started at daybreak and got to Watervaal drift at dark, with our men very tired. Gen French came the next morning and we made a demonstration against the waterworks and got out all our wounded about 37. We were then ordered to return to Bloemfontein.

---

11   The Battle of Stromberg
12   Capt W.J. McWhinnie, Royal Irish Rifles.
13   *Royal Irish Rifles losses at Reddersburg, South Africa* <https://www.royal-irish.com/events/royal-irish-rifles-losses-at-reddersberg-south-africa> (accessed 11 July 2023)

We thought we were going to have a rest. But the next morning we suddenly got an order to march to Rietfontein about 13 miles SE of Bloemfontein. The intelligence Department had heard there was going to be a meeting of Boer generals on the top of a hill. So the next day we made a reconnaissance round the hill with Porter's 1st Cavalry Brigade (2), saw about 200 Boers who were dispersed by the Horse Batteries, and went back to our bivouac, where we were rained on from 2 p.m. to 8 p.m. This morning we again marched back to Bloemfontein, having marched some 90 odd miles in the week without much result. Now all we want for the division is a little rest, all the men are nearly shoeless and though we have been here 3 weeks we are again in just the same state as when we arrived. We have had another small disaster near Reddersburg where about three companies got surrounded and it is believed they have all been made prisoners. It is most annoying having all these petty disasters. I think the general opinion out here is that we have got a rotten HQ staff who mismanage details. As long as our troops keep concentrated no Boers have come within 10 miles, but if we push small bodies out they only get cut up. Hamish turned up with his battalion and bivouacked about 50 yards from me, and Geordie is still on the other side. Isn't it curious that we should have been plumped down so close to one another. Unfortunately before Jimmy had been here more than a day, he was suddenly ordered off in the middle of the night and I believe he marched with Gatacre to try and relieve these companies at Reddersburg. Geordie came with us to Rietfontein. He is now very well and though we got a good ducking yesterday, and he a very bad one as he had to go on outposts, he says he is none the worst this morning.

I hear some ladies have come up here, Lady Edward Cecil (3), Lady Hampton, which I am very sorry to hear as at present Bloemfontein is not the place for ladies. Wounded men are continually being brought in and the sanitary arrangements in camps are not nice for lady's eyes. I must now leave off, darling one, I have just had time to do my official writing since we marched in and to write this before the mail goes. I have not changed my clothes or washed for 3 days. I have never yet attempted to grow a beard but sometimes I don't get time to shave for 2 or 3 days. The old Boers have cut off the water supply so it is very difficult to get any water at all, and it is rather funny – we cannot have tea this evening as the water has been forgotten.

Goodbye my precious,

Ever your most loving Harry

Note
1. Major General Gatacre had fought with Kitchener in the Sudan. After the disaster at Reddersberg, he was sent back to England.
2. Brigadier General T C Porter, 6th Dragoon Guards (Carabiniers)
3. Lady Cecil nee Violet Maxse, wife of Lieutenant Colonel Lord Edward Gascoyne-Cecil, Grenadier Guards. On 3 July 1899, Colonel Baden-Powell was informed by Wolseley at the War Office that he should leave immediately for Mafeking taking Lord Edward as his Chief Staff Officer. They sailed on 8 July, Cecil taking Violet with him.

Harold writes wrote again on 11 and 14 April respectively.

11 April 1900
Bloemfontein

My own darling wee one,
I have been thinking about you a great deal, and all my letters by the last mail have gone wrong and I have not heard a word about you. So I am now on the point of wiring every day. But I hope you have been going on alright, and by this time are able to get about again.

Since I last wrote we have been sitting quietly in camp, resting men and horses, and awaiting drafts to file up. The Highland Brigade is only about 1500 strong instead of 4000, and I am glad to say that a lot more men are arriving today. The Boers seem to have plucked up courage again and are all down the line on the East. I expect we shall have to wipe them up before we advance. We hear that the 8th Division is coming up here and I hope it is as I want to see Frankie and hear all about you. The latest arrival is Jonah Bailey, who has come in with some of his Imperial Volunteers. Hamish is still away down at Kaffir River, but 3 companies of the Camerons are back here. There is great grief in the Guards Brigade as they have taken away Pole Carew and given him a division and our friend has been given command of the Guards Bds. He is very lucky I think, dropping into a nice command like that. The latest excitement was that one day it appeared in orders that Gatacre had been 'ordered to England'. I can't help feeling very sorry for him, but at the same time he has made such costly mistakes and is such a gasbag that he richly deserves it. Mum darling, it is a long war isn't it? and I am afraid we shall be here a long time yet before we go on. Did you send me some shirts from Thresher and Glennie? I got two very nice ones and some khaki handkerchiefs, and I can't imagine who sent them.

We have got quite a decent mess going on now, a private soldier as cook and Holmes does butler. We are able to buy bread and butter so I am quite happy. I don't care much for the rest of the staff except Ewart

(Camerons) and Browne (H.L.I.). They are regular 'blatherers' and talk too much. It is now getting very cold at nights and I roll myself up tight in my blankets and think of my precious mum.
Ever your most loving
Harry

14 April 1900

My own darling wee one,
I have just got your two letters of the 16th and 23rd. I was mis. for a whole week as I had not heard from or about you and I am so thankful to hear that you are going on alright and I do hope you have been careful with your dear self and not caught cold.

I have written twice to Frankie to thank him very much to have looked after my precious mum. I can't hear where the 8th Division is going to, but I think they will have to clear the country east of the railway and perhaps join us later. Anyhow they are certain to have quite enough marching and fighting to satisfy anybody. We are leading a very quiet life here now, getting up drafts and fitting the men with boots and clothes. All the Guards Brigade and the Camerons are still away, but Geordie is still next door and welcomed young Fraser on his arrival to join the Black Watch. You will have heard that Pole Carew is going to leave the Guards Brigade.

I have just had a glance at the Magersfontein dispatch and it seems more of an apology than a narrative of the action. I see he mentioned me again, but I am inclined to think that he has mentioned me quite enough and perhaps will begin to say so. Two or three of the old Boers who have surrendered have said that Methuen's column fought much the hardest.

Have I been writing rotten letters lately, mum, as you call them 'scrimpy' but I am always thinking about you.
Look after your precious self
Ever your most loving Harry

Dertha kept the Duke abreast of developments including her disapproval of certain appointments.

16 April 1900
King's Hotel, Brighton

Dearest Father,
I am sending you back Geordie's letter which I got two or three days ago from Kitty. He must have spent all his time writing! I wonder what you

are doing about all the back papers he asked to be kept for him? What I do myself is that I have kept every number of the Weekly Times; they contain all the war news articles and general digest of the Times and are in a handy form to keep, not being newspaper shape.

Cousin Emily wrote and asked if she could see anything of Harry's letters, so I referred her to you, if by any chance you had kept them. I am writing another now of the two last. They are certainly not generally interesting enough to send to anyone else, but they may amuse Cousin Emily so could you send them to her? I have suppressed a certain amount of personal matters. Apparently they are all perfectly furious at having Col Bar (1) foisted on them. They would like to have the extra two battalions of Guards but they don't want Bar – so it is a question what is to be done. The last idea is that Col Bar is not to be allowed to go beyond the Orange River, but there is a rumour in London that they have gone to Bloemfontein. If the first is the case, it is rather hard on the men under him. I wonder what possessed the authorities to give it to such an unpopular man?

Mamma has had a bit of a cold the last two days, but she wouldn't have gone out anywhere as it is raining. She has stayed in bed today but so far I don't think it really bad. Aunt Georgie was here from Saturday to Monday.

Your affectionate daughter Dertha

Note

1.   Presumably Dertha is referring to Major General Barrington Campbell, whose 16th Brigade, part of 8th Division under General Sir Leslie Rundle, consisted of the 2nd Grenadier Guards, 2nd Scots Guards, 2nd East Yorkshire Regiment and 1st Battalion Leinster Regiment (Prince of Wales's).

Harold was now assigned to Major General Pole-Carew's new 11th Division. Colvile was sorry to lose him 'not only as an old friend, but as a Staff Officer of the highest calibre'.

Throughout their time together, Colvile had consistently acknowledged Harold's contribution and mentioned him twice in despatches which were passed on to Lord Roberts by Methuen.

There was no greater compliment for a brigade commander to bestow on a staff officer.

5

Back With the Guards in 11th Division

As with Colvile, Harry's new divisional commander, Reggie Pole-Carew, was an experienced Victorian soldier well versed in expeditionary force warfare. One of seven children of William Pole-Carew, MP for East Cornwall, he had grown up in the idyllic surrounding of Antony House, a Queen Anne mansion on the west bank of the River Tamar overlooking the sea. After Eton and Christ Church Oxford, he was commissioned in the Coldstream Guards in 1869 and served as the private secretary to Sir Hercules Robinson, Governor of New South Wales, from 1876 to 1877. Appointed ADC to Lord Lytton, Viceroy of India, he left after only six months to join the staff of Lord Roberts (Sir Frederick Roberts as he was then) in the Second Anglo-Afghan War in 1878-1880.

Already having had his horse shot under him in the Chadreh Valley, for the young Guards officer the contrast to ceremonial duties in England and Delhi could not have been greater than the moment he rode with Roberts through the streets of Kabul[1] at the head of his invading army, 'the bazaars and dead walls echoing to the music of the bands and wild scream of the bagpipes'.[2] Then followed the eight-day siege of the Sherpur Cantonment on the outskirts of the city when Mohamed Jan and his 40,000 tribesmen attempted to invest Roberts's army without success. In July 1880, Ayoub Khan inflicted a devastating defeat on the British at Maiwand just to the west of Khandahar. Out of a force of 2,476 men, 946 were killed, 167 wounded and 201 horses lost. With Pole-Carew as his Orderly Officer (ADC), at the head of 10,000 men Roberts set off from Kabul on his famous march to Kandahar. They covered 303 miles in 20 days. By 9 September, the city was once more safely in British hands and Pole-Carew and Roberts sailed for England from Bombay on 30 October.

---

1   *The London Gazette*, MID by Roberts 16 January and 4 May 1880
2   Forbes, Archibald, *The Afghan Wars 1839-42 and 1878-80* <https://www.gutenberg.org/ebooks/8428>

Two year later, Pole-Carew was back on active service, this time with the 2nd Battalion Coldstream Guards in General Sir Garnet Wolseley's Egyptian Expeditionary Force. He also acted as orderly officer to Queen Victoria's son the Duke of Connaught, who was in command of the Guards Brigade. On 13 September 1882, Wolseley advanced by night and attacked Arabi Pasha's lines at dawn. The thousands of fellahin manning the defences were completely taken by surprise as four battalions of Highlanders hurled themselves over the ramparts. To their chagrin, the Guards Brigade remained in reserve. It was all over in 35 minutes and two days later Wolseley was in Cairo. Egypt was no longer 'for the Egyptians'.

In 1885 Pole-Carew became Military Secretary to Lord Roberts in the Madras Command and continued in the same position when Roberts became Commander-in-Chief India in November. In October 1886, Roberts together with his wife and some of his staff including Pole-Carew started from Simla on a trip across the Hills, with the object of inspecting the stations of Dhurmsala and Dalhousie before it was cool enough to begin his winter tour in the plains. When they arrived at Palampur, a telegram awaited them that his great friend General Macpherson had died of fever in Burma. A second message then arrived from the Viceroy Lord Dufferin, telling him to transfer his HQ to Burma and to remain there until 'the neck of the business was broken'.

The business Dufferin referred to was the fallout from the Third Anglo-Burmese War. The previous year, Anglo-French relationships had taken a turn for the worse when it was revealed that the ministerial council of King Thibaw of Burma had written to the French government suggesting a bilateral treaty, a gambit construed by the British as a serious threat to their commercial interests. Equally alarmed by the treatment of the Bombay Burmah Trading Corporation which had recently been fined by the council for underreporting its timber extractions, the Viceroy despatched the Burma Expeditionary Force under General Sir Harry Prendergast VC with orders to occupy Mandalay. The annexation of Upper Burma was duly announced on 1 January 1886, bringing to an end the Konbaung dynasty and Burmese independence and the beginning of armed resistance to British rule. Roberts hurried to Calcutta and landed at Rangoon on the 9 November. For the next three months, Roberts and Carew-Pole remained in Mandalay, working closely with Major General George White, a veteran of the Second Afghan War, to create the Upper Burma Field Force.

Made a CB for his work in Burma, Pole-Carew returned to England and took command of the 2nd Battalion Coldstream Guards. In the autumn of 1899, on his appointment as Commander-in-Chief South Africa, Roberts asked Pole-Carew to join him as the commandant of his headquarters in the post of Assistant Adjutant General. He then took over the Guards Brigade from Colvile in

November. Equally experienced as Colvile, arguably even more so, intelligent and thoughtful, Pole-Carew had the confidence of the Commander-in-Chief unlike his predecessor.

21 April 1900

My own darling wee one,

I wrote you a line last night as I was under orders to march at daybreak this morning, but the move was countermanded and we do not go off until tomorrow.

As I told you, I have been transferred DAAG to the 11th Divn which include the Guards Brigade. Pole Carew asked for a Guardsman on his staff, and so Colville was asked if he would mind my coming. As he did not mind, I went. I am very glad to get back again to the Guards Brigade, as it makes all the difference and Pole Carew is a very nice general to serve under – a model Guards General – in this way rather different to Colville. However the latter has been awfully good to me, and I am very grateful to him for it. I do not think he has improved since he got a division as he lives more and more by himself. I suppose he tells Lady C. that he wins all the battles – from what she told you – but all the same he has done everything for me, and so you must stick up for him too. Poor little wee complains that I do not tell her about the battles, but I do not know what more I can tell her, as they are on such a big scale that I really don't see very much myself, but I will try next time.

The Boers are giving a bit of trouble in the East. They have now got round some of Buller's force at Wepener (1), so Rundle (2) and the 8th Divn have been sent against Dewetsdorp to try and relieve the pressure and we are going to march South East tomorrow to guard Gen Rundle's right flank. I do not suppose we shall have much fighting but there are a lot of small bodies of Boers in front of us who I think will retire. I am afraid Frankie got up too late to take part in Rundle's advance as I hear only 1/2 the second Battn had arrived at Edenburg when they started (3).

There is a lot of sickness among the men, chiefly enteric fever, and some of the older men have caught it too, but I keep most fit and flourishing. It was rather sad to see poor Trotter today with his arm off. He however is in very good spirits and is going to Cape Town at once and hope to go straight back to England. Old Crabbe is going on very well with his arm in a sling and is as cheery and busy as ever. Col Codrington has gone down to Cape Town and probably will go back to England, as the Drs. are afraid of his riding.

You naughty mum, you never said a word about your throat in your last letter, and you ought to have told me how it was.

Colvile wanted a galloper (4) and he has taken Geordie – which was very nice of him. Luckily there are now plenty of officers in the Black Watch so he could be spared. And Cuthbertson of the Black Watch has taken my place as DAAG of the 9th Divn. I have no more to tell you darling one, with all my love,
Ever your most loving Harry

Notes
1.   A town eighty miles southeast of Bloemfontein.
2.   General Sir Henry Rundle, GCB, GCMG, GCVO, DSO (1856 – 1934)
3.   Lieutenant Colonel Frankie Lloyd and the 2nd Battalion Grenadier Guards sailed from England in March and moving up from Capetown reached Bloemfontein on 23 March where by chance the 3rd Battalion were out on an excursion. On that day, the two Grenadier battalions were within eight miles of each other but for the rest of the war they never came so close again.
4.   A kind of mounted ADC who could give and take messages to other commanders.

On 16 April, the Guards Brigade War Diary records 'troops in terrible conditions… rain incessant for twenty hours … bivouacs shuffled daily as ground becomes quagmire'. By the end of the month, the division had assembled at Kareefontein near Leeuw Kop. Serge khaki was now the order of dress except for 200 men of the Coldstreams and Grenadiers who had only received trousers! On 2 May, it moved up to Karree Siding and followed the railway line up to Brandford and Smaldeel.

The big picture was vividly described by Sir Arthur Conan-Doyle.

'In the early days of May, when the season of the rains was past and the veld was green, Lord Roberts's six weeks of enforced inaction came to an end. He had gathered himself once more for one of those tiger springs which should be as sure and as irresistible as that which had brought him from Belmont to Bloemfontein, or that other in olden days which had carried him from Cabul to Candahar. His army had been decimated by sickness, and eight thousand men had passed into the hospitals; but those who were with the colours were of high heart, longing eagerly for action. Any change which would carry them away from the pest-ridden, evil-smelling capital which had revenged itself so terribly upon the invader must be a change for the better. Therefore it was with glad faces and brisk feet that the centre column left Bloemfontein on May 1st, and streamed, with bands playing, along the northern road.[3]

3   Conan-Doyle, Arthur, *The Great Boer War* <https://www.gutenberg.org/files/3069/3069-h/3069-h.htm#link2HCH0025>

On 3 May, the day of the advance from our most northern post, Karee, the disposition of Lord Roberts's army was briefly as follows. On his left was Hutton, with his mixed force of mounted infantry drawn from every quarter of the empire. This formidable and mobile body, with some batteries of horse artillery and of pom-poms, kept a line a few miles to the west of the railroad, moving northwards parallel with it. Roberts's main column kept on the railroad, which was mended with extraordinary speed by the Railway Pioneer regiment and the Engineers…This main column consisted of Pole-Carew's 11th Division, which contained the Guards, and Stephenson's[4] 18th Brigade (Warwicks, Essex, Welsh, and Yorkshires). With them were the 83rd, 84th, and 85th R.F.A., with the heavy guns, and a small force of mounted infantry. Passing along the widespread British line one would then, after an interval of seven or eight miles, come upon Tucker's[5] Division (the 7th), which consisted of Maxwell's 14th Brigade (formerly Chermside's—the Norfolks, Lincolns, Hampshires, and Scottish Borderers) and Wavell's[6] 15th Brigade (North Staffords, Cheshires, East Lancashires, South Wales Borderers). To the right of these was Ridley's mounted infantry. Beyond them, extending over very many miles of country and with considerable spaces between, there came Broadwood's cavalry, Bruce Hamilton's 21st Brigade (Derbyshires, Sussex, Camerons, and C.I.V.), and finally on the extreme right of all Ian Hamilton's force of Highlanders, Canadians, Shropshires, and Cornwalls, with cavalry and mounted infantry, starting forty miles from Lord Roberts, but edging westwards all the way, to merge with the troops next to it…'

This was the army, between forty and fifty thousand strong, with which Lord Roberts advanced upon the Transvaal'. Events continued apace including the capture of over 15,000 sheep, cattle and horses.

4 May 1900
Brandfort

My dearest Mums,

I had not time to write to you last week as we were on the march very often from daylight to dark, so I just scribbled a line to Dertha and asked her to write on to you. We had a longish march for a week, marching every day to a place called Dewetsdorp through a nice grass hilly country, with plenty of water which was a pleasant change. Our march had the

---

4   Brigadier T.E. Stephenson, CB (1856-1928)
5   Later Lieutenant General Sir Charles Tucker, GCB, GCVO (1838 – 1935)
6   Major General Archibald Wavell (1843-1935), father of FM Lord Wavell.

effect of making all the Boers bolt away as hard as they could and we only saw their backs when we got to our turning point. So we had to march back again to Bloemfontein but we left our mark on the country as we brought back with us over 14000 sheep, 700 cattle and about 600 horses. We arrived in Bloemfontein on Sunday morning and thought they would give us some rest. But we suddenly got the order to start on Tuesday due north to Karree Siding, and we had to march 20 miles or so on a very hot day. The men lasted better than our transport animals as some of the latter died and we got into camp that night, so we had to rest the next day. On Thursday we were ordered to march on Brandford where the Boers were supposed to be going to make a stand but as usual they bolted when they saw us, though their commander in chief was here in person. We got into Brandford about 4pm and secured a nice house for our residence. The owner of the house was at once put into prison as we found a Mauser rifle in the house. This is the first time since I have been in South Africa that I have had a nice bed and room to myself. In fact I have hardly slept under a roof at all. We have had a further day's rest today which I have enjoyed. This is quite a small country town with two good hotels and a large Dutch church. Most of the men here are English or Scotch, and all the Dutchmen we have clapped into prison. The Irish Brigade (1) were to have fought us, but they all bolted except one man who we caught and handcuffed. I am afraid we have to treat these people harshly as they only mistake our kindness. I did not get a letter from you last mail but I expect it went wrong as I changed my Division. Remember to address me now as 11th Division. No more to say, with best to all,
Your most affectionate Harold
I am still flourishing

Note

1.   The Irish Transvaal Brigade was established days before the outbreak of the Second Anglo-Boer War and initially consisted of Irishmen who worked in the Witwatersrand. The volunteers were given full citizenship and became Burghers of the Boer republics. The brigade was formed by Colonel John Blake, an Irish American former officer in the US Army, who was later succeeded by John MacBride. Under the leadership of MacBride, the brigade was strengthened by volunteers travelling from Ireland who entered South Africa via Portuguese Mozambique.

Two days after this letter, Harold learnt of the death Captain Edward Verschoyle who died from wounds received when commanding No.3 Company of the 2nd

Battalion[7] at Thaba'nchui. An exact contemporary who had joined the regiment the same year as Harold, Edward was the son of a famous Crimean Grenadier, Captain Edward Verschoyle who had carried the regimental colour during the Battle of Inkerman when surrounded by the enemy.

The record of the Division's advance is now geographical more than military as it marched northwards through the huge clouds of smoke for the Boers had set fire to the dry grass, partly to cover their own retreat, and partly to show up the British khaki on the blackened fields. On 11 May, Roberts's army advanced 20 miles to Geneva Siding, where it paused to prepare for battle for it was thought certain that the Boers would defend their new capital, Kroonstad. However, there was no stand and Roberts rode into the town the next day. The Division had now accomplished half its journey to Pretoria and after an eight-day halt, the advance resumed on 22 May. The country through which they passed swarmed with herds and flocks, but, with as scrupulous a regard for the rights of property as Wellington showed in the south of France, Roberts forbade his men to take so much as a chicken as they passed. They crossed Rhenoster River, then the Vaal River at Viljoen's Drift and by 28 May, they had reached the Klip River without fighting.

Roberts's infanteers had covered 130 miles in seven days and by 30 May, they were camped outside Johannesburg. Two days were spent there while supplies were brought up, and then a move was made upon Pretoria 30 miles to the north.

For a time it appeared that the entry would be bloodless, but the booming of cannon and the crash of Mauser fire soon showed that the enemy was in force along the ridge for Botha had left a strong rearguard to hold off the British while his own stores and valuables were being withdrawn from the town. It seemed for a time as if a real battle was at last about to take place. The Guards' Brigade, Stephenson's brigade, and Maxwell's brigade streamed up and waited until Hamilton, who was on the enemy's right flank, made his presence felt. The heavy guns had also arrived, and a huge cloud of debris rising from the Pretorian forts told the accuracy of their fire.

About 2.30 p.m., the Boer fire slackened and Pole-Carew was directed to push on and his infantry swept over the ridge, with some 30 or 40 casualties, the majority of which were Warwicks. The position was taken. In the early morning of 5 June, the Coldstream Guards occupied the hills which overlooked the town. That afternoon, in the town centre's square, Roberts took the salute as the men who had followed him so far and so faithfully—the Guards, the Essex, the Welsh, the Yorks, the Warwicks, the guns, the mounted infantry, the dashing irregulars,

---

7   The 2nd Battalion along with the 2nd Battalion Scots Guards, 2nd East Yorkshire Regiment, and 1st Leinster Regiment, formed 16th Brigade under Major-General Barrington Campbell, part of General Rundle's 8th Division

the Gordons, the Canadians, the Shropshires, the Cornwalls, the Camerons, the Derbys, the Sussex, and the London Volunteers – marched by in waves of khaki. For Pole-Carew and Harold, it must have represented a milestone in the progress of the war.

The Boers may have retreated but they had not surrendered and were still determined to fight. So Roberts began an advance to the east in order to push Boer forces away from the Pretoria region to the Portuguese East Africa border. Weakened by the long march to Pretoria and the loss of horses and sick men, the British force mustered only 14,000, a third of whom were mounted on sickly horses. The Boers, hidden in the hills at Donkerhoek, were ready for battle. On 11 June, French's cavalry with Hutton's infantry brigade[8] attacked on the left in an attempt to outflank the Boers to the north, while Hamilton's infantry attempted an outflanking movement on the right. Pole-Carew's division advanced towards the Boer centre. After intense cavalry action which proved indecisive, Roberts decided to make a frontal attack on the next day. Artillery fire from guns in forward positions enabled the infantry to capture Diamond Hill and on 13 June Botha's army retreated to the north. Although Roberts had removed the threat to his eastern flank, the Boers were unbowed despite their retreat. Jan Smuts wrote that the battle had 'an inspiriting effect which could scarcely have been improved by a real victory'.

On 19 June Harold wrote to Dertha and included a single violet which is still in the letter in the Archives at Blair Castle. This was not to be the only occasion when Harold would send his wife a flower from the battlefields although he would have had no reason to think that one day he would swap the dusty plains of South Africa for the fields and mud of France and Belgium.

> 19 June
> Pretoria
>
> My own darling wee one,
> I do not quite know what I am to write about but there is a chance of sending a letter by a doctor who is going home and I can't help thinking of you all day long, so I has to write. Hamish's Bn came in here two days ago and he and I saw a good deal of one another. He is extraordinary fit and well and I have never seen him look better. He is off again this

---

8   Later Lieutenant General Sir Edward Thomas Henry Hutton, KCB, KCMG, DL, FRGS (1848-1923). As commander of the 1st Mounted Infantry Brigade, a formation made up of Canadian, Australian, and New Zealand troops, he was actively engaged both during Roberts's advance from Bloemfontein and after the fall of Pretoria. When the brigade was broken up in November 1900, he returned to England where he was awarded a KCMG.

morning under General Ian Hamilton. I fancy the 11th Division are going to remain near Pretoria for Lord Roberts to do what he likes with. I have not heard anything of Geordie for a long time. You will have heard that Colville and the Highland Brigade were shut up and that he telegraphed 'If I am allowed to eat the mules I can last 8 days longer'. It was then thought about time to do something and Lord Methuen was sent off post haste to relieve him. You will have heard that the railway line has been smashed up in the Free State. They have burnt all the warm clothing and I believe a lot of mail bags and I shall be angry if they have burnt my Wee's letters.

We had a great dinner last night at the Pretoria Club, given by Abe Bailey (1) who was going home after being attached to this division as intelligence officer. Unfortunately he was stopped going but we had our dinner all the same. Do you know, darling mum, I have not heard from you for two months and I am beginning to fidget and I do dream about you so at night. I heard a good deal about the cavalry charge of the 12th Lancers. Unfortunately the squadrons were very weak, but they saved the guns (2).

Take care of your precious self during the hot weather in London. Ever your most loving Harry

What do you think of Pretoria violets? It is now midwinter here, but still a nice sun in the middle of the day.

Notes
1. Sir Abraham Bailey, 1st Baronet KCMG (6 November 1864-10 August 1940), known as Abe Bailey, was a South African gold tycoon, politician, financier and cricketer. He was with the City of London Imperial Volunteers.
2. At Diamond Hill (11-12 June 1900), a charge of the Household Cavalry and 12th Lancers saved Q Battery, but they lost Colonel the Earl of Airlie 'who fell at the head of his regiment'. Lieutenant Wright was also killed, and the regiment had a dozen other casualties.

Late June found Harold camped at a whisky distillery.

25 June 1900
About 11 miles E of Pretoria in a whisky distillery
Close to Erste Fabricken Station

My own darling wee one,
I have at last got a letter from you and am comparatively hap again. You know that that rascal De Wet looks up the line behind us and burnt two weeks mail so I shall never get your dear letters of the 27th April and 3rd May. Since I last wrote to you there was the usual scare and Botha

was supposed to be advancing on Pretoria. So off we were bundled and marched to a place called Marks Farm, and now the Guards Brigade are at Donkerhoek and the 18th Brigade are at Edendale and Divisional Hd Qrs are just in rear of the centre at a whisky distillery owned by a Jew who is called Marks (1). He is not a bad fellow and puts up the General in his house and I went to dine with him one night. However we have shifted now and are living in a house owned by the manager of the whisky distillery. The last few days I have been reconnoitring the country which is very hilly and very rough with stones. At the same time I think it is the nicest part of the country I have been in; nice springs of water and the country would grow anything if trouble was taken. Unfortunately we had two days of rain but otherwise the climate is perfect and just what you would like, Mum – a blazing hot sun by day and cool at night, and on the low ground we get frost. I had a long letter from your mother who was full of your praises - and I was so proud, Mum, and she said you were looking much better since your operation – and I is prouder than ever, mum. I suppose you are staying with Mrs Frankie and I am afraid you must be having a very anxious time since he was wounded (2). I have not heard how he is, but I trust he is alright or nearly so … (remainder of correspondence missing)

Notes

1. Samuel Marks (1844-1920) was a Lithuanian-born South African industrialist and financier. Marks built a grand 40-room Victorian mansion, Zwartkoppies Hall, on his farm near Pretoria, and entertained on a lavish scale. Pole-Carew would have dined well! Besides President Kruger, Marks enjoyed the trust of the Boer Generals Botha, De Wet, and de la Rey, and the respect of Roberts, Kitchener, and Lord Milner. He played a not inconsiderable part in the negotiations for the cessation of Anglo-Boer hostilities at Vereeniging on 31 May 1902.

2. Frankie Lloyd was badly wounded during the Biddulphsberg fight. *The Times* War correspondent was on the spot: 'The scene on the battlefield at this moment was one of the most awful descriptions. The battle had now fully developed. From the front, where the Grenadiers had disappeared in the smoke, the crackle of bullets was deafening … Ten guns on our side and two on the Boers' added their roar – the bursting of shells and the demoniac scream of shrapnel made up a perfect pandemonium of sound. Over all, and dominating all, was the dreadful popping crackle of the burning grass, while the smoke hid everything. Biddulph's Berg, the Boer guns, our own guns, the Grenadiers and the Scots Guards, who had moved up in support of them, had all vanished. One saw nothing but vast rolling billows of thick blue-white smoke … Out of this great pall that hung over the battlefield came the dreadful din, and from under its edge crept stricken and bleeding figures, groping along in the semi-darkness, or staggering feebly, supported between blackened and dishevelled comrades towards the busy doctors at the rear. It was bewildering, it was terrifying, it

was horrifying….. no realism of art could equal the awful realism of the pallid, drawn, blood-smeared faces and swaying, tottering steps of the ghastly figures that now, in a steady stream, staggered out of the hell in front of me….'. Lloyd later wrote: 'At the next halt my right-hand man was hit, my left-hand man was hit, I was hit … There were a few ant-heaps, but they were rotten and useless. I was behind one on my back with Drummer Haines and Fruin of No. 6 … Drummer Haines had got his arm over me, drawing me to him for protection, I suppose (I was a bit silly, but not very), when bang came a bullet that hit me on the stomach, but it was covered by his arm, which it broke, and I was only bruised fearfully. This, no doubt, saved my life. I tied him up with a handker-chief, and he put some stuff on my wounds, and there we lay.' When the order was given to retire at 3 p.m., Lloyd, assisted by Haines and Fruin, stumbled through the fire and was taken to the Dressing Station.[9]

By now, the state of the division's footwear was dire. On 3 July, Pole-Carew sent a telegram to the Military Secretary – 'can anything be done to expedite supply of boots? 3,000 urgently required here – have tried Ordnance frequently, with no effect – please help us or we shall be unable to move'.[10] The division was in contact with Botha who used Pole-Carew as a conduit to Roberts to protest about 'the inhuman removal of families from their homes' and holding the British government responsible for any fatal consequences.

Using the halt in Pretoria to take stock of his army, Roberts told his Military Secretary to arrange a Report on the Organization and Equipment of Infantry. Under the Presidency Brigadier General Inigo Jones, Harold and his staff sought the views of the commanding officers of the eight infantry battalions in the division. Such exercises are usually treated with due deference but little enthusiasm for soldiers know only too well that few if any changes will result. Little of interest emerged and in Pole-Carew's submission of 17 July 1900 the main recommendation was that 'the present cut of tunic and trouser (which are too tight) is thoroughly impractical and an impediment to freedom of movement'. He agreed with the commanding officers that entrenching tools were best carried on mules rather than the man but did not endorse their suggestion[11] that company commanders should be mounted in battle for 'horses get in the way'.

9   Lloyd, Brigadier-General F. and Russell, Brevet-Major Hon. A. (Comp), *First or Grenadier Guards in South Africa 1899-1902*, (London: J.J.Keliher & Co., 1907), pp.34-38.
10   TNA WO 105/7 Lieut. General R. Pole-Carew - Dewetsdorp, Reitfontein, Paardekraal, Springfield and Leuwkop (126/56)
11   TNA WO 108/253 Infantry, 11th Division: Report on Organisation and Equipment

21 July 1900
Near Pretoria (1)

My own darling wee,
I got your two letters today of June 22nd and I is more hap. We are on the eve of a move but where to I cannot find out. Lord Roberts sent all his horses and wagons out here so I should not be surprised if we are off tomorrow.

I hope you did not knock yourself up at the bazaar, little one, and had someone to look after you. I am sorry that Mrs Mackinnon made a stupid of herself, but she always does. I was very surprised to see in a Cape newspaper that Kitty had started for the Cape. Did you know she was going? I wish she hadn't as Durban the same as Cape Town is in a state of confusion and she will have nobody to look after her, as I suppose Bardie is somewhere near Standerton. Besides the great difficulty will be to get home comfortably after the war is over as the rush will be terrific.

I sometimes despair at the war being finished for a long time. At one time I thought that if they could capture Steyn (2) and De Wet, the Transvaalers would give in too. But now the Free Staters have burst through, I am rather despondent. But I ought not to write like this to you as really every day we get stronger and the Boers weaker and I hope the end will come suddenly.

You must not mind my leaving off now, darling one, and mind you write letters all about yourself and every little ache and pain.
Ever your most loving Harry

Note
1. Wolmaran's Farm
2. Martinus Steyn (1857 – 1916) was a South African lawyer, politician, and statesman. He was the sixth and last president of the independent Orange Free State from 1896 to 1902.

Harold wrote home to Dertha the following month concerning pressing domestic matters that could not be ignored from a far-flung battlefield.

7 August 1900
Waterval Onder

My own darling wee one,
I got your nice letter of August 10th and I only long darling mums to get back to my little wee. But I suppose I shall have to wait till the war is over or until they break up the 11th Division which I am afraid they won't do

until the end. I have already written to Gen Trotter about the Brigade Majorship so it is practically settled that I take it when I come home.

About the house – I am very annoyed that the agents behaved so badly to you, but you must not be angry, mum, and don't bother your dear little self about looking out for another one until I come home and I will look after you and help you. The little house you chose sounded nicer than I could imagine and I am very sorry, mum, we have not got it. But I am sure we shall be able to find another for a little home for us and we have got a little money to make it nice with.

Hamish turned up the day before yesterday on his way to join his brigade the 21st. He had been away for three weeks in Bloemfontein with slight fever and dysentery. He is alright again and says he is very well indeed though he looks a bit thinner but that is no doubt from having to drink milk and nothing to eat. I have heard nothing about Geordie….

The nights are bitterly cold with hard frost but luckily I have plenty of warm things including a Balaclava woollen night cap sent by my dear cousin Miss Bowyer-Smyth. However I have been sleeping in a house this last week. I have kept my door and window open so as not to get too soft. I was delighted to hear from Spains Hall that my darling mum was so well and in good spirits and I long to get back to her – you don't know how much. I am afraid the war will drag on a long time but when we get to Pretoria I think a lot will be sent home and I hope I may be among them. But, darling mum, I does want to be with you again. When we have to stop like we have done I get so impatient and cross and my temper is quite ruined … The orders have just come in so I must go and leave off. Take good care of your darling self,
ever your most loving Harry

Boer guerillas had been attacking the railway with the assistance of farmers resulting in the British burning the farms but having to house the women and children left homeless. Camps (concentration camps) were established but a scandal developed as conditions in the camps worsened. Crops were destroyed and herds seized.

15 August 1900
Middleburg

My own darling wee one,
I was very much disappointed at not getting a letter from you last mail (July 13) so I am looking forward to 2 by the next, which ought to be here soon. We are leading a very quiet life here; the division is still scattered all along the line from Bronkhuist Spruit up to Wilge River railway

station about 12 miles east of this. Everyone's attention is devoted to the De Wet chase which is taking place on the west of Pretoria. I think there is a chance of catching him, or at any rate most of his men. Buller has at last moved up from the south and French is in communication with him. Buller is now named the 'sitting bull' as he won't move. When he gets near enough to us, I suppose we shall cooperate with him and have another go at Botha, Kruger and Co who are supposed to be some 20 miles East of Belfast. Have you seen a book called the Absent Minded War? (1) It is rather good but I think it is a pity to publish it during the war. The Boers get hold of these books which may encourage them. They have made a great deal out of the hospital row and issued proclamations to say that the British army is dying off like flies. I see Geordie's Battn is ordered to hold itself in readiness to go to China (2), so I am afraid you won't see very much of him. I wonder if Bardie has come up with old Buller. Some well-informed people say that the Boers will not fight again after Machadodorp and that the war will be over in September, but I am rather incredulous, and I am half afraid we shall have to follow them up to Lydenburg which is a beastly hilly country and full of kopjes and valleys covered with bush, but I think it is fairly healthy. I saw my wee had been at the Buckingham palace garden party (3) and she never told me about it, and I hope she did not find an old codger to bother her. I wonder if you got any of my letters from Pretoria – we have not heard of any of the home mails being taken, and I got all your letters at once, so I think they may be alright – Goodbye my precious mum, and longing to come home to you.
Ever your most loving
Harry

Notes
1. The full title was *An Absent-Minded War: Being Some Reflections On Our Reverses and the Causes Which Have Led To Them.* Published anonymously in 1900, the author was identified only as 'A British Staff Officer' and it referred to the ongoing war in South Africa.
2. The reference to Geordie's battalion and China is likely to refer to the Boxer Rebellion of 1899-1901.
3. Dertha had been to Buckingham Palace twice within the last three months, first to a Drawing Room on 14 May hosted by the Princess of Wales, and secondly to the Queen's Garden Party on 11 July together with her parents and Edward Ruggles-Brise.

On 18th August, Harold wrote to his sister Florence.

18 August 1900
Middleburg

My dearest Flo,

I am afraid I have been a very bad correspondent, but you have been a very good little girl to write to me so often. We are still dawdling along but I hope we shall be on the move again in a day or two.

This is a regular Dutch town and very healthy as it stands very high with plenty of good water. There is hardly a man in the place and the ladies are very bitter against us and say they would rather have all their husbands and brothers killed than they should surrender so it looks as if we are going to be out here for some time and I only hope we shan't. I think our next move will be down the railway line and release a number of our prisoners. The country all around here is as black as your hat as the Boers have burnt all the grass. Consequently our poor animals get nothing to eat and die by the scores. I have been lucky with my two original horses. The one I brought from Gibraltar has done very well. It suffered a bit from starvation. The other is all shaken and stumbles nearly every step it takes. I have now got a third which I am certain is a London bus horse. Every step it sends one's stomach into one's mouth and it is uncommon short of wind too. So it is not much pleasure to ride any of them but still they save me having to walk.

We are having a most luxurious stay here in a comfortable house and I have got a bed and we can buy all sorts of vegetables. I am afraid we shall not like roughing it again but as we get nearer the sea the ground gets barer and it gets much hotter.

I suppose you are all getting tired of the war and so are we. These Boers will not stand up but one has to be as careful as ever. I see the price of wheat has gone up again so I hope the squire is putting thousands into his pocket. I think Dertha must be at Spains now so I shall expect a letter. She is very naughty in London and will give a hand for too much. There is an old millionaire who says the war to be over the first week in September so I may be home before too long.

With love to all,

Your most affectionate Harold

20th August 1900
Middleberg

My dearest Mums,

I think we shall be on the move again shortly so I must send you a line to say that I am still flourishing but rather tired of this place. I do not know

quite where we are going to. I expect we shall keep along the railway line. We are only having lovely weather but it is inclined to be windy and dusty. It is distinctly warmer again and then grass is beginning to grow. We do not seem to be getting much further in finishing the war, do not foresee the end yet and people here say that old Kruger will never give in. It is such an enormous country that it will take a long time to subdue properly. Yesterday we took possession of a Dutch Reformed Church for a service and our Canon Knox Little (1) preached a very good sermon. Considering he is a man of seventy years I think he is a wonder. We do not hear much news of what is going on elsewhere and we cannot get our mail up. Some of the Boers amuse themselves by shooting at the train so nothing is allowed to travel except in daylight. Luckily we have managed to get up most of our stores and provisions so we are living quite luxuriously.
With best love to all,
Your most affectionate Harold

Note
1.   Canon William John Knox-Little (1839-1918). Born in County Tyrone and Cambridge educated he was mentioned in despatches during the Boer War in his capacity as an army chaplain. He was widely published and made Canon of Worcester Cathedral in 1881. He was a few years younger than Harold though.

Harold maintained his correspondence with home.

31 August 1900
Waterval Onder

My own darling wee,
We are halted here today so I must send you a line and chance it ever getting to you. We left Belfast on the 22nd and went to Wonderfontein and the next day but one marched to Belfast without any fighting until we arrived there and we could not put our noses over the skyline beyond without being shelled. Belfast is a rotten little place with a few tin houses. We stopped there for a day and gave the Boers plenty of shells whenever they showed themselves and the next day we moved out to the north about 4 miles, the Boers shooting at us a good deal especially with their Long Tom but luckily doing very little damage. The 28th we started off with French's cavalry and marched to a place called Middlepunt (1). There were some Boers in front of us but we avoided them on the 29th and turned more to the East and marched to where we came up with Buller's force. On the 29th the Guards Brigade came out here on the hills overlooking Waterval Onder. There were a lot of Boers the other side of

the valley yesterday but we could see them all trekking off this morning. You will have seen all the accounts of Buller's fight at Bergendal (2) which was close to Belfast. I saw with my glasses all his shells bursting and he seemed to be giving them a real doing. The Boers since then have as usual been on the run, but luckily all our prisoners of war were brought in yesterday except officers who have been taken down to Barberton. The railway here runs through a sort of valley like an enlarged glen, the country on both sides being horrible and rocky with steep precipices. How we are going to get on I don't know as we must make a long detour to get on to a road. We all hope that the weather would have given in when we got hold of Machadodorp, but I despair of it now. I'm afraid it will still take us a long time to get to Barberton as the country is so rough. However I don't think it suits the Boers any better than it does us.

I wonder what my darling mum has been doing and where she is and if she has gone to Scotland after that hot dusty London. I don't know when I shall hear from you again but you must keep on writing and the more letters I get in a heap the happier I is. The railway here runs down such a steep incline that it has rack engines that the Boers have all taken away (3). So we shall be in rather a fix how to get up our food. Take care of your dear self my precious mum,
Ever your most loving
Harry

Notes
1. Under Elandsfontein.
2. The Battle of Berg-en-dal (also known as the Battle of Belfast or Battle of Dalmanutha) 21-27 August was the last set-piece battle of the war. Although British casualties were 385 and the Boers's only 79, the Boer line of defence had been breached and on 28 August Buller's troops marched into Machadodorp. The ZAR government, meanwhile, had decamped to Nelspruit. A few days later, on 1 September, Lord Roberts proclaimed the entire South African Republic British territory.
3. The four rack locomotives were stored at Waterval Onder. When working a train up to Waterval Boven (Watervalborn), a 32-ton engine would be coupled to the rear end of a train as banking engine. When working a descending train, the order of assembly was reversed, with the train's locomotive at the rear end and the rack locomotive in front to act as brake.

8 September 1900
Waterval Onder

My dearest Mums,
Very many thanks for your letter of August 9th. We arrived here about a week ago, having made a detour to the north so as to fall on the

unsuspecting Kruger but the old man had fled before our arrival. We are now encamped on the high ground overlooking the valley through which the railway, river and road pass which is 144 feet below us. The country is rather pretty but very rough and not at all suited to our advance but now we have got hold of Lydenberg we hold all the high ground and the Boers will have to skip down below which they won't like as the country is feverish. I hope we shall be able to battle old Kruger unless he runs away to Delagoa Bay (1) but it will be a slow process as the country is very difficult and the roads bad.

Last night the General gave us all a dinner in the hotel down below kept by a Frenchman and we fared very well but the walk up the hill after a good go at plum pudding was rather a trial. Dorothea enjoyed her rest at Spains hall tremendously and I hope she is now recuperating in Scotland as I do not think that awful heat in London does anybody any good. This morning we had a regular Scotch mist and it feels horribly cold. Yesterday we had one of the hottest days we have had lately and it reminded me of the Modder. I only hope we get out of this country before the summer comes on again. We are all most flourishing and the outdoor life and the hill climbing makes us all ravenous but I am quite ready to come home and only wish the war would end.

Your most affectionate Harold

Note
1. Kruger fled the Transvaal for Mozambique by train on 11 September 1900. He planned to board the first outgoing steamer but was prevented from doing so when, at the behest of the local British Consul, the Portuguese Governor insisted that Kruger stay in port under house arrest. About a month later Queen Wilhelmina of the Netherlands concluded a deal with Britain to extricate Kruger on a Dutch warship and convey him through non-British waters to France. On arrival in Marseilles on 22 November, he received a rapturous welcome —60,000 people turned out to see him disembark.

Since 4 September, Pole-Carew had been trying to persuade Roberts to let him find a different route to Komatipoort for 'the country is infinitely more difficult than it looks and we found that to get to the top of some of the hills from below is practically impossible...and that to occupy the lower slopes with the enemy of top is in many cases useless...Well-wishers in these parts strongly urge that we should have nothing to do with these hills...is it is not too to risk a possible misfortune...My experience of yesterday has entirely altered my opinion of the possibilities of the rote, and the views I have expressed are shared by men who were through Tirah'.[12] This last reference must have rung a bell with Roberts for by 13 September Pole-Carew was in Godwaan from where he planned to go to Alkmaar and Nelspruit via Kaapsche Hoop.

As soon as he arrived in Kaapsche Hoop, Pole-Carew ran into another problem, this time with Hutton. He had asked him to send all of Henry's Mounted Infantry to join him, only to discover that Hutton had told Roberts that Pole-Carew had given his consent that they were to remain under Hutton's orders. He blew his top, respectfully suggesting to Roberts that this was 'a case of insubordinations and flat disobedience of orders on the part of Hutton' and that he considered that 'he had behaved in an untruthful and unsoldierlike manner'. The next day he wrote to Roberts 'I am extremely obliged to you for ordering Henry's Corps to rejoin me as they will be of the greatest assistance to me in the country which I will have to work between here and Kamrudin'[13].

On 24 September came the last chapter of the campaign in the Eastern Transvaal, when at 8 a.m. Pole-Carew and his Guardsmen occupied Komatipoort. They had made desperate marches, the last one through thick bush where they went for nineteen miles without water. To them fell the honour of entering and occupying the ultimate point which the Boers could hold. Although resistance had been threatened and prepared for, hardly a shot fired and the town was occupied. Although the bridge which enabled the British to receive supplies from Lourenço Marques had been mined and guns placed in position, fate decided otherwise and it was still intact. General Pienaar[14] and the greater part of his force, amounting to over two thousand men, had crossed the frontier and had been taken down to Delagoa Bay.[15] Other small bands had slipped away to the north and the south, but they were insignificant in numbers.

12   TNA WO 105/18: C-P telegram Roberts.
13   Ibid.
14   Benjamin Pienaar was an officer in the Boer Forces; he was on the staff of General Cronje and latterly with General de la Rey. For his services in the Anglo-Boer War, he was awarded the War Decoration for Loyal Service and the War Medal. Following the Union of South Africa, he was the Potchefstroom Member of the Transvaal Provincial Council. He was also General Agent and Appraiser to the Land Bank, Potchefstroom and a Member of the District Bestuur of 'Het Volk'. In 1937 as a Senator, he was awarded the Coronation Medal.
15   Pienaar, Philip: *With Steyn and De Wet* (London: Methuen, London, 1902), passim.

29 September 1900
Komatipoort

My own darling wee one,
I got your nice letter of Aug 17th yesterday, and I have not had a moment
to write to you since I left Waterval Onder. We started from there on the
12th and marched to Nooitgedacht where the Boers had been keeping
all our prisoners in a kind of barbed wire cage (1). Ennismore (2), whom
I daresay you remember, was one of them, and he joined our intelligence
staff as guide and kaffir interpreter. But I don't think he is much good.
We next marched to Godwaan River, and the following day up an
enormous hill called Kaapsche Hoop, we went up 2400 feet in one day
up a very steep road, and the next day we came down about 2000 feet on
the North Kaap River. We then turned off in the direction of Barberton
and went through Jamestown (about 6 tin houses and a mine) to North
Kaap Station, past Avoca and finally got to Kaapmuiden junction, and
then followed the main line until we got here. We luckily had no fighting
but we had a very hard march with practically no road, and one had to be
made by the engineers and infantry. Besides as we got into lower ground
it became very hot, and the day we did our longest march it was 102
in the shade. There was also very little water in places, and one's thirst
is awful from coming suddenly into the heat. We are now occupying a
house on some high ground overlooking the junction of the Komati and
Crocodile Rivers, the country is all covered with prickly bushes with the
result that all my clothes are torn to ribbons. The river is full of crocodiles
and hippopotami, there are a few birds with very brilliant plumage and
some beautiful butterflies. The actual village consists of a few tin houses,
and the Boers burnt everything they could before leaving. However there
is no end of flour, sugar, coffee and ammunition left and we are getting
up stores from Delagoa Bay and yesterday we had champagne for dinner.
It is a curious sight.

Notes
1.   Since the start of the campaign in South Africa, according to War Office
      returns, 259 officers and 6,840 officers, NCOs and men had, been taken pris-
      oner. Of these 182 officers and 4,037 men had been released or had escaped,
      and one officer and 85 men had died. When the Boers evacuated Pretoria they
      took some 900 of their prisoners with them to Nooitgedacht, in the Eland's
      Valley. As early as 30 August, Pole-Carew reported 'the prisoners from
      Nooitgedacht have been walking in all day and we are doing all we can to
      provide them with food, rum and blankets, and our doctors and ambulances are

out to-night picking up the sick and footsore, of which there are many; some are half-starved and very badly clothed'.[16]

2. Richard Granville Hare, 4th Earl of Listowel (1866 – 1931), known as Viscount Ennismore from 1866 to 1924, had been commissioned as a lieutenant into the Grenadier Guards in 1890. He later transferred to the 4th (Militia) Battalion of the Royal Munster Fusiliers and in February was appointed a lieutenant of the 45th (Dublin) Company attached to the 13th Battalion, Imperial Yeomanry. The company left for South Africa in the middle of March 1900. Their first battle was their last for they were defeated by the Boers at Lindley on 31 May 1900, when Lords Longford, Ennismore, Leitrim and Donoughmore were all captured, while Sir John Power of the Irish whiskey family was killed.

Harold was clearly pleased when Kitchener sent them back to Pretoria.

4 October 1900
Pretoria

My dearest Mums,

I am afraid I have not written to you for a long time, but we have been busy marching without a moment to spare.

When we left Waterval Onder, we marched down the Eland valley to a station called Nooitgedacht we then rode off towards Barberton and made a circle back again to the line at North Kaap Station and followed the railway down to Low's Creek Station. It was a very hard march; the road had not been used for years and was quite overgrown with bushes and washed away by the rains so it had to be remade. Besides, there were some very high hills to get over, one day we went up over 2000 ft, and the next day we had to come down the same height, so you can imagine the difficulty with our guns and waggons. The heat too was awful, on the worst day on which we did our longest march it was 102 degrees in the shade, and I do not think I was ever so thirsty in my life. As usual the Boers ran away whenever we got near them and destroyed everything they could and nearly every railway bridge was blown up. We saw the remnants of a great many guns and we brought back as a relic the remainder of 'Long Tom' which I believe Lord Roberts was going to send back to England.

After we had been at Komatipoort a day or two, Lord Kitchener came down and said we are to go back to Pretoria at once and we are delighted. So we got into the trucks we had captured, put some of the soldiers who said they know how to drive engines to drive and started off. However it took us nearly 4 days to get back the 300 miles, as our amateur drivers did not know much about their job. The brutal Boers upset a train

16 TNA WO 105/18: C-P telegram Roberts.

full of Coldstream and then fired into them in the dark and killed five and wounded 15 (1). We are all very much put out about it and as usual 'somebody blundered'. We all hoped that when we got here we might be told that we could go home but so far they have not said so but hint that we may be kept here another two months, but I hope that is not so.

I think all my letters must have gone missing as I have not heard from you the last 3 mails and I have only had one letter from Dertha. Perhaps they will turn up in a day or two. I hope you have had some decent weather for the harvest, we could spare you some sun from here. The only interesting thing about our visit to the tropics was that we saw some new animals – crocodiles, hippopotami, baboons and several birds with most brilliant plumage.

With best love to all.

Your most affectionate Harold

Note

1.   The Guards Brigade Diary for 2 October 1900 notes: 'train left Waterval Onder at 7.30 a.m., being taken up incline and through tunnel by special engine. Reached Machadodorp at 11 am and heard that line had been cut near Pan last night, a train with part of the 2nd Battalion Coldstream on board having been derailed and five men killed and fifteen wounded. There were no reports of an ambush. This account is at variance with Pole-Carew's telegram to Pretoria in which he reports 'I have visited the hospital at Middleburg today (2 October) … some of the men are I regret to say very seriously hit and almost all with soft nosed bullets…it is evident the Boers fire from a distance of little over 60 yards and from the manner in which the grass was eaten down and from remnants of food it would appear that they had been in the immediate vicinity for some hours.[17]

4 October 1900
Pretoria

My own darling wee one,

I got your nice letter of Sept 7 – but I was very unhap. at not getting a letter from you the two previous mails. I wrote a long letter to you from Koomatipoort which I hope you have got alright, and we were soon bustled back here. We took nearly four days as the trucks and engines had not been used for a long time, and we only had amateur engine drivers. The brutes of Boers lay in wait for the trains and derailed and then fired into a Coldstream train which was just in front of us. They killed 5 men and wounded fifteen, and it was the greatest luck in the world it did not happen to us as we had very few men on board. We eventually got back here though we had to stop about 3 times up every hill and we did not go at night. We came back in a guard's van and thought it quite luxurious. We all hoped that we should be told that we are to go home but they will not say so. Darling mum, I does want to get back to you, and really now I am not doing much good out here. I think that the Guards Brigade have done its fair share of work, and they are all sick to death of marching about the country. Besides our Division is broken up and we have left the 18th Brigade behind to garrison the railway line and we have only the Guards Brigade left in addition to some mounted infantry and a battery of artillery. We are now living in a house again with a bathroom, so all quite luxurious. If I don't hear in a day or two what they are going to do with us, I shall try and get home by saying that I am badly wanted in London and that if I don't go home my place will be filled up. If only Gen Trotter would get the War Office people to wire for me as I am afraid if I push too much here they will give me a black mark. Pretoria is a most delicious place after Koomatipoort and is quite like coming back to civilisation again. Since they have started the hospital commission (1), the place is full of beautifully kept hospitals and there is plenty of accommodation for the sick, which was unheard of before.

Dearest one, I am very sorry you are going away from Blair to London in September. I know how unpleasant it is for you when they are not nice to my darling wee – but London is so trying and horrible in September and I am sure it is much better for you to keep out of it if you can, so you must go and stay quietly in the country with some peops. until I come home, and I am still full of hope that it may be soon. Don't stay in nasty London, darling, I don't like to think of you all alone in Eaton Place.

I had a letter from Geordie who told me all about the shooting at Blair, it really seems as if there were more grouse about. I saw a Cameron Highlander who told me that when last he heard from his regiment Hamish was alright and was somewhere near Kroonstadt All the people here are getting frightened about the Free State again, they say the Boers are working down to the south and they are bustling troops down as fast as they can but infantry are no good to try and catch a mounted man. Goodbye my darling one, don't stop in London when it is hot and longing to be with you to look after you.

Ever your most loving Harry

Note

1.   Some 22,000 troops were treated for wounds during the war and some 28 field ambulances, five stationary hospitals and 16 general hospitals were established. Many voluntary organisations set up further facilities. Mahatma Ghandi, a Durban lawyer, was one of the volunteers. Following the British occupation

of Bloemfontein significant concerns about treatment and facilities for the sick and wounded resulted in a Royal Commission to consider and report on the treatment of the sick and wounded during the war. The Commission, led by Lord Justice Romer, visited Bloemfontein. It is this Commission to which Harold refers.

Pretoria
Date Unnkown

My own darling wee one,
I am afraid I can't get away by the next mail but I am in great hopes that they will let me go by the boat leaving about the 25th and I hope before you get this I shall have word to you. I think my darling one had better stop in London, as the times of arrival of the boats are so uncertain, and your coming to Southampton would only make a very long tiring day for you. Besides if the boat stops at Plymouth I shall be extrav. and come by train from there but I will wire everything. I can hardly believe there is a chance of coming home to you and I am so afraid something may turn up to stop me. I am too excited to write any more. Longing to see you again darling one.
Ever your most loving Harry

Harold sailed back on the *Manchester*. When he arrived at Southampton on 20 November, Dertha was waiting on the quayside.

20 November 1900
84, Eaton Place

My dearest Mums,
I got to Southampton alright this morning and the first person I saw was my little wife standing on the quay. So you can imagine how delighted I was. I will come down with Dertha to see you all tomorrow by the 4 o'clock train as already arranged, and till then all news.
Your most affectionate Harold
I am afraid I must come back the next day as I have business to do and clothes. I am afraid I shall only have very scratch garments to come in tomorrow.

Harold left South Africa before war's end but with his head held high having played a significant part and having learned a great deal about soldiering and warfare. His qualities and values had shone through. Harold was to have fourteen years of peace and many happy days with Dertha before he was to return to a far bloodier and more terrifying battlefield. His *Army List* biography now read.

S. African War, 1899-1900 – On Staff. Advance on Kimberley, including actions at Belmont, Enslin, Modder River and Magersfontein. Operations in the Orange Free State, Feb. to May. 00, including operations at Paardeberg (17 to 26 Feb); actions at Poplar Grove, Dreifontein, Vet River (5 and 6 May), and Zand River. Operations in the Transvaal in May and June, 00, including actions near Johannesburg, Pretoria, and Diamond Hill (11 and 12 Jun). Operations in the Transvaal, east of Pretoria, July to 29 Nov., 00, including action at Belfast (26 and 27 Aug.). Despatches, Lond. Gaz. 26 Jan.00 (Lord Methuen, 26 Nov. and 1 Dec. 99), and Lond. Gaz. 16 Mar. 00 and 8 Feb. 01. Brev. Of Maj. Queen's medal with 7 clasps (Belmont, Modder River, Paadeberg, Bloemfontein, Dreifontein, Diamond Hill and Belfast).

The war was from over and mention must be made of Bardie's extraordinary achievements with the Scottish Horse. In November 1900 Kitchener asked him to raise a new regiment to be known as the Scottish Horse. He started promptly recruiting Scotsmen or men of Scottish descent in South Africa, chiefly in Natal; by early February 1901 he was ready to take to the field with three squadrons.

Recruiting was not confined to South Africa. Great Britain and the other Colonies were appealed to and the Highland Society of London sent out 386 officers and men in February and March 1901; his father the Duke of Atholl personally raised 831 men before the war was over. In Australia, the Society in Melbourne enthusiastically joined in and some 300 men joined in March.

With his flair for organization, Bardie set up depots for his new force. A central headquarters depot for both regiments, with a convalescent camp for sick men and overworked horses, was established in Johannesburg, and there were advance depots for each regiment near the railway in the district in which each might be trekking. At these advance depots were remount establishments. Thus sick men could go to the regimental camp rather than get lost in the labyrinth of army hospitals. Horses needing a rest could also be sent in to the rest-camp at the depot.

In selecting his officers Bardie picked wisely – the commander, second in command, and adjutant of each regiment were all experienced regulars. 'From first to last I had 157 officers: 14 were killed or died; seven were invalided; 11 were removed or resigned at my request; 107 served to the end of the war, and the remainder resigned for private reasons. 22 officers were supplied from regular army; 78 were appointed in South Africa from outside the regiment; 46 came up through the ranks; and 11 came from Perthshire.

The 1st Regiment, commanded by Bardie, served in the Western Transvaal but did not see any serious fighting till the action at Vlakfontein on 29 May 1901. When the battle commenced, the Scottish Horse were detached but they rejoined in time to assist the infantry in driving off one of the fiercest attacks of the war. The next serious fighting was at Moedwill in September and Witpoort in December. In the early months of 1902, the regiment captured the whole of Commandant Sarel Albert's commando - seven Boers were killed, 132 prisoners taken, 11 of whom were wounded, together with 130 rifles and their ammunition, and a large number of horses, mules, cattle, and waggons taken. The regiment took part in another battle at Rooival on 11 April 1902 where Bardie claimed for the Scottish Horse the capture of two guns, one pom-pom, one ammunition-cart and 10 waggons.

The 2nd Regiment, under Major Murray, Black Watch, quickly became one of the best corps in the country, fighting at Roodekrantz (April 1901), Eland's Hoek and Dullstroom (July 1901), Tautesberg, Wagen Drift, Brugspruit, and Bakenlaagte. It was here that the Regiment incurred its worst losses of the war when trying to save the guns of Colonel Guinness. Out of 93 engaged in the action, five officers including Colonel Benson and Major Murray and 28 men were killed, and four officers and 36 wounded. Of the 73 who reached Gun Hill, only six were unscathed at the close of the day.

On 20 December 1901 Major Jennings Bramley (19th Hussars), who had succeeded Major Murray in command of the 2nd Regiment, and Lieutenant John Dow were killed at Lake Banagher. Brought to Pretoria after the declaration of peace, the Scottish Horse, along with the Imperial Light Horse, Johannesburg Mounted Rifles, and Kitchener's Fighting Scouts, marched past Lord Kitchener on 17 June 1902, and the Commander-in-Chief intimated that arrangements might be made under which these corps would be placed on a permanent basis.

The Second Anglo-Boer War finally ended on 31 May 1902 and both former Boer Republics were incorporated into the Union of South Africa in 1910 which became a self-governing dominion of the British Empire. Louis Botha, the Boer Leader, became Prime Minister. Independence and reconciliation paved the way for South Africa's entry into the Great War as an ally of Britain and Jan Smuts who led a Boer commando for the Transvaal was destined to lead South African forces during the Great War, becoming a Field Marshal in the British Army in 1941.

Located at the South Africa Gate (Commoner Gate) at Winchester College is a memorial to the 32 Wykehamists who died in both Boer conflicts. On the second tablet are inscribed words from John Bunyan's *Pilgrim's Progress*. When one thinks ahead to Harold's battles and scars, the words appear particularly apt:

> Then said he, my sword I give to him that shall succeed me in my pilgrimage, and my courage and skill to him that can get it. My marks and scars I carry with me, to be a witness for me that I have fought His battles who shall now be my rewarder. So he passed over, and all the trumpets sounded for him on the other side.

6

Home From the Wars

After they had met up in Southampton, Harold and Dertha travelled to London and after a short stopover, headed for Essex by rail. Their first stop was Braintree where 'a grand reception' awaited them. In the large crowd which has assembled to welcome them was Pte Franklin who had been Harold's signaller in the Guards Brigade before being invalided home. To the tune of *See the Conquering Hero Come*, their brougham was drawn through the streets by an enthusiastic crowd to watch a display of fireworks on the Fairfield.

There was more to come for they were soon on their way in a two-horse brougham to Finchingfield where every window had at least one lighted candle in it. On the village green, to the prolonged peal of church bells, fifty farm workers from the Estate waited for them, each carrying a flaming torch. Archie Ruggles-Brise now took over the proceedings. The horses were removed from the brougham and under the direction of the head gamekeeper, the villagers gathered up their ropes and to the music of the Finchingfield Brass band, Harold and Dertha began their journey to Spains Hall.

The lodge gates were covered in laurel leaves and hung with Chinese lanterns; likewise the park was lit by lanterns suspended from trees and the lawns covered in various colours of lights in glass. When they reached the entrance, Harold leapt out and hurried into the Hall to greet his mother. He then returned to the lawn where a great crowd, together with members of his family, eagerly waited. Standing on a large stone near the lawn, Harold addressed his well-wishers. After thanking them for 'the hearty and magnificent reception', he recalled how 'we marched thousands of miles from the Orange River to Komatipoort…and eventually we drove old Kruger (loud laughter) and his foreigners to Delagoa Bay (applause and laughter)'. The band struck up the National Anthem, cheers followed and then the villages were 'regaled with refreshments'. The family returned indoors and sat down to dinner at a table decorated with large knots of blue and red silk, the colours of the Guards, and laurel wreaths with mottos worked in ivy berries. It was a memorable homecoming.

29 November 1900
Spains Hall, Finchingfield

Dearest Father,
I am writing to tell you that I propose taking out my £2000 to buy a house with. Is it convenient to you? What had I better do about it? Shall I write to Jamieson and ask him to transfer it to the bank? We have settled on a house in Regents Park, for which after a good deal of haggling they have accepted £1850, but new drainage and odds and ends will bring it to £2000.

We should have had a good shoot here, but yesterday's bad weather spoilt it; however they got over 600 head and should get a good deal more today. We go down to London tonight, just to see Geordie off.
Your affectionate daughter, Dertha

The war in South Africa still dominated domestic news. In February the House of Commons vote of censure over the government's handling of the Second Boer War was defeated by a majority of 213. Dertha in her typically forthright way wrote to her father with news and views. London papers had been reporting on Lord Methuen's disagreement with his officers including Colonels Gough and Paget, suggesting that the latter had been ordered to 'take their men to certain death'.

6 December 1900
84 Eaton Place, SW

Dearest Father,
I tried to send you this several days ago but I had to make another copy and it took so dreadfully long. I should have sent it off by this post, only Neil Menzies (1) came in and interrupted. He has honoured me a good deal with his company.

The rumours about lord Methuen's eccentricities have now taken shape. Colonel Gough (2), 9th Lancers, who has been sent home in disgrace says he and Lord M had a row because he was ordered to charge and he says his horses were absolutely done – they couldn't even walk, so Lord M flew at him. The other retaliated – all this before the men – and Lord Methuen said: 'Sir I have no confidence in you.' Col G said, 'Then I had better leave?.' 'Yes, and the sooner the better!' and so he did and he is now at home. Though Lord Methuen was wrong, Colonel Gough seems to have been insubordinate and he has no business to go screaming this all over London. He asked for an interview with Lord Wolseley and sat with him for two hours, and as Lord Wolseley hates Lord Methuen it has done him a great deal of harm.

Then Lord Wolseley and the 'civil side of the War Office' are dead cuts and Lord Wolseley states as an absolute fact that he was never told that Lord Roberts and Kitchener had been appointed, and he is hatching up many things and has a very strong case for the future and as he is the cleverest man of the lot he will make it extremely nasty. Then to go back to Lord Methuen, when he was wounded, for two days or more he was incapable of doing anything, but absolutely refused to let Sir Henry Colvile do anything or anybody else, till they actually forced him to.

To go to more cheerful things than squabbles, somebody has written down that old Col Codrington walked about in the water because Captain Nugent told him the General wanted him to, and that Harry on his own responsibility got him back again. There is absolutely no news about Buller, except they say Tugela was not his fault, and that General Hart let him in for it (3).

Johnnie Moncreiffe has enlisted as a trooper in the yeomanry. I should think it will kill him, but it is the only time I have respected him.

I really can't write any more – I am so sick of my pen.
Your affectionate Dertha

Notes

1.   Sir Neil Menzies of that Ilk, 8th Bt, a Captain in the Scots Guards and a neighbour of the Atholls at Weem in Perthshire.
2.   Colonel Bloomfield Gough (1852-1904) was killed in a carriage accident in June 1904. *The Times History of the War* (1900-1909) stated that the cavalry at the Battle of Enslin, 'weak in numbers, and with worn-out horses, could do little to turn the [Boer] retreat to advantage … Once more Methuen had cause to regret the absence of a cavalry brigade. Whether the mounted troops present could have done more is doubtful, but Lord Methuen was not satisfied with the leading of Colonel Gough, commanding the 9th Lancers, and that officer was succeeded by Major Little'.
3.   Major General Fitzroy Hart's 5th (Irish) Brigade attacked the next high ground to the northeast, Hart's Hill, on 23 February 1900. Not waiting for all his battalions to arrive, Hart sent his troops up piecemeal and they were repulsed with almost 500 casualties. Two battalions of reinforcements arrived in time to prevent a rout. Two colonels were among the dead and the Royal Inniskilling Fusiliers lost 72 percent of their officers and 27% of their rank and file. Curiously, Dertha referred to an action that took place ten months earlier.

Sad news was only just around the corner for Harold's mother Marianne died suddenly on 12th December when he and Dertha were in Perth.

14 December 1900
7 Barossa Place, Perth

Dearest Father,
All our plans are now upset, as Harry got a telegram yesterday to say his mother had died suddenly. We have settled to stay here till just after Christmas, and then come to London. Harry passes through on Monday to go to the funeral and will call about seven o'clock in the morning for some clothes. He goes on with his brother and has breakfast with him. I have come to Perth for the day to buy some common black clothes and am having luncheon with Cousin Emily. Mamma is in bed with a cold.
Your affectionate Dertha

As it transpired, Dertha rather had her eye on Harold's 'Long Tom' souvenir:

15 December 1900
84 Eaton Place, SW

Dearest Father,
Harry has just come across this beautiful effusion in his desk. I am sending it to you in case you would like to keep it – if not, burn it. I meant to see you this morning but I slept badly and didn't think you would be gone so early. We are going to Blair on Saturday and will pick up Helen. I think I shall have to come back to London on the 20th, when we take over the house. We go to Longleat for Christmas week, and then we could arrange to live somewhere else in London till Regents Park is ready – I doubt it being done before February.
    I hear Harry has given you his piece of 'Long Tom'(1) – I am not very pleased as I wanted it myself as an ornament! He has a Transvaal flag taken from a fort in Pretoria (he saw it there himself); I suppose you wouldn't rather have that than the Long Tom would you? He says if you do, you can certainly have it. Harry says he hears they are to give 12 clasps for the war – three for the defence of Ladysmith, Kimberley, Mafeking, three for relief of ditto, one each for Cape Colony, Free State and Transvaal. one for Pretoria and one for Bloemfontein. I think it is a pity they didn't have them for particular battles, anyway for Paardeburg … remainder of correspondence missing.

Note
1.   The 155 mm Creusot 'Long Tom' was a French siege gun (artillery piece) manu-factured by Schneider et Cie in Le Creusot, France, and employed by the Boers as field guns. Four guns, along with 4,000 common shells, 4,000 shrapnel shells and 800 case shot were purchased by the South African Republic in

1897. With a 10,000-metre range and rate of fire of 20 rounds an hour, it was a formidable weapon system.

On 23rd December, Dertha received a letter from Colvile's spouse Zelie,[1] with the dramatic news that he had been sent home. The long running saga of the Spragge incident had finally come to an end, albeit an ignominious one for Colvile. According to Gleischen, on 7 May 1900, he had been handed a note by 'two strange Englishmen in nice new uniforms' supposedly from Colonel Bragge,[2] the commanding officer of 13th Battalion Imperial Yeomanry. The message read: 'Found no one in Lindley but Boers – have 500 men but only one day's food, have stopped three miles back on Kroonstadt road. I want help to get out without great loss'. On questioning the men, Gleichen established that the battalion was comfortably encamped some way out of Lindley and had not had any fighting at all. Their wagons were intact and they had their rations. When Colvile had been apprised of the note and the verbal report of the messengers, he had to make a decision as to whether to turn back to rescue Spragge or follow Roberts's order to advance to Heilbron the next day as part of the general advance. He chose the latter and reached Heilbron on time after two days of hard fighting. His division, in spite of being dead tired and short of food, and in spite of determined opposition, had carried out its orders.

Meanwhile it transpired that Spragge's entire force of 468 men had shortly afterwards been surrounded and taken prisoners. Roberts attributed the whole disaster to Colvile, who on arrival in Pretoria was carpeted by the Field Marshal and sent back to Gibraltar. He could forgive once (Sannah's Post), but Colvile was suspended for having twice shown a 'want of military capacity and initiative.' It was only later that a Court of Enquiry was held into 'the Spragge affair' at which Colvile was not represented. At this point, Gleichen comes up with a surprising twist to the story. In November 1900, he had met an officer who had been with Spragge. He told him that on 23 May Spragge had received a telegram signed by Colvile telling him to come to Lindley at once. He had accordingly hastened to Lindley. Something was very fishy for Colvile did not know Spragge's name; he had expected him at Ventersburg, not Kroonstadt; the 9th Divisional HQ did not reach Lindley until 26 May and critically there was no telegraphic equipment at the Post Office and the telephone lines had been cut. The telegram was therefore clearly a forgery or the story was fiction.

1   Zelie was born in Orthez, France. Her father Richard de Preville married Georgiana Mowbray, the daughter of a Royal Navy Captain.
2   Lieutenant Colonel Basil Spragge, DSO: 51st Foot or Yorkshire Light Infantry Jowaki campaign (1877); 51st Foot and Superintendent of Army Signalling Afghan War (1878-1880); DAAQG Burmese campaign (1886-1889) and Gentleman-at-Arms.

The officer also told Gleichen that Spragge, ignoring his officers, had insisted on remaining just outside Lindley when the Boers began to surround him. After three days fighting, the British surrendered. British casualties amounted to 80, of whom 23 were fatal. Amongst these was Lord Craigavon and Sir John Power, a whiskey baronet. Of Spragge's men, 379 were marched into captivity, three managing to escape. There were 28 British wounded left in hospital in Heilbron, seven of whom died from their wounds. Somewhat uncharacteristically, Roberts's previous close relationship with Spragge in Afghanistan and Bruma seems to have clouded his usual objectivity in judicial judgement.

23 December 1900

My Dear Dertha,

Misfortunes come in wars but it seems to me we are having more than our share. A few days ago I was very down about our moving matter … but now that all seems very small trouble compared to this thunderbolt that fell on us two days ago … anyway I send you the copy of the letter ….they cannot degrade him more than they have done – insult after insult has been showered upon him – but now thank goodness they have made it possible for him to speak and speak he will and they won't find him easy with his clear clever brain. Why, he is treated worse than a vagabond for at least with the law of the country no one can be tried twice for the same offence. They begin by having a board on him which did not even see him. They find nothing to prevent him taking up his appointment and secretly and by telegraph without a word to him undermine him and hunt him down. Surely there is some justice left somewhere.

He is starting for home next Tuesday and I shall try to get off on New Year's Day. What a beginning of a New Year! But Dear Dertha I have a strong feeling that this is the best thing that could have happened … for now he can make for home and clear himself. That Kitchener is at the bottom of this mischief I have not much doubt, but still he can't do it without Roberts. I am wondering if they have told Roberts that board sat on the case. I have no doubt it is quite possible Lord Roberts was not told of all the mistakes his HQ made – so he may only know part of the yeomanry business. But I never can forget that was one of the very last incidents and that he hunted down my Harry long before that. Why heavens only knows. It is rather funny that Bobs will still find me in possession here when he comes and spends the day in Gib. We have made no secret of all this here…..you can tell everyone that Harry has come home to defend himself having been told to resign and he having flatly refused to do so. Sir GW (1) is furious about the whole business…what will become of our English army if our officers are to be tricked like this in the dark and made to resign as if it were of their own free will.

He has been proud to defend himself before, but now he is roused. He says he has nothing more to lose ….but what fools to think that a strong head like Harry would chuck his career that he has loved for years. He has his wife and son (2) to think of too. He can't throw away the one means he has of making a livelihood without a struggle. The expense of it all appals me but I would rather find myself penniless at the end of it than rather than that he should spare expense to right himself. I think his case will help others. For I believe there are others who are being kicked in the dark corners …

I have so much to do and to think of so must stop. I hope to see you both soon.
Yours affectionately,
Zelie
I think I have every right to be bitter now. Don't show the letter out, say what I have said above.

Notes
1. General Sir George White VC (1835-1912).
2. Gilbert Colvile (b. 1887).

Included with Zelie's letters is a copy, in her hand, of a letter her husband had received from the War Office.

War Office
16 December 1900

My Dear General,
In the temporary absence of the Military Secretary an unpleasant duty devolves on me.

The Secretary of State having discussed by telegraph the incidents of the surrender of the XIII Imperial Yeomanry batt. concurs with Lord Roberts that you were mainly responsible for the surrender and has reluctantly come to the conclusion that you cannot be permitted to retain your command.

I am directed to request that you will hand in your signature to General Sir G White on receipt of this letter and quit Gibraltar.

I am sending a copy of this letter to Sir George but do not propose to write through the usual channel as it may be less vexatious to you if the resignation appears to be voluntary.
Yours truly,
Evelyn Wood

The story continues in Dertha's letters to her father.

31 December 1900
84 Eaton Place, SW

Dearest Father,

First of all a happy New Year to you. Secondly a 'Cow Gun' is a 5-inch siege gun drawn by sixteen span of oxen, throwing a 50lb lyddite shell – range 1000yds. Thirdly I am glad you like the chairs. I thought they were particularly nice. Fourthly, what do you think of old Colvile? Harry and Count Gleichen have been putting their heads together. The latter was intelligence officer to the division and knows more about it than Colvile himself. He says he has an absolutely unanswerable case, even stronger than he made out – but of course he has utterly done for himself by publishing the whole thing (1). Brodrick (2) wanted to kick him out, and deservedly, for other things but he has made a perfect ass of himself by picking on the one thing that Colvile had not done. Gleichen says it would have been perfectly impossible for them to have gone back. Brodrick has his facts all wrong. I am very sorry for Lady Colvile. It will all recoil on her.

I see the 'Times' says Bardie has telegraphed to the Caledonia Society to send him recruits.

Your affectionate Dertha

Notes

1. Colvile resumed his command in Gibraltar on 1st October 1900, having already reported back to the War Office to state his case. Under the impression that matters had been resolved, it came as a shock to learn that a Board of Enquiry had found against him. Little wonder that when he next landed in Plymouth, he gave an interview to the *Reuters* correspondent, blaming the fate of the Imperial Yeomanry Battalion on poor staff work.

2. St John Brodrick, later 9th Viscount and first Earl of Midleton, Secretary of State for War, 1900-1903. The issue of a miscarriage or misapplication of justice refused to go away. On 11 March 1903, a debate on 'The Removal Of Army Officers' took place, the main thrust being to challenge the practice of using secretive Boards of Enquiry, where the defendant was not represented, to dispense justice rather than Courts Martial.[3]

---

3   *Hansard* <https://hansard.parliament.uk/Commons/1903-03-11/debates/42786185-beea-49ba-a71b-995998d18490/TheRemovalOfArmyOfficers> (accessed 12 December 2022).

19 January 1901
84 Eaton Place, SW

Dearest Father,

Everybody seems to be in a great state about the poor old Queen. It does sound rather serious, as apparently her heart fails. It would be a bad thing if she were to die now, but I can't wish her to live long and lose her powers.

You will have seen General Colvile has been kicked out. They have told him it is entirely on account of his having published and nothing to do with his 'case', so he has certainly given them the weapon they wanted. I am afraid he is going to rake up Sanna's Post and I am afraid of Harry being dragged into it as a witness.

We were given a present of game, on the strength of which we asked Bill Mansfield (1) to dinner last night. What a lot he drinks!

Your affectionate Dertha

Note

1. William Murray, 4th/5th Earl of Mansfield (1860-1904). He had been a Captain in the Grenadier Guards.

As Brigade Major to Sir Henry Trotter,[4] the Major General commanding the Brigade of Guards and GOC Home District, Harold was responsible for implementing the military ceremonial aspects of all state occasions in London. On 3 January 1901, Field Marshal Lord Roberts returned to England and received a hero's welcome in London. Welcomed by the Prince of Wales at Victoria Station, he rode through the streets to Buckingham Palace. Over 14,500 troops were on parade, including 1,200 mounted.

The death of Queen Victoria at Osborne House on the Isle of Wight three weeks later triggered a series of ceremonial events. On 24 January, four battalions of Foot Guards lined the streets between Buckingham Palace and the Royal Exchange. Passing standards, colours and drums draped in black, the Royal Procession reached Temple Bar at 9.30 a.m. where the Lord Mayor of London read aloud the Order in Council requiring the herald to proclaim His Majesty within the jurisdiction of the City of London.

4   Henry Trotter (1844-1905) was commissioned into the Grenadier Guards in 1862. Promoted to Major General in 1895 and appointed Major General commanding the Brigade of Guards and General Officer Commanding Home District in 1897, his military career ended in1903.

27 January 1901
84 Eaton Place, SW

Dearest Father,
I have seen no snow here except once about a fortnight ago.

Harry has to do a deal of running about arranging for the procession on Saturday. He is going to hire a charger as at present he has nothing but his little Gibraltar pony which he keeps in barracks. There won't be much for one to see, as unless one stands in the park, which is impossible, there will be nowhere else. Harry has begun badly. On the morning of the 'Proclamation' at St James's Palace he had left word overnight that he was to be called at 6 a.m. and have breakfast at 6.45. His servant called him at quarter to seven so he had no breakfast and he had to rush into his uniform. He split his breeches and then found he couldn't draw on a new pair of boots over his leg. He hammered his legs in with some difficulty, and the result was that after half an hour on his horse he had to fall out and leave the work for someone else. He is furious with himself and said it was the first time in his life he has ever fallen out.

Did you notice the other day that the Duke of Westminster (1) was gazetted out of the Blues almost as soon as he had been gazetted in? As far as I can make out Lord Wolseley (2) said if he wanted to marry, he must wait a year, as he couldn't have any more married subalterns. His Grace said he wouldn't and the result was as above. He now says (I suppose following Colvile's example) that he refuses to resign, but I don't think anybody pays attention to him.
Your affectionate Dertha

Notes
1. Hugh Grosvenor was commissioned in 1900. Aged 22, he married Constance Cornwallis-West in 1901, the first of four marriages.
2. Wolseley had been Colonel of the Royal Horse Guards since 1895.

The funeral arrangements for Queen Victoria were complicated by the fact that she died at Osborne. In what must have been a major staff operation, Harold burnt the midnight oil to mastermind the military component of the state funeral from Osborne to Frogmore. On Saturday 2 February, Guards of Honour were mounted at Victoria and Paddington Stations and Buckingham Palace. A small party of 12 Grenadiers and an officer had already been sent to Osborne to carry the Queen's coffin and escort the gun carriage to Cowes. From there, the catafalque moved by train to Victoria and then by carriage to Paddington via Buckingham Place and onto Windsor by train until it arrived at St Georges Chapel for the state funeral service until the Queen reached her final resting place at Frogmore House in the grounds of Windsor Great Park. Now General Trotter and Harold turned their attention to planning the military ingredients of the Coronation.

One interlude from work at the end of Court mourning was the marriage on 19 February of Major General Pole-Carew to Lady Beatrice Butler, the eldest daughter of the Marquess and Marchioness of Ormonde. It was fitting that the best man was Colonel Vesey Dawson, a fellow Coldstream officer, who had been made the first commanding officer of the Irish Guards in 1900.

18 September 1901
19, Hanover Terrace
Regent's Park

My own darling wee,

I got a little letter from you this morning, for which many thanks.

I really had no time to write a line to you today. I was running about every moment, and as we have got a field day at Wimbledon tomorrow, I am writing this after my dinner.

You will have seen in the paper that poor Gurdon-Rebow has been killed (1). I am afraid it looks as though he had got careless and was caught in a farmhouse. He was a very gallant boy, but most stupid. He was very badly wounded – to all appearances – at Belmont, but the bullet had only scratched his head. Anyhow he had a near shave and it seems very cruel that he should be killed just at the end, after all he went through. I am very sorry for his people as he was, I think, the only son. I daresay you remember his mother from when he used to work at the Staff College. I went and saw Cuthbertson (Black Watch) today in York Terrace. He has been in bed for three weeks with jaundice and is rather bad. The Doctor says he will have to spend another fortnight in bed, so when you come back we will get him to come round here.

I think I have squared my leave alright for November, but I see the Duke of York comes back about the 2nd. I daresay however I could shirk that if necessary. Write and tell me who you have got staying at Blair and if there is anybody who goes out stalking, and if your little wee self is flourishing.

I am sorry Geordie has got to go to South Africa again as I am afraid it will worry the Duchess.

Goodbye my darling mums. I is looking forward to seeing you again, and it is only a week next Friday. Meanwhile take the greatest care of yourself.

Ever your most loving Harry

Note

1. The only son of Hector Gurdon–Rebow, the head of a prominent Essex family, Martin went to South Africa with the 3rd Battalion Grenadier Guards and was present at the action at Belmont, where he was wounded, and then at Modder River. The day he was killed, he was in charge of a patrol of Grenadiers. Kitchener in referring to his death observed: 'I must also make allusion to the very gallant stand made on 16 September by nine men of the 3rd Battalion Grenadier Guards, under Lieutenant Gurdon–Rebow, who found themselves attacked by some 30 to 40 of the enemy near Cyferkuil, ten miles north of Riet Siding. A summons to surrender was refused by Gurdon–Rebow, and he and one man were killed and two others dangerously wounded. The Sergeant of the patrol was drowned in a gallant attempt to swim the Carolus River in order to get assistance'.

Around this time, efforts were made, unsuccessfully, to secure Harold greater recognition of his courage, work and leadership in South Africa. It is not clear who the recipient of the letter was.

31 October 1901

My dear General,
Yours of today. I fear it is quite hopeless about Ruggles-Brise. The reason I say this is that his case has already been specifically considered both by Lord Roberts and the Secretary of State and they decided that it did not come into a very small and exceptional category of men who were given double rewards.

I will however file your letter with a mass of correspondence I have in similar subjects which are to be brought up at the end of the war, so that in a way your protégé will have one more chance for consideration,
Yours sincerely
Ian Hamilton

Attached to this correspondence is the following which is in a different hand and unsigned:

1. Major Ruggles-Brise, Gren Gds, was four times mentioned in dispatches for good work in action - at Belmont where he led the night attack, at Modder, at Magersfontein and at Paardeberg and was on the staff of the 11th Division during its march from Bloemfontein to Komatipoort (medal with 7 clasps).
2. He does not in the least consider that his services merit a double reward, and while most grateful for the honour of a brevet majority, he points out that it was given to him when third senior Captain of his Regiment (1) and has made no difference to him in the position he now holds, nor will it make any in the future, whereas a reward that is more appreciated is either a tangible and permanent one, or one that will assist the recipient in further advancement.

Note
1.   Promotion in the Army was governed by the regimental system where progress was dependent on vacancies triggered by retirement, resignation or death, irrespective of achievement in the wider Army.

Harold attended the King's first Levée at St James's Place on 11 February 1902. Two days later he was present at a memorial service in the Guards Chapel for Kenneth Meeking, a young officer in the 2nd Battalion who had died of enteric fever while serving in the Orange River colony. The war remained as close as ever and in April, Harold was among other officers who bid farewell to the 255 members of the Coldstream Guards who entrained at Nine Elms for Capetown. At this stage, the Brigade of Guards was already planning a memorial in the Guards Chapel to all those who died in South Africa.

The coronation of King Edward VII was scheduled for 26 June 1902. With meticulous preparations in place all around Britain, the King was suddenly taken ill just two days before Coronation day and had to have an emergency operation. He reluctantly accepted that the Coronation would have to be postponed to 9 August. This last-minute change of date meant that foreign dignitaries and military contingents had to leave London and were unable to return for the rescheduled date, the former delegating to their ambassadors. For the Atholl family, this turned out to be a blessing in disguise for the Duchess died in Italy on 9 July whilst taking thermal waters at Salsomaggiore. Her body was returned to Scotland where she was buried at Blair Atholl on 17 July.

On the day of the Coronation, although the procession still included representatives of the British Army, Royal Navy, Royal Marines and Colonial, Dominion and Indian forces, the public event was low-key.

On 10 August 1902, Harold wrote of the coronation of Edward VII and of his meeting with the new Monarch.

10 August 1902
19, Hanover Terrace
Regent's Park

My own darling little one,
I am all alone again without you, but I must not grumble. I am very anxious to hear what they do to you, as I can't bear your being bullied.

We got over the coronation alright and everything went very well, and the King was not a bit the worse. I kept down by Westminster Abbey all the time, which was by far the most amusing place. (1) I saw all sorts of funny people and I did not get home till half past four. Most of the people in the Abbey saw nothing, but the Peeresses and the House of Commons had the only place from which the ceremony could be watched.

I suddenly got a letter today that I had to go and see the King at 5pm this afternoon to settle about the medal parades. I had to wait about an hour but he was very nice and sensible when he did come. I am going to dine with Bob tonight and meet Kitty. I did not go to St Paul's with her after all, as I could not spare the time. She went with her pal Miss Antrobus (2).

I must go now and dress, my precious. Do anything you can to get well quick.

Your most loving Harry

Notes

1. If Harold had been inside the Abbey, he may well have found it more amusing! The service was conducted by the elderly and infirm Archbishop of Canterbury, Frederick Temple, who had to be supported throughout by two other bishops. Because of his failing eyesight, the text of the service had to be printed in gigantic type onto rolls of paper called 'prompt scrolls'. He was unable to rise after kneeling to pay homage and had to be helped up by the King himself and several bishops He then placed the crown back-to-front on Edward VII's head, and when a colleague enquired after his well-being, he was told to 'go away!' in a loud voice that was plainly heard by the congregation. The King also deviated from the order of service; when the Prince of Wales touched the Crown and kissed his father's left cheek in the traditional gesture of homage, the King rose to his feet and threw his arms around his son's neck in an unusual display of affection. Another disruption came from the King's sister, Princess Beatrice, who accidentally (but noisily) dropped her service book from the royal gallery onto a gold-plate table.

2. Colonel Sir Edmund Antrobus,4th Bt. (1848-1915) was a colonel in the Grenadiers and would have been well known to Harold. His only child, also called Edmund, was killed in October 1914 when serving with the Grenadiers in France. Miss Antrobus may have been a cousin , either Blanche (1858-1954) or Dora (1865-1919)

The reconstituted Coronation Procession took place in October 1902. As *the Times* reported 'there was no galaxy of foreign guests...no Princes of India and Premiers from the colonies' but even so there were 28,000 British soldiers on parade including nearly 5,000 from all ten Guards battalions. Covering   eight miles in all, the Progress left from Buckingham Palace, down Pall Mall, then across Trafalgar Square, up the Strand and Ludgate Hill until it reached the Guildhall. The route back went along the Victoria Embankment. One wonders what Harold was thinking when he rode past the stands in front of the National Gallery from where Botha, De Wet and De la Rey watched their former enemies march past.

As there had been no King's Birthday Parade in June, on 27 October the king reviewed all the Guards regiments on Horse Guards Parade. By now gazetted a major in the Grenadier Guards[5], Harold was on parade.

If 1902 had been a busy year for the Brigade Major, 1903 was equally hectic. The routine commitments such as the inspection of all the individual Guards battalions by the Major General and the King's Birthday Parade (that year the 2nd Battalion Coldstream Guards trooped their colour) were supplemented by two state visits, President Émile Loubet of France in July and the King and Queen of Italy in November. Both required intricate ceremonial programs for Harold to execute. His tenure as Brigade Major ended on 22 January 1904 and he joined the 1st Battalion.

Understandably there is far less correspondence to rely on in interwar years as Harold was able to spend considerably more time with Dertha. On 25 April 1904, Dertha wrote to her father with two significant pieces of news.

25 April 1904
19, Hanover Terrace, Regents Park

Dearest Father,

Thank you for the piece of salmon which arrived two days ago. We are still feasting on it.

Harry has been given the Secretaryship of the Manoeuvre Committee. The work lasts from now till the end of the manoeuvres. He will have a room in the War Office and will have to take journeys into his native county Essex to arrange for ground to be used. One advantage is we won't have to go to Pirbright for two months which was rather troubling to me, and also he gets £2 a day instead of one and we want it badly just now.

I have had rather a nasty thing happen to me. A large bull terrier pinned Towser down by the throat and I thought was killing him so I tried to haul him off by the collar and choked him. He then turned his attentions to me and bit me in both hands, the left one badly so. Some workmen beat him off with an iron bar. I had to have the bites cauterised, but it is going on alright – only I shan't be able to use my left hand for some time as it is nearly bitten through.

Nothing more to tell you,

Your affectionate Dertha

The outcome of Harold's work was a large military exercise commencing on 7 September in Essex which was designated a 'foreign country' to be invaded by

---

5   *The London Gazette,* 24 October 1902.

troops under Sir John French. Rumoured to be indisposed on account of having caught a chill, Sir John appeared 'in the best of trim' at Avington Park, Sir John Shelley's magnificent 17th mansion and park outside Winchester which had been designated the 'concentration area'. Wining and dining continued on board one of His Majesty's cruisers as the ten transports gathered round Spithead. The next morning, the invasion fleet lay some 2,000 yards off Clacton-On-Sea. Fortunately, the placid state of the sea enabled the disembarkation of men and horses to proceed uninterrupted and the troops, including Frankie Lloyd's 1st Guards Brigade, pushed forwards and took Colchester. The manoeuvres, involving some 12,000 men, 3,000 horses and 60 guns, were observed by Prince Arthur (third son of Queen Victoria and Prince Albert), Inspector General to the Forces, and a host of military attachés as well as crowds of excited members of the public. Little did Harold nor anyone else know that in 1914 the British Expeditionary Force would be landing in France and Belgium and yet again in 1915 at Gallipoli.

Before long Harold was transferred at short notice to 3rd Battalion Grenadier Guards at Blenheim Barracks, Aldershot, which meant letting their London home.

16 May 1905
Ellesmere
S. Farnborough

Dearest Father,
I wonder whether you would care to come here for the big review – I think on the 9th for a couple of nights or so? Let me know as I have just one spare room and otherwise will put someone else into it. I rather enjoy being here now and am having a lot of riding and going about generally.

Great excitement over the 'new probationers' just come down. They haven't settled yet what uniform they are to wear so they are walking about in flannels.....
Your affectionate daughter Dertha

20 May 1905
Ellesmere
S. Farnborough

Dearest Father,
The Review is now fixed for the 9th. It is the ordinary sort of annual review here, nominally this time for the King of Spain (1). It will be on Laffan's plain (2), about a mile from here. Perhaps you would like to come for the day? There are two battalions of Scots Guards here who may

amuse you. I think their piping is not up to the mark. Nobody takes any interest and it is only looked upon as an 'infernal row' … I see the worm in the shape of Lord Stair (3) has at last turned, and Neil (4) is to be run in over Lady Stair (5). I am sorry as it will make an ugly scandal (6), and I suppose there were some people in his part of the world who still believed in him.

Your affectionate Dertha

Notes
1. In 1905 Spain's King Alfonso XIII set off on a tour of Europe which, among other purposes, was aimed at finding himself a wife. In London he thought he had found someone: Princess Patricia of Connaught, one of Queen Victoria's granddaughters. She turned him down. However, he did manage to attract the attention of Victoria Eugenie of Battenberg (1887-1969), daughter of Princess Beatrice. They married the following year.
2. The Annual Review by the Sovereign took place on Laffan's Plain, a parade ground in Aldershot that was named after Lieutenant General Sir Robert Laffan (1821-1882), former Commanding Royal Engineer at Aldershot.
3. John Hamilton–Darlrymple, 11th Earl of Stair, a Major in the Ayrshire (Earl of Carrick's Own) Yeomanry who was granted the honorary rank of lieutenant colonel in 1902.
4. Sir Neil Menzies of Castle Menzies, Perthshire.
5. In 1878, he married Susan Grant-Suttie, the grand-daughter of the Duchess of Roxburghe, a friend and Lady of the Bedchamber to Queen Victoria.
6. The scandal broke in *The Times* on 26th June 1905. The Earl brought an action for divorce against the Countess on grounds of her alleged adultery with Sir Neil Menzies. She had previously raised an action on grounds of desertion when the Earl had relocated from London to Perthshire. Although they were legally separated in 1893, the Earl produced witnesses that she and Menzies had been openly living together in a house in Maidenhead. A decree was granted. Neil and Susan married two weeks later. Sadly he died without issue in 1910 and his baronetcy became extinct.

The year 1907 got off to a busy start with Harold destined for higher rank.

1 January 1907
19, Hannover Terrace
Regent's Park

Dearest Father,

I am writing to wish you a happy New Year. We had a very good time in Wales and beautiful shooting. I came back yesterday and Harry comes tomorrow. I have just heard from him that he is to go on to the 'Economic School' (1), whatever that is, in London for six months. That is rather a relief as we shan't have to let our house and will get off Windsor. We have let our stables to Mitchell of Bond Street (2); he seems rather a lunatic as he is to pay us a good rent for two years, build a motor garage and fit out the coach house, put in electric light and do up the rooms and stables all at his own expense!

We go tomorrow to shoot in Essex and that will be the finish up.
Your affectionate daughter Dertha

Notes
1. The brainchild of Sir Edward Ward, the Permanent Secretary at the War Office, 31 students, including Harold, attended the first Army Administration Course at the London School of Economics from January to July 1907. Lectures were given on 14 subjects covering six broader areas: accounting and business methods, commercial law, statistics, transport, banking and economics. They were supplemented by numerous 'observation visits' to such enterprises as the offices of *The Times*, the Great Western Railway Works, the London Docks, the London Omnibus Works, the Railway Clearing House, the Houses of Parliament and Lloyds. Eminent experts in their fields who were drawn from business, the universities and government instructed students. Haldane was a frequent lecturer and several others were politically from the radical wing including Webb, who lectured on the organisation of trade unions, Hastings Lees-Smith on economics (later a Labour Cabinet Minister) and the Fabian Socialist Graham Wallas, one of the seminal figures in the development of social science (on public administration).[6]
2. Possibly the family of John Mitchell, publisher and bookseller to Her Majesty the Queen.

Harold was promoted to Colonel on 20 July 1907 and took command of the 3rd Battalion Grenadier Guards at Victoria Barracks, Windsor. His adjutant was Lieutenant the Hon Arthur Weld Forester. The hierarchy of the regiment now consisted of HRH Field Marshal The Duke of Connaught as the Colonel, Colonel John St.Aubyn as the Regimental Lieutenant Colonel Commanding, and the three commanding officers, Robert Scott-Kerr, William Cavendish and Harold. In the 3rd Battalion, there were some familiar faces from South Africa like Noel Corry, Maxwell Earle, George Jeffreys, Alexander Russell, Charles Corkran and Wilfred Abel-Smith. The younger officers included John Vereker, Viscount Gort, a future VC and Field Marshal. Of the officers who passed through the battalion during Harold's command, ten would be killed during the Great War including Arthur Weld Forester; five would win DSOs.

6   Grant, P., 'Learning to Manage the Army: The Army Administration Course at the London School of Economics 1907-1914' in LoCicero, M., Mahoney, R. and Mitchell, S. (eds.), *A Military Transformed? Adaptation and Innovation in the British Military, 1792-1945* (Solihull: Helion & Company, 2014), pp. 99-111.

Harold's parents and siblings c.1885-1886. (Ruggles-Brise family)

Second Lieutenant Harold
Ruggles-Brise c.1886-1887.
(Ruggles-Brise family)

Captain Harold Ruggles-Brise in
South Africa 1900. (Ruggles-Brise
family)

Lady Dorothea Stewart-Murray,
5 February 1895. (Atholl family)

Lady Dorothea Ruggles-Brise c.1910.
(Atholl family)

The Duke of Atholl and his sons L to R: Lord George (Geordie), the Duke, Lord James (Hamish), Lord Tullibardine (Bardie)

Wentworth Castle, Harold back row second from left; Dertha in front of Harold; Duke of Atholl back row fifth from left, 1890

Blair Atholl in the 1880s. (Atholl family)

Harold en route to South Africa on Ghoorka 1899. (Ruggles-Brise family)

Deck cricket. (Ruggles-Brise family)

3rd Battalion officers South Africa 1900 . Harold seated on L; Lieutenant-Colonel Crabbe on far right. (Grenadier Guards)

9th Division staff officers South Africa 1900: Back (L to R): Nugent, Cuthbertson, Browne, Raymond, Bordon; Seated (L to R): Johnson, Ewart, Colvile, Barker, Mr Makins; Sitting (L to R): Gleichen, George Murray. (Gleichen, *A Guardsman's Memoirs*)

3rd Bn Staff Group London 1909: Front row: Sergeant Major Wall, Captain & Adjutant Pike, Lieutenant–Colonel Ruggles-Brise, Lieutenant & Quatermaster Cook, QMS Acock. (Grenadier Guards)

Lieutenant-Colonel Ruggles-Brise leading the 3rd Bn on a route march at Aldershot, 1908. (Grenadier Guards)

Hythe officers c. 1912. Commandant Ruggles–Brise centre. (Ruggles–Brise family)

Dertha fetching water 1914. (Ruggles-
Brise family)

Major-General Ruggles-Brise
c.1916. (Ruggles-Brise family)

Harold on Laffans Plain c.1916. (Crown copyright)

King George V inspection, Aldershot, May 1916.

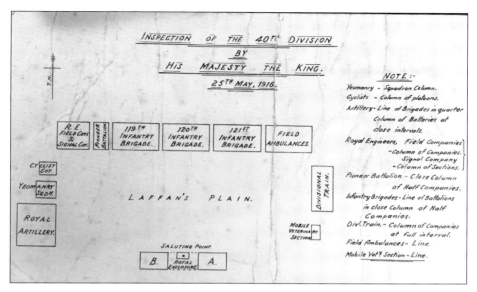

Inspection parade plan.
(Ruggles-Brise family)

British 14.5 inch howitzers
in support of Harold's
division c.1916. (Grenadier
Guards).

Field Marshal Sir
Douglas Haig, 1918.
(Ruggles-Brise family)

La Vacquerie from
the air, 1917. (Crown
copyright)

Harold arrives to open Finchingfield War Memorial 27 June 1920. (Ruggles-Brise family)

Unveiling of Finchingfield War Memorial. (Ruggles-Brise family)

Grenadiers line Harold's graveside at Finchingfield Parish Church, June 1927. (Ruggles-Brise family)

Floor Memorial to Harold in the Guards Chapel. It was destroyed by an enemy bomb in 1944. (Author)

Harold's approach to leadership at senior rank included keeping close to his men and trying to keep his hand in at cricket.

6 August 1907
St. Leonards Lodge,
Clewer Green, Windsor

Dearest Father,

I am so sorry I am a day too late to wish you many happy returns of your birthday. I propose coming to Blair a little before the gathering. Harry says he won't get away much before the last week of September, but he doesn't expect stalking. I shall be at Windsor most of this month. I am really having rather a nice time in some ways. Harry insists upon dining and sleeping in barracks as he says he wants to keep people together, but I don't suppose the subalterns look at it from the same point of view! As you know, he rather fancies himself at cricket. They have a bowling sergeant who succeeded in getting 15 runs. Harry (having made 0) congratulated him. The sergeant smiled sweetly and said: 'I try my best, Sir, but you are no use now, you are past your time!'

I had a good time fishing in Norway. I was very lucky as the more I fished the more I found out how badly I did it.

Your affectionate daughter Dertha

In November, an unsavoury regimental affair came to light when a Court of Inquiry was convened at Chelsea Barracks to investigate claims by Lieutenant H.C. Wood of the 2nd Battalion that he had been pressured to resign his commission by Major Corkran, Captain Garthorne–Hardy and Lieutenant Colonel Cavendish. There was undoubtedly some truth in his allegations as he was a far from popular officer. However, after his silk, Rufus Isaacs KC, MP, later Marquis of Reading, had finished summing up his defence in an impassioned speech that lasted three and a half hours, the Grenadiers came out badly.

News came of the tragic death of Sir Henry Colvile in a motorcycle accident. Approaching Heatherside Corner crossroads near Bagshot at high speed, he collided with a car slowly emerging from the Aldershot direction and was thrown clear of it into the middle of the road. The driver of the car, Brigadier General Sir Henry Rawlinson, got down and ran to his assistance; to his consternation and grief, he found it was his old friend Henry Colvile. The funeral took place at Lullington on 28 November. A Grenadier Sergeant Major and 12 sergeants escorted the body from the station to the Parish Church where two Grenadier officers were waiting. Harold was the senior Grenadier at the service for the remainder of the regiment remained in London to attend the memorial service at the Guards Chapel that afternoon. Both Field Marshal Earl Roberts and General Lord Methuen were there to pay their respects to the man who had served them both well.

November also found Dertha at tea with the former French Empress Eugenie.

18 November 1907
Blenheim Barracks,
Aldershot (1)

Dearest Father,

Yesterday the Empress Eugenie (2) sent for me and I had tea with her and a long talk. She said she would like very much to see you. If you come south soon you might try and fit it in. I think she goes abroad some time in December but I will find out exactly what are her movements. She said: 'Tell him that I look very old.' When she goes out she always has her face covered with a very thick veil and never lets her portrait be taken. She has extraordinarily bright eyes and though very wrinkled she is still very graceful and handsome. She is full of life and asked about all sorts of people.

Harry has been laid up with his bad leg, ever since he left. I had no idea at the time that it was so bad. The doctors won't let him walk at all. He is due at Wentworth next week so he is getting rather anxious.

This house is extraordinarily nice – a long way the best house we have had in our wanderings …

Your affectionate daughter Dertha

Notes
1. The 3rd Battalion had moved back to Aldershot where it would remain until November the next year when it returned to London, first to the Tower, then Chelsea Barracks followed by Wellington Barracks.
2. Maria Eugenia Ignacia Augustina de Palafox y Kirkpatrick, known as Eugénie de Montijo, wife of Emperor Napoleon III and the last Empress of the French. She would have been 81 years old when Dertha met her. The Second Empire had been overthrown following France's defeat in the Franco-Prussian War of 1870-1871 and she and her husband took refuge at Chislehurst, Kent. Napoleon III died in 1873 and their son died in 1879 fighting in the Zulu War in South Africa. In 1885 the Empress moved to Farnborough Hill house in Hampshire. This presumably was where Detha was summoned.

Battalion life ticked along with spring drills preceding the Major General's inspection and the King's Birthday Parade, guard mounts in London and Windsor, state ceremonial occasions and the two-month annual summer training camp.

Despite the lessons learnt in the Boer War, the Guards continue to wear their tunics on field training!

In March 1910 Harold was offered an instructorship at the Staff College.

26 March 1910
Shavington,
Market Drayton (1)

Dearest Father,

I have been here all this week … Harry has just been offered an instructorship at the Staff College from 1st April. He isn't wildly keen to take it and is going back to London to see about it. It depends a good deal on whether they mean it as a substantive Colonel's job or not – only it is rather dangerous refusing things. I am careful not to prejudice him one way or the other.

We are playing lawn tennis here out in the sun. I hadn't been away from London since Christmas and felt I needed it.

Your affectionate Dertha

Note

1. Shavington Hall was originally built in 1506 by the Needham family (later the Viscounts Kilmorey and Earls of Kilmorey) who had acquired the Shavington Manor in 1461. Rebuilt on a grander scale in 1685, it was sold together with its 600-acre park by the third Earl in 1885 to Arthur Heywood-Lonsdale. The Heywood-Lonsdales improved the house and grounds and bought several adjoining estates. Alas, the hall was demolished in 1959 as it was too expensive to maintain.

Harold refused the Staff College post because it would not count as a substantive Colonel's job and in a year's time he would probably have had to go on half pay. Promotion was, however, just around the corner. Harold and Dertha bid farewell to the Grenadiers on 30 August 1911 before setting off for Hythe in Kent where he was to become Colonel and Commandant of the School of Musketry. The importance of this command should not be underestimated for musketry and tactics were synonymous; Hythe was both author and implementer of the doctrine and training needed to prepare the British infantry for the modern battlefield. Arguably Harold assumed one of the most important roles in the British Army.

17 July 1911
19, Hannover Terrace,
Regent's Park

Dearest Father,
Would you be inclined to have us both at Blair about the 10Th of August? Harry doesn't want any shooting, but he wants to get away and he is happier at Blair than anywhere else. He would come back to manoeuvres at the end of the month.

We have had a horrid week saying goodbye to the battalion. I made a speech to the married people and Harry made various orations the next day. We shall be at Aldershot from 28th till 9th.

Your affectionate daughter Dertha

7

Bulls-Eyes and the School of Musketry

An 'Establishment for the instruction of the Army in rifle and target practice' with its attendant ranges extending across the sand dunes between Dymchurch Redoubt and Hythe in Kent was formed in 1853 and soon became known as The School of Musketry. It owed its origin to the introduction of the Minié rifle.[1] The Commander-in-Chief, Field Marshal Viscount Hardinge, judged that, if it were left to the commanding officers of regiments to see that the men under them were properly instructed in the use of the new weapon, he would fail to secure uniformity of practice throughout the army and hence he advised the creation of a special establishment to serve as a training school for infantry and marines.

The school's staff and students were housed in the Napoleonic barracks built during 1807-1808. This area of Kent, on the edge of Romney Marsh, has a long and proud association with the British Army. The first Commandant was Colonel Charles Crawford Hay, a formidable shot, and his leadership is credited with laying the foundations that ensured generations of soldiers benefitted from the very best training delivered by first rate instructors.

On 6 December 1911, Harold took over as Commandant from Colonel Walter Congreve VC of the Rifle Brigade. A contemporary at Sandhurst, Congreve completed two tours in India and spent three years in South Africa where he had the distinction of being shot through the leg, though the toe of his boot, grazed on his elbow and shoulder, and his horse shot in three places all on the same day and lived to receive a VC. He went on to become a Corps commander on the Somme in 1916. He was but one of other illustrious predecessors such

---

1   Following the French invention of the Minié ball that allowed rapid muzzle loading of rifles, the Pattern 1851 Minié rifle was in use by the British Army from 1851 to 1855. Some 34,000 of the guns were manufactured under the formal name of Regulation Minié rifle. In practice it was found that only about 12 musket balls could be fired before it became impossible to reload.

as Colonel, later General, Charles Munro, commandant from 1903-1907 who commanded 2nd Division of the British Expeditionary Forces (BEF) in 1914. An early Commandant was Colonel Sir Ian Hamilton who had an extensive military career including both First and Second Boer Wars, and the Russo-Japanese War. Monro and his contemporaries, responding to the experiences of South Africa, had sought to develop training that better combined fire, movement, and cover, and in this they had been largely successful. The 1909 Musketry Regulations, the result of their endeavours, remained, in amended form, the basis for training until 1924.

There were two distinct but complimentary roles of the School. The first one was to train officers and non-commissioned officers throughout the infantry and cavalry to instruct the men of their own regiments in the use of small arms, primarily the short magazine Lee-Enfield Mk III bolt action rifle (SMLE) that had been adopted by the British Army in January 1907. With a calibre of .303 inches, the forty-four-inch long SMLE weighed 8.62 lbs and was effective up to 550 yards with a normal rate of fire of ten rounds per minute[2]. Fitted with the 17-inch blade of the Pattern 1907 bayonet, the length of the rifle extended to five feet two inches, just five inches shorter than the average height of a 21-year-old male at the time. The SMLE went on to be the staple infantry weapon of the British Army throughout the Great War with over five million produced.

The range training package needed constant tweaking. The design of the outline and size of figure targets and their colours, the variables of their dynamics e.g. static, moving or vanishing, selection of fire positions e.g. lying, standing, sitting, kneeling in the open or behind cover, short- or long-range distances, types of fire e.g. rapid, snap or magazine, rounds allowed, all combined into an extraordinary mesh of intricate programming. Musketry merged with tactics and vice versa which meant that the School had responsibility for both the theory and practice of 'fire direction by leaders', target indication, individual and section battle drills such as moving after firing and advance to contact using fire and movement.

The modern machine gun had been in development since 1862 when the hand-operated crank Gatling gun entered service with the US Navy. Twenty years later, the American inventor Sir Hiram Maxim introduced the first practical self-powered water-cooled Maxim machine gun with a rate of fire of 550-600 rounds per minute. Adopted by the British Army in 1888, it was widely used in the colonial wars of the late nineteenth century including the Second Anglo- Boer War. Vickers, who had bought the Maxim company in 1896, refined the design and the new variant, the Vickers Mk I .303inch machine gun came into service on 26 November 1912.

---

2   Italians up to 10; French approximately five and Germans seven.

Captain Reginald Applin set out the machine gun's stall in his book on machine guns tactics in 1910: 'For machine gun fire has special characteristics that are entirely its own. It can be concentrated like a jet of bullets on a single oval area, or by traversing the gun on its pivot it can bring sweeping fire to bear over a wide front. Thus the machine gun gives a small group of men the power of either keeping up a slow deliberate rate of fire or delivering sudden gusts of fire, turning it rapidly on a diversity of targets or directing it on one narrow space of ground, or again sweeping the front with a rain of bullets ... *feu fauchant* – a mowing down fire'. [3]

Maxim gun courses for Junior Officers were run at Hythe between 1890 and 1914 and the first School of Musketry Vickers Mk I course took place at Aldershot in the late autumn of 1913. [4] Based on the use of two guns which were allocated to each pre-war infantry battalion, in hindsight it seems somewhat irrelevant when compared to the later organisation of Machine Gun Battalions with sixty-four guns each and using barrage fire on regular occasions. It was at Hythe though that those ideas of concentrated machine gun fire and machine gun tactics were first explored and the potential acknowledged but not, until much later, realised. Campbell and other School instructors regularly participated in discussions at the Aldershot Military Society[5] and the Royal United Services Institution to keep the debate well informed. The official history of the First World War military operations recognizes the school's efforts: 'The rapid fire of the British infantry was introduced as a substitute for additional machine guns that were refused to it. In 1909 the School of Musketry urged that each battalion should have six guns instead of two; the suggestion was declined for financial reasons, and subsequent reductions of the Army Estimates and Vote made any such addition impossible. It was therefore decided to increase the rate of fire of each rifle by the special training of the men.[6]' The individual record for the most rifle rounds fired in a minute was 38!

So Practice 22 was introduced by the School in 1909 to focus on firing a maximum of fifteen rounds in 'a mad minute' – a figure that was far higher than that of any other European army – which required revised drill practices to attain the necessary level of efficiency. It should be noted that there was considerable discrepancy between British and continental estimates of the fire equivalent of

3   Applin, Capt. RVK, *Machine Guns Tactics* (London: Hugh Rees Ltd, 1910), passim.
4   The German Army had been training with the MG 08, its own version of the Maxim, since 1908. When the war began in August 1914, 4,411 MG 08s were available to battlefield units.
5   Campbell, Lt Col J., 'Fire Action', AMS Paper CXII, 14th Mar 1911, passim.
6   Edmonds, Brig-Gen. J.E. (ed.), *Military Operations France and Belgium 1914*, Vol. II (London, Macmillan & Co., 1925), p.463.

machine guns. The French plumped for 150/200 rifles, the Germans 80 rifles and the British as low as 20 in the 1911 Infantry Training manual.

It was Harold's job to ensure that these two weapon systems, the SMLE and the Vickers Mk I machine gun, were supported by the highest standards of instruction for their users throughout the Army and to this end he had a remarkably small staff[7]. The Chief Instructor and his senior Staff officer, Lieutenant Colonel John Campbell, Cameron Highlanders, had an impressive career to date. He served in the Sudan in 1898 and had been present at the actions of Atbara and Omdurman, being mentioned twice in Despatches. In South Africa, as Adjutant 1st Battalion Cameron Highlanders, he had seen action at Vet River, Johannesburg, Pretoria, Diamond Hill, Wittebergen and Ladybrand and would have known Lord James Stewart-Murray well. Mentioned in Despatches, he was made a Companion of the Distinguished Service Order in recognition of his services on operations. On return to England, he attended Staff College and after two years as a Staff Captain at the War Office, he became Brigade Major, Aldershot. He would go on to command a division in the Great War.

Under Campbell, were two instructors, Captain L. Brandreth, Royal Fusiliers, and Captain de Putron, Lancashire Fusiliers, and four Assistant Instructors, Lieutenant R.G. Clarke, West Surrey Regiment, Captain H.F. Somerville, Rifle Brigade, Captain C.H. Marsden, Yorkshire Regiment, and Lieutenant H.C.B. Kirkpatrick, King's Own Scottish Borderers (KOSB). All had served in South Africa. During Harold's tenure, there was a full schedule of courses planned at the School of Musketry. Two types of courses were offered: Qualifying and Refresher. These were then separated by the different subjects: Rifle; Machine Gun; Range-Taking; Senior Officers' Course and a Special Course.

The second role of the School came under the broad heading of research, trials and development (R&D). It was headed by the Experimental Officer, Major George Browne of the Suffolk Regiment, supported by the Officer for Technical Duties, Capt Vivian Thompson, RE,[8] who had invented the Vivian Thompson Stereo-Plaingraph at his previous posting to the School of Military Engineering where he was Assistant Instructor in Chemistry and Photography. These two officers provided Harold with the scientific knowhow and research disciplines that were crucial to the credibility of the School.

---

7   In the small headquarters, Harold's Quartermaster and Adjutant was Hon Lieutenant Quartermaster I. Oborn and, given the hazardous nature of live firing, Surgeon Captain R.C. Wilmot, RAMC, was on hand to deal with any casualties.

8   Thompson was later awarded the DSO for reconnaissance work during the battle of Loos (September-October 1915) and was three times mentioned-in-dispatches. He died in October 1917 of wounds whilst in command (as acting Lieutenant Colonel) of a battalion of the Essex Regiment.

Harold inherited from his predecessor the ongoing R&D on the Pattern 1913 rifle as it became known which had started in 1908.[9] In addition, there was a school of thought that the age of the automatic rifle was nigh and over 27 designs were trialled by the School before 1914, none of which were satisfactory.[10] This proved a mixed blessing for, while on the one hand an improved or fully automatic rifle had obvious benefits, the time required for its development detracted from the School's argument for the urgent need for additional machine guns and it was only in 1911 that a Vickers Mk I was sent to Hythe for testing.

The sheer weight of the Vickers presented the infantry with a conundrum. Was it a solely a defensive weapon system or could it also be used in the advance? Harold with his experience of the South African war was sceptical about the latter. Although it had a three-man crew, the combined weight of the gun components (gun tripod, water and spare barrel) was nearly 100 lbs and a belt of 250 rounds without a 5 lb box came in at 17 lbs. Given that each gun needed at least sixteen belts apart from the 15,000 rounds in the two-gun ammunition cart, the sheer weight of the ammunition required ruled against quick deployment during a rapid advance. Its role was therefore limited to supporting an attack with direct or indirect fire from fixed positions for which it was ideally suited.

The War Office infantry training manual of 1914 stated that a large number of machine guns, strangely deemed 'a weapon of opportunity', could not be permanently allotted to the defensive line, because this would destroy their offensive mobility. 'For these reasons it should be exceptional to employ more than a limited number of guns with the firing line in defensive positions'. Equally, the machine gun should 'rarely' open fire, except at critical moments, since opening fire lost 'the advantage of surprise…' Such muddled thinking continued until May 1915 when Sir William Robertson finally set out some clear principles for the role of the machine gun in defence[11].

In contrast, the American-designed Lewis Mk I light machine gun, the nearest equivalent to an automatic rifle, weighted only 28 lbs and thus allowed individual soldiers to take the fight to the enemy. With a rifle-style shoulder stock, pistol grip, and carrying sling, instead of a water-filled barrel jacket, the Lewis was air-cooled

---

9   Designed as a replacement for the SMLE, the rifle had an advanced chamber allowed for a high-velocity .276 Enfield rimless round, which was more powerful than the service-issued .303 British cartridge.

10   TNA WO 163/16 Minutes and Precis, 1911 Mar 28-Dec 18; TNA WO 163 17 Minutes and Precis, 1912 Feb 26-Dec 20: Brigadier GeneralHenry Wilson (the Director of Military Operations) and his automatic rifle committee had trialled four but with the exception of the Farquahar-Hill version, found the others 'thoroughly unsatisfactory'.

11   Travers, T.H.E, 'The Offensive and the Problem of Innovation in British Military Thought 1870-1915', Journal of Contemporary History, Vol. 13, No. 3, 1978, pp. 531–53.

using a finned radiator fitted beneath a steel shroud. The belt feed system of the Vickers was replaced by a rotating pan 47-round magazine, keeping the gun light and easy to handle. Importantly, a clamp-on bipod was also designed to allow a stable firing platform, replacing the fixed tripod mount of the heavy machine guns.

Its inventor, Colonel Lewis, frustrated with trying to persuade the US Army to adopt his design left the United States in 1913 and went to Belgium, where he established the Armes Automatique Lewis company in Liège to facilitate commercial production of the gun. With the full support of Harold and the School, Lewis also worked with the Birmingham Small Arms Company Limited (BSA) and, in 1914, he moved his factory to England, away from possible seizure in the event of a German invasion. Despite costing more than a Vickers gun to manufacture (the cost of a Lewis gun was £165 v. the Vickers cost about £100), it was about 80% faster to build. The British government placed orders for 3,052 guns between August 1914 and June 1915

The remit of the School extended as to how to counter advances in technology on the battlefield, the most pressing one being the development of military aviation. Charged with the task of measuring the effects of infantry fire against aircraft, at a conference on 30 July 1912 it was decided to trial shooting by skilled shots at a balloon target and by a Maxim machine gun at a 45-degree elevation[12]. When Harold asked the question 'as it appears impossible, at present at all events, to distinguish between friendly and hostile aircraft till they disclose themselves by shooting or dropping explosives on the troops on the ground, is it advisable to provide facilities for shooting them down?' Assured by the War Office that 'means are being devised which will enable troops to distinguish between our own and hostile aircraft', the trials went ahead.

Working with the Superintendent of Experiments at Shoeburyness, a system was devised to use railway engines to tow kites up to 30 mph at a height of 600 feet. The results in May 1913 were disappointing. Machine gun fire at an elevation of between 38 and 50 degrees scored two hits after firing 250 rounds. The forty-eight infantry riflemen, shooting at an elevation between 30 to 45 degrees, fared worse. After four runs, they scored a meagre eight hits after expending 1,587 rounds. Clearly these were early days and much work needed to be done, particularly on the weight of the Maxim's high elevation mounting with the School submitting that 'no mounting which exceeds over 50 lbs in weight is worth considering'.

---

12   TNA WO 32/9089: GENERAL AND WARLIKE STORES: Guns (Code 45(H)): Use of machine guns and rifle fire against aircraft. Trials at Hythe and Shoeburyness, with diagrams

The list of trials did not stop there. Tests of foreign weapons included the US Springfield rifle, the Danish Madsen Rexer and the new Russian rifle, the barrel of which 'got very hot and barrel ruinage was worse that has ever been experienced in such a short duration of fire'. Sights such as Gilbert Russell's Aim Corrector for two eyed shooting, Baron de Bertouch's Foresight & Protector, Major Muller's Trigger Controller – 'a device without any practical value whatsoever' – Hensoldt's Small Rangefinder were all subjected to strenuous testing. Web equipment, magazines, loopholes, capes, gloves, magazines were likewise scrutinized. Barbed wire used to create obstacles during the Russo-Japanese War soon found a place in the training manuals of all major armies and the bayonet wire-cutter and other designs soon appeared on the list. The wire cutter of the Rev T.R. Price met short shift for 'a man using the cutter is very likely to get his fingers caught between the lever and its recess in the butt'[13].

Harold was also President of the Small Arms Committee which reported to the Master General of Ordnance who had the final say on all procurement of weapons. Ex-officio members were the Chief Inspector of Small Arms and the Chief Instructor Woolwich. The other members were Lieutenant Colonel M.L. MacEwen, 16th Lancers, Major B.W. McMahon, Durham Light Infantry[14], and Lieutenant Colonel the Hon T.F. Fremantle, Oxfordshire & Buckinghamshire Light Infantry.

The Duke was to be an early visitor to Hythe.

4 June 1912
Commandant's House,
Hythe

Dearest Father,
We both want you very much to come down and stay for two or three days......if you came on a Friday Harry would like to show you his work. Anyway do try and manage it. I could put up Seaton or whoever you bring. Or I could put you up Ascot week. I shall be frightfully offended if you don't come.
Your affectionate Dertha

---

13   TNA WO 140/13: Report of Trials March 1911-December 1912, Report of Trials January 1913 to April 1914.
14   A leading authority on machine gun tactics.

18 June 1912
Commandant's House,
Hythe

Dearest Father,
I am glad to hear you are coming on Friday. General Haldane (1) is coming to dinner – also Colonel Campbell, who gets a battalion of Camerons next year and is now chief instructor here. Harry will be away next week and I want very much to spend a few days in London, as, unlike Helen, I think it is a necessity for me!
Your affectionate Dertha

Note
1.   General Sir James Haldane, GCMG, KCB, DSO (1862 – 1950). Haldane was a Gordon Highlander who had served in South Africa. As an observer on the Japanese side during the Russ-Japanese war, his views on the new technologies and their impact on tactics were much in demand.

One imagines Harold and Dertha having a very happy time at Hythe and enjoying the sea air and some bracing walks but it was about a very different story that Dertha wrote to her father.

26 March 1914
Commandant's House
Hythe

Dearest Father,
Thank you for remembering my birthday and for the excellent photograph you sent. I am almost getting to the age of wanting to forget my birthday.
       We are certainly living in extraordinary times (1). One certainly can't blame General Gough under all the circumstances but though it may have 'saved Ulster', it will probably have a very bad effect on the army as a whole. We hear very well authenticated rumours of the wholesale provisional resignations of the General Staff at the W.O. in the case of Gough & Co having been kicked out and Sir John French has taken a heavy fall as it was in defiance of him. I don't know what old Lord Roberts was doing in that group; he would have been better left out of it. I suppose it will have an adverse influence on any future scheme of Universal Service. I gather from private sources that old 'A.P.' (2) made an awful muddle of it – but it isn't fair to make him a scapegoat.
       It is rather comical the way everyone offers themselves up as a scapegoat in turn, and then suits up again! But it is a shocking business altogether.
Your affectionate daughter Dertha

Notes

1. The Curragh Mutiny of 20 March 1914 took place in the Curragh Camp of the British Army in County Kildare, Ireland. At that stage in Irish history, Home Rule was expected to become law and it was anticipated that the Ulster Volunteers would rebel. Many officers (particularly those with Irish Protestant connections) threatened to resign or accept dismissal rather than put down the Ulster Volunteers. The officers included Hubert Gough.

2. General Sir Arthur Paget, GCB, GCVO, PC (Ire) (1851-1928). Well known to Harold for he had commanded the Scots Guards at Belmont and Modder River. He had certainly 'made a muddle' in offering officers a choice whether to obey orders in the event that they were issued.

They were certainly extraordinary times. Historian Frank Fox captured the mood perfectly: 'the year 1914, up to the declaration of war against Germany, was singularly quiet for the soldier, but it was hardly a happy quietness. The kingdom was tossed and vexed by many unhappy dissensions. In Ireland civil war was threatened. In England serious labour strikes, the Suffragette disturbances, and an unexampled bitterness in party political strife, seemed seriously to threaten social order. The general vexation and dejection of the public mind had naturally its reflection in the defence forces. As the clouds of the Great War began to gather few were fully confident that their country could meet the coming crisis with resolution and dignity'.[15]

The trumpet of war was soon to sound.

30 July 1914
Commandant's House
Hythe

Dearest Father,

Leave being stopped. Harry cannot come tomorrow and I thought it better not to start without him. I could come with or without him on Monday or Tuesday as I suppose you will get your garden party over in any case – or I would come earlier if Helen wanted me for anything. Everybody is in a very jumpy state and we get woke up by telegrams recalling certain officers. On Wednesday night at 11.30 a telegram was sent to Harry asking for a marine officer to take a motor and go at once to rejoin his ship at Weymouth. He was living in lodgings and they sent to the wrong marine and I think they woke up half Hythe before they got the right one. I hope everything will be all settled before next week. Your affectionate daughter Dertha

15   Fox, Frank: *The History of the Royal Gloucestershire Hussars Yeomanry 1898-1922* (London: Philip Allan & Co., 1923), passim.

On 1 August 1914, the Germans declared war on Russia. Three days later they invaded Belgium in order to attack France. This violation of Belgian neutrality led to a British declaration of war on Germany on 4 August and mobilisation of its armed forces. Britain went to war with a small, professional army that was primarily designed to police its overseas empire. The entire force consisted of just over 250,000 Regulars. Together with 250,000 Territorials and 200,000 Reservists, this made a total of about 700,000 trained soldiers. This was tiny when compared to the mass conscript armies of Germany, France and Russia.

Harold was confident that the British Expeditionary Force (BEF) that went to France was, in his assessment as Commandant of the School of Musketry,[16] as well trained as any that had gone before it. 'It was not perfect, and had war come later many things might have been different about that force, both in terms of armaments and training. But this does not mean that they were felt to be underequipped or poorly trained by the majority of officers. On the contrary, the comments from Hythe suggest that they were improving on an already good standard, and one which they felt was equal if not superior to any European army. If described in modern terms of 'force multipliers', the training allowed a relatively small force to operate successfully in the face of numerically superior opposition and gave the country time to begin the long and arduous process of equipping for the entrenched warfare that followed. Although this approach has been criticised, the training had succeeded in creating a successful expeditionary force, but those behind it understood that it was not designed to operate in the field for extended periods of time. Once the new realities of warfare took hold, and tactics adapted from open to entrenched warfare, the training was changed to allow for the greater usage of new attack plans and weapons, including machine guns and grenades.'[17] As to his future, Harold's letter to the Duke carried the news that he was to become Commandant at Sandhurst on promotion to Brigadier General.

4 Aug 1914
Harold to the Duke

I have had a worrying time as I do not know what is going to happen to me after mobilisation. All my staff and students disappear and I shall be left alone in my glory. I think very likely that I shall have to go and work

---

16   War Office, *Report by the Commandant, School of Musketry, Hythe, on the School of Musketry, Hythe, and on Musketry Training during the musketry year ended 31st December 1913* (London, Harrison & Sons, 1914), passim.

17   Harlow, Nicholas, 'ASI VIS PACEM PARA BELLUM: MUSKETRY TRAINING IN THE BRITISH ARMY, 1884–1914', Doctoral thesis, University of Huddersfield, 2019. p.222

in the War Office. I shall hate being left behind, if the army goes abroad, but I suppose I shall have to grin and bear it. I heard this morning that, if I am still available, I am to go to Sandhurst as Commandant of the Royal Military College in January. I become a Brigadier General, General Staff, with a larger house and income . It is an important place and an honour to be offered it. Until the war is over, will you keep this confidential ? I am afraid that we are bound to go to war, as Germany will never climb down. Soldier as I hope I am, I think this enormous war horrible – and all about nothing really too. But it was bound to come, so it is as well to get it over. Yours affectionately,
Harry

The call of war, however, fell on Harold's shoulders and he was instead promoted temporary Brigadier-General on 15 September and given command of 20th Brigade.

8

To War With 20th Infantry Brigade

Like many of his military colleagues, Harold was quick to put his affairs in order:

13 August 1914
Hythe

My own darling,

When I first talked to your mother about our marriage, I gave her a guarantee that, so long as I was alive, your life should be a happy one. I hope that I have kept my guarantee and that your life has been as happy as mine.

You know that during my lifetime it has always been my one wish that my old home, Spain's Hall, should not fall into the hands of strangers, and that I have never asked my Brother to pay me the full amount, which he ought to annually. If he is unable to do so after my death, I hope that you will not push him, but – to make up any deficiency of income – buy yourself an annuity with a portion of the ready money, which will be available from my life insurance.

I also ask you – as my last request – to leave at your death to my eldest Brother or to his heirs the mortgage which I hold on the Spain's Hall property, also any of my belongings which may be of interest to the family. I ask you, however, in case any of my brothers or sisters have an insufficient income, to stipulate that in return for the capital a sufficient income is allowed to them, to admit of their ending their days in comfort.

No husband has ever loved his wife more than yours,

To my executors:

1. So far as I know at the present moment I owe nothing
2. I am insured in the London Life Association. One policy is for my marriage settlement, the other to repay money in which I had a life interest and which passes at my death to my Brother Evelyn. From

this second policy there should be a small surplus which should pass to Lady Dorothea.

3. If I am killed in action, would you take steps to process the regulated pension for Lady Dorothea.

4. Enclosed are receipts for three guns and one rifle.

In gratitude,

H Ruggles-Brise

On 2 September Dertha wrote to the Duke with what she knew of Harold's whereabouts.

Commandant's House
Hythe

Dearest Father,

This is the first September since I was born that I have not spent at Blair. I am living here alone, but I am so busy that I have not time to worry. Last week Harry spent at Felixstowe. On Monday he left here to go to Portsmouth, but this morning I have a letter to say he is at Cromarty! Possibly he may pay you a flying visit, but I know nothing about him. You probably heard the rumour about troops of Russians having come over from Archangel via Aberdeen. One has heard accounts from all over the country from people who say they have seen trains full of them, and they are supposed to have gone to Cherbourg. All I can say is that Mr Asquith spent last weekend with his brother-in-law Mr Tennant near here (1). Miss Tennant was given authority by her uncle absolutely to contradict the rumour, and that there was no truth whatever in it. He might be lying from motives of policy, and I only hope it is true.

The principal feature of this place now is the thousands of Belgian refugees who have come over (2). I spent yesterday afternoon in the hall in Folkestone where they receive them and find them lodgings or send them elsewhere. Most of yesterday's lot seemed fairly well-to-do and wanted to pay for their lodgings when they were ever able to get hold of their money. They usually want to stick at Folkestone but the place won't hold them, and train after train takes them up to London. But they are being well looked after. There are also many destitute ones – and they say that some of the women had nothing on but a nightdress and a cloak. We are being asked to give bundles of old clothes, specially boots. The other day they brought in 12 Belgian soldiers who were leaving Shorncliffe to go back to Belgium. Their trousers were torn and mended up with string. They brought them to the 'Hythe Bureau' and we bought them 12 pairs of blue overalls like the fishermen wear here. I have nothing personally to do with the refugees as I have many other things. Shorncliffe Military Hospital and the General Hospital at Folkestone are filled with wounded – partly Belgians and partly men from Seaforths, Dublin Fusiliers, 16th Lancers, Yorkshire and artillery. They have told the Sandgate V.A.D.(3), where I shall be, to get ready for overflow – I should think probably the lighter cases. Please tell Helen not to forget to tell me any news by the next post.

Your affectionate Dertha

Notes
1. Emma Tennant (1864-1945), known as Margot, was married to H. H. Asquith, Prime Minister of the United Kingdom, from 1894 until his death in 1928. Her brother, Jack Tennant, was Under-Secretary of State for War and lived at Great Maytham Hall at Rolvenden, Kent. It is not clear who Miss Tennant is. There were indeed rumours circulating about phantom Russian soldiers landing in Scotland and heading south to cross to France to fight the Germans.
2. One million Belgians fled to the Netherlands, some 250,000 to France and another 250,000 to England. It is still the largest refugee movement in British history.
3. Started in 1909, the Voluntary Aid Detachment (VAD) was a voluntary unit of women civilians providing nursing care for military personnel in the United Kingdom and various other countries in the British Empire. They were not military nurses unlike the Queen Alexandra's Royal Army Nursing Corps. By summer of 1914 there were over 2,500 Voluntary Aid Detachments in Britain and of the 74,000 VAD members, two-thirds were women and girls. Sandgate is adjacent to Folkestone and was home to the Bevan Hospital which opened just after the outbreak of war and was home to a VAD detachment, later becoming an annex of Shorncliffe Military Hospital at Folkestone.

Dertha wrote to her father that she was keen for Harold to go to the front.

11 Sept 1914
Commandant's House
Hythe

Dearest Father,

Harry has had a telegram to say he will probably be given a brigade 'for the war very shortly – no further details but they are I think sending out two more guards battalions and they would join two line ones with them. I am very glad as I want him to go.

Meanwhile he is still running around the British Isles but spends Sunday here. We are absolutely crowded out by Belgian refugees. Every house except this one is crowded with them.

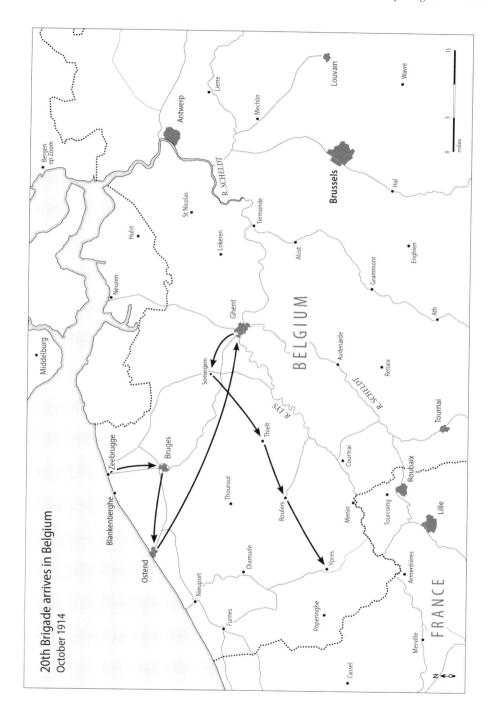

20th Brigade arrives in Belgium
October 1914

14 Sept 1914
Commandant's House
Hythe

Dearest Father,

Harry has got his orders. He is to command the new 20th Brigade comprised of 1st Grenadiers, 2nd Scots Guards, 2nd Gordon Highlanders, 2nd Border Regiment. He is to start tomorrow to Southampton or Beaulieu and expects to be abroad in about 10 days. General Capper (1) has the Division, but I don't know what the other brigade is composed of. Major Cator (2) is to be Harry's Brigade Major and he has asked for an officer from here as A.D.C.

Would you ask Helen to write by this post to Bardie as I don't know where he is.

Your affectionate Dertha

Notes

1. Major General Sir Thompson Capper, KCMG, CB, DSO (1863-1915) was a highly decorated senior officer who served with distinction in the Second Boer War. At the Battle of Loos in 1915, Capper was shot by a sniper as he reconnoitred the front line during an assault by the 7th Division on German positions. He died the next day in a Casualty Clearing Station from wounds to both lungs.
2. Major Albemarle Cator, Scots Guards, an experienced soldier of the South African War. Later, Major General Cator, CB, DSO (1877-1932).

An infantry division typically consisted of three brigades commanded by brigadier generals (each consisting of four battalions and in some cases a territorial battalion) and a variety of support units including artillery, ambulances, engineers, signallers, transport and headquarters staff. In 1914 a Division numbered in the order of 18,000 men. British plans to send troops to Europe in the advent of war with Germany included a British Expeditionary Force (BEF) consisting of six infantry divisions and five cavalry brigades under the command of Sir John French. The BEF was made up of I Corps under Lieutenant-General Sir Douglas Haig and II Corps under Lieutenant-General Sir James Grierson. The 7th Division was not part of the original BEF and was formed in September 1914, drawing on units returning from garrison duties across the Empire which included the army in India and British troops in South Africa (the only self-governing colony garrisoned by Regulars).

Dertha wrote to her father about her concerns for 'Bardie'.

17 September 1914
Commandant's house
Hythe

Dearest Father,

Just got your telegram about Bardie. All one can say is, that if he is slightly wounded and gets sent home, all is well (1). He has not been strong for a long time and what I have most dreaded for him is the effect of all this strain and hardship. The wounded are now getting very well cared for in the French hospitals. I am going today to Southampton for two or three days, but letters and telegrams here are forwarded to me at once. Tell Helen to wire any news.

Your affectionate Dertha

Note

1. Bardie, now a Lieutenant Colonel, had gone to Scotland in late August to raise another regiment of Scottish Horse. There is no evidence that he was in France or Belgium. He deployed to the Dardanelles in 1915. More likely, Dertha meant Geordie who was with the 1st Battalion Black Watch in France.

Dertha was still living in the Commandant's House at Hythe although she was not entirely pleased with the experience.

19 Sept 1914
Commandant's House
Hythe

Dearest Father,

Here the School of Musketry left in charge of the quarter master is being almost destroyed – they are billeting 800 of Lord Kitchener's New Army in or around it (1). They are under one of the new 'Generals' – he cannot be found on the army list. I think he has come from India and whatever else he is he is certainly not a gentleman!(2)

Your affectionate Dertha

Notes

1. By the end of September 1914 there were nearly 20,000 recruits of Kitchener's First New Army in training at Shorncliffe. Most were from the Eastern Division commanded by Major-General James Spens, CB, CMG (1853-1934).
2. Since Spens was a famous first-class cricketer, he is unlikely to have been the target for Dertha's verbal arrow. However his father had been in the Bengal Engineers!

The good news was that she was able to join Harold for a few days in Hampshire:

21 September 1914
Beaulieu, Hants

Dearest Father,

I don't know whether you know, what I have just found out for myself, that all wounded officers, on arrival in this country, are still under military orders and are sent at once to whatever hospital is thought best suited to them. They cannot go to their homes, and perhaps that is a good thing in a way. On arrival in London, the matter goes through Frankie Lloyd's hands and he said if Geordie and Hamish (1) arrived in London he would take care they were sent to the best hospital there was. They have had a good deal of trouble over Miss Keyser's Hospital (2), which is overcrowded and Miss Keyser has been so troublesome that the War Office may have to run the hospital without her – but there are several others just as good or better. It is a relief to me to think that Geordie and Hamish are somewhere being taken care of, instead of being in this dreadful fighting when one never knows from hour to hour what might happen.

I'm staying at Beaulieu (3) to see what I can of Harry. He will not get off till the end of the month.

Your affectionate Dertha

Notes

1. 'Geordie' (Lord George Stewart-Murray, her eldest brother, serving with the Black Watch) and 'Hamish' (James Thomas Stewart-Murray, her youngest brother, serving with the Queen's Own Cameron Highlanders). On 19 September, Geordie and Hamish were both reported wounded. On 2 October, *The Times* reported that Hamish had been wounded in the forearm but had returned to Blair to recuperate. In the same notice, Geordie is described as 'doing well in hospital'. It was only on 19 October that he was officially posted missing and it was not until 3 April 1916 that the War Office declared him dead. He is commemorated on the La Ferte-Sous-Jouarre Memorial to the Missing on the south bank of the River Marne.
2. Agnes Keyser, courtesan and mistress to Edward VII, and her sister Fanny used their house in London to treat soldiers wounded during the Second Anglo-Boer War. In 1907 it became King Edward VII's Hospital for Officers and in the Great War was located in Grosvenor Gardens.
3. 7th Division had assembled at Lyndhurst in Hampshire including Harold's 20th Brigade which consisted of 1st Battalion Grenadier Guards from Warley in Essex, 2nd Battalion Scots Guards from the Tower of London, 2nd Battalion Border Regiment from Pembroke Dock and 2nd Battalion Gordon Highlanders from Egypt. Artillery came from Canterbury, Woolwich and

Chatham. Alongside the 20th were 21st Brigade under Brigadier General
Watts and 22nd Brigade under Brigadier General Lawford.

Crowds gathered to cheer the 7th Division on its way to embarkation at
Southampton on 6 October on 14 transports. From Southampton they steamed
to Dover where they were joined by their pilot. The voyage to Zeebrugge was
far from easy as they had to avoid the mines the Admiralty had laid from the
Goodwin sands to the Belgian coast. 20th Brigade arrived off Zeebrugge at 3.30
a.m. on 7 October but a lack of capacity at the port meant that half the Division
landed there and half at Ostend. 20th Brigade's war diary suggests that German
submarines had attempted to attack the transports and that when they docked
guns could be heard booming around Antwerp.

The situation was very different to that of August 1914. The British, after
resisting the attacks of six German divisions in the Battle of Mons, on 24 August
began to fall back from the Belgian frontier toward the Marne. The French had
abandoned their planned offensive into Alsace and Lorraine and Joffre had formed
a fresh Sixth Army to enable the retiring armies to return to the offensive. In
the first half of September, the French stopped the German advance at the First
Battle of the Marne (6-12 September) and the Germans began a general retreat
that ended north of the Aisne River, where they dug in (First Battle of the Aisne
13-15 September), and the trench warfare that was to typify the Western Front for
the next three years began.

On 17 September, the Germans switched their right flank in what became
known as 'the Race to the Sea'. As the 7th Division assembled at Lyndhurst,
it was decided to transfer the original BEF from its position on the Aisne to
Flanders, a move beginning on 1 October. It made sense, strategically, practically
and politically to have the British divisions operating together. Under siege by the
Germans, the situation in Antwerp was deteriorating rapidly and the fall of the
city became inevitable, necessitating the withdrawal of the Belgian Court and
Government.

General Capper resisted pressure from local Belgian military authorities
to entrain to Antwerp for fear of becoming trapped in the city and followed
Rawlinson's orders to go to Bruges some 15 miles distant. By late afternoon on 7
October the whole Division was at Bruges where it received a very warm welcome
from local people. That evening there was a 'procession of humiliation' through
the streets, a long train of old men and women following in the wake of priests,
who were headed by acolytes swinging their censers. As they walked slowly

through the streets, chanting a litany, they made an odd contrast with the masses of fighting men, and their array of wagons and guns.[1]

The Division then headed to the port of Ostend to cover the landing of 3rd Cavalry Division. This entailed a difficult 13-mile march on cobbled streets with full kit and many men missing out on their rations. A defensive position was taken up at Lellinghe on the outskirts of the city but at three feet below the surface, the infantry hit water. 20th Brigade set up its headquarters at Steene, three miles from Ostend, having had no contact with German forces save observation by a German Taube aircraft. The 20th and 22nd Brigades were then ordered to entrain at Ostend on 9 October, their destination being Ghent; the 21st Brigade followed on foot in reserve. The 20th Brigade War Diary[2] records some 2,000 wounded Belgians in Ostend and 'many thousands of refugees, all fever-stricken, wandering aimlessly about, making the streets almost impassable'.

Harold and 20th Brigade finally arrived in Ghent by 1a.m. on 10 October and were deployed to mask the east of the town. Terror-stricken Belgian refugees streamed out of the town all night long. The following day reports came in of increased German activity; the brigade outposts spotted snipers and patrols, one of which was engaged by Private Reay of the Scots Guards who claimed a hit. A troop of the Northumbrian Hussars obtained firsthand accounts from fleeing civilians of German troops across a wide front heading in the direction of the brigade.

Back in Hythe, Dertha was coping with a range of emotions. On the one hand she had wanted Harold to go to France and be part of the action, but now casualties were coming home, more was known about the German advance and she was worried about her brother Geordie.

6 October 1914
Commandant's House
Hythe

Dearest Father,
I am very strongly of the opinion that you ought to send a notice to the Times correcting their mis-statement of a few days ago and saying that he is wounded and missing. It might bring in some information and also stop the flow of letters that arrive here by every post (as I have no doubt they do to you) saying 'that they are so delighted to hear the good news of George'. Also if I have to depend on Helen for news, I hear absolutely

1   Ponsonby, Lieutenant-Colonel the Rt Hon Sir Frederick, *The Grenadier Guards in the Great War*, Vol. I (London: Macmillan & Co, 1929), p.89.
2   TNA WO 95/1650/1: 20 Infantry Brigade, Headquarters, War Diary 1914.

nothing. I have repeatedly asked her to telegraph to me any definitive news and to send me copies of any letters. Her first letter saying that 'we have heard unofficially that he is in hospital in Versailles' took three days to get to me. Then another letter reached me at Lyndhurst on the 5th (after Harry had gone) saying 'that we had heard from Major Murray that Geordie cannot be found'. Harry is just as annoyed with her as I am. Her only other remark in her first letter was that she had 80 letters to write – but surely there are telegraphs and typewriters – and I don't like to be considered as one of the 80. You can show her this. I am afraid I have written a lot about it but it does make me feel rather bitter.

I have Harry's niece (1) who lives with us coming here and I have had rather a bad time with her already. She was to have been married from our house, but the man who was to have married her has been killed. He had been here a great deal.

It is rather encouraging to know Major Nicholson (2) is a prisoner and one hopes the same for Geordie, if they do not find him. Harry's brigade is a magnificent one. I am afraid they will be plunged straight into the fighting – two of Lord Saltoun's sons are in that battalion of Gordons (3), and as you know the eldest one as a reserve man with the other battalion was wounded and missing – but they have now pretty good evidence that he is a prisoner. They seem to treat their officer prisoners pretty well. Your affectionate Dertha

Notes

1. Marian Ruggles-Brise, daughter of Edward Cecil, Harold's elder brother, and her fiancé, Oswald Sanderson. He had transferred to the 4/7th Dragoon Guards from the East Riding of Yorkshire Yeomanry in June 1910.[3] The regiment had been in France since August 1914 and had almost immediately been deployed as a reconnaissance force on the border with Belgium. In the Retreat from Mons, Regimental Drummer Edward Thomas is reputed to have fired the first British shots of the war and Oswald's fellow officer, 'Butcha' Hornby, had the distinction of being the first British Tommy to kill a German Kuirassier, using a cavalry sword as his weapon of choice.[4] Oswald was in fact a POW and they married after the war.
2. Major Arthur Nicholson, QOCH, was wounded and captured. He died in September 1915 in a POW camp near Cologne.
3. The Hon Simon Fraser was killed on 29 October 1914; his eldest brother, the Hon Alexander Fraser, survived the war as did his younger brother, the Hon William Fraser, who served with the Grenadier Guards.

---

3   TNA WO 76: 4th Dragoon Guards.
4   Gibb, The Rev Harold, *Record of the 4th Royal Irish Dragoon Guards in the Great War 1914-1918* (London: Saward, Baker & Co., 1923), passim.

On 10 October Dertha received her first letter from Harold since his embarkation:

On Active Service
The Lady Dorothea Ruggles-Brise
Commandant's House, Hythe

My own darling one,
I am getting on first rate. Hard at work with very little sleep. So far our friends the Germans have not had a shot at us or us at them, we thought they would come on this morning. We had a long dawdling embarkation and sea voyage.
From your most loving Harry

On the night of 11 October, 20th Brigade moved nine miles to Somergem, arriving at daybreak the next day. The weather was bitterly cold and news came that the Germans had occupied Ghent and that Antwerp had fallen. The next day, 20th Brigade marched to Thielt in the general direction of Ypres, having covered more than 26 miles in twenty-four hours. Harold's men were hungry and fatigued, their feet aching from pounding along the cobblestone roads.. The Grenadiers formed the rear guard and the march was carried out in strict silence. If the enemy was encountered, he was to be tackled with the bayonet. Congestion caused by guns and wagons on the road resulted in frequent delays and it was not until 10 p.m. that the brigade arrived at its billets.

At 7 a.m., the division was on its way again, this time to Roulers. The Germans, sensing that this was an isolated formation, were right behind them. Taking precautions against being rushed by large numbers of enemy, the rearguard felled trees to block roads. As the march continued in heavy rain along muddy tracks, news arrived of a German advance from the north and northeast but there was no engagement and the 20th Brigade arrived in Roulers at 10 p.m. 'in excellent spirits'. Roulers was bustling with people who had come to give apples and cigarettes to what they regarded as an army of deliverance. On 14 October, once again in pouring rain, Harold and his men along with rest of 7th Division resumed their march to Ypres and arrived at 2 p.m. although a few men had fallen out of the line of march, never to be seen again, and others limped in having taken off their boots and tied their puttees round their feet. Some German uhlans had managed to slip into Ypres before the Division arrived but the Yorkshires took one prisoner and the remainder were captured in a nearby wood by 10th Hussars.

15 October found Harold's men busy entrenching south of the town and he snatched a moment to dash off a short note to Dertha.

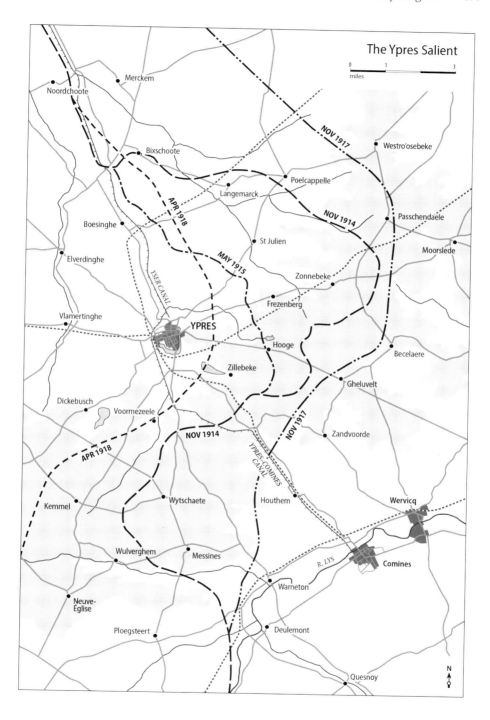

The Ypres Salient

0   1   3
miles

NOV 1917

Merckem

Noordchoote

Bixschoote

Westro'osebeke

APR 1918

Poelcappelle

Langemarck

NOV 1914

Passchendaele

Boesinghe

St Julien

Moorslede

Elverdinghe

MAY 1915

Zonnebeke

ISER CANAL

Frezenberg

Vlamertinghe

YPRES

Hooge

Becelaere

Zillebeke

Gheluvelt

Dickebusch

Voormezeele

NOV 1914

Zandvoorde

APR 1918

NOV 1917

YPRES-COMINES CANAL

Kemmel

Wytschaete

Houthem

Wervicq

Wulverghem

Messines

R. LYS

Comines

Neuve-
Èglise

Warneton

Ploegsteert

Deulemont

N

Quesnoy

My own darling one,
Just got your letter of the 10th and much distressed to hear about Geordie
but someone told me that he had now been reported as wounded and
prisoner – I just hope that is true. We have had so far no serious fighting
but have accounted for several odd Uhlans and patrols. The weather is
getting cold and wet.
From your most loving Harry

Ypres (Ieper), a prosperous Flemish city in the Middle Ages, was famous for its
linen trade with England. In the centre stood the magnificent Cloth Hall built
in the thirteenth century and almost totally destroyed nearly seven hundred years
later by German shell fire. Like a phoenix from the ashes Ypres would rise again
and the Cloth Hall would be rebuilt and once again dominate the market square.
Ypres held a key strategic position as it stood in the path of Germany's advance
into France. Ypres, or 'Wipers' as it became known to the Tommies, was also
symbolic – much of Belgium was in German hands but Ypres and the little of
Belgium that remained was not to be surrendered however costly the defence of
the Ypres Salient. Belgium was a country whose neutrality Britain had guaranteed
and her coastline was precious – the more of that coast that Germany held, the
greater the threat they posed to the Channel and shipping.

Ypres is often referred to as the 'Holy Ground of British Arms' because of the
scale of commonwealth losses in the three Battles of Ypres - some 500,000 British
empire troops.[5] The First Battle of Ypres (19 October-22 November 1914) lay
ahead for Harold and his men, many of whom were destined to remain forever
within sight of the spires of Ypres in the beautifully tended Commonwealth War
Graves Commission Cemeteries or beneath the fields with their names being
amongst the 185,000[6] Commonwealth missing and remembered for evermore on
the Menin Gate, Tyne Cot and other memorials.

Ypres was to be held at all costs: those were Sir Henry Rawlinson's orders for
four German Army Corps were estimated to be operating somewhere in Belgium
but where exactly no one knew. The 7th Division was ordered to advance and
occupy a line between Zandvoorde and Zonnebeke either side of the soon to be
infamous Menin Road. 20th Brigade was to hold the line between Zandvoorde
and Gheluvelt. On 16 October the brigade proceeded to Zandvoorde, the
Grenadiers forming the advanced guard as Harold's men marched along the main
road. Despite the fog and the need to clear every wood, at 11 a.m. they took up the
line without too much difficulty with the Scots Guards to the left (Gheluvelt) and

---

5   https://www.oxfordreference.com/display/10.1093/oi/authority.20110803125646762
     (accessed 1 November 2023)
6   Commonwealth War Graves Commission

the Grenadiers to the right (Zandvoorde). The rest of the day was spent improving and strengthening trenches and in the afternoon two companies of Scots Guards were ordered to occupy a 'commanding ridge' at Kruisek, an isolated position vulnerable to snipers and enemy patrols. Visitors to this area will know that 'ridge' (implying some spectacular vantage point) is a relative term in the context of the low lying and flat land of the Salient and often amounts to little more than a gentle rise in the landscape.

The advance to Kruisek was intended to drive back German snipers but the position itself amounted to a salient and was hard to defend. 7th Division was being shelled from a farm beyond Kruisek known as 'America'. Despite the very real difficulties of advancing and then entrenching, Sir John French ordered the Division to attack Menin, some four miles beyond Kruisek, which he considered 'a very important point of passage (which) would much facilitate the advance of the rest of the Army'.[7] On 18 October, 20th Brigade was ordered to advance and occupy the forward ridge at America, 'bending' to Zandvoorde on the right and Kilo 9 on the Menin Road to the left. Well aware of the vulnerability of its position for the front was much too long for a brigade to hold and the salient a source of great weakness, the brigade was soon under accurate artillery fire, the Gordons particularly hard hit.

The attack on Menin started at 6.30 a.m. on 19 October. Then news came in of a large enemy force of all arms advancing from the direction of Courtrai. Rawlinson suddenly realised that it was madness for a single infantry division to attack Menin and the advance was countermanded. 20th Brigade returned to its former position, a semi-circular line running from Zandvoorte through Kruisek to the cross-roads at Kilo 10 on the Ypres-Menin Road. The Grenadiers and Borders were in the trenches, and the Scots Guards and Gordons in reserve at Reutel. That night, the role of the division was switched from the offensive to the defensive

The Scots Guards and Gordons returned to the front line the following day to make a reconnaissance towards Gheluwe (in German hands) during which they were heavily shelled. 20th Brigade was ordered to hold its trenches with 21st Brigade to their left. Then, to Harold's dismay, 5th Cavalry Brigade to their right was ordered to withdraw, leaving his right flank exposed until the arrival of 3rd Cavalry Brigade. At 3 p.m. on 20 October the Germans advanced to a point 200 yards from Harold's lines albeit this was regarded as more of a German reconnaissance in force than their main effort. That said, it was little comfort that two companies of the Scots Guards had been sent to Veldhoek as divisional reserve.

---

7   Sir John French, *The Despatches of Sir John French* (London: Chapman & Hall Ltd, 1914), p.131.

It was on the afternoon of 21 October that the enemy attacked all along the line. The Gordons reported they were under attack and the Scots Guards now deployed at Zandvoorde as divisional reserve reported that they were under heavy shellfire. An hour later, two companies of Grenadiers were sent to support 21st Brigade who were under heavy attack, leaving Harold's brigade with no reserve battalion. The Grenadiers and Borders were being shelled heavily whilst the Gordons were being 'much troubled' by enemy machine guns. At 3 p.m. the Grenadiers reported that they were under heavy attack with German machine guns a mere 150 yards away. 20th Brigade suffered some 150 casualties that day. Although the British artillery and rifle fire had been effective, the German army was pressing home with repeated assaults and in growing numbers.

22 October saw another day of fighting with 21st Brigade being troubled by sniping from their rear. German heavy artillery destroyed trenches and men were repeatedly buried and dug out. Soil choked rifles and machine guns. Conditions experienced by the Scots Guards were typical with trenches only some four feet deep and on a forward slope. Harold's men were facing 15 German battalions and some Germans were reported to have got behind Harold's lines and caused confusion by shouting 'retire' in English. Casualties in 20th Brigade increased steadily and included Major Lord Esme Gordon-Lennox (badly wounded) and Captain Thomas Rivers-Bulkeley (killed).

The position of the 7th Division was becoming increasingly precarious as it doggedly held on to a seven miles line with everyman in the trenches. 24 October brought another costly day with 20th Brigade suffering a further 200 casualties including the deaths of Major Lawrence Colby and Lieutenant Antrobus who had led a successful counter-attack by the Grenadiers. Brigade HQ was at Kruisek and Harold was very close to the front line. Put bluntly, he was 'in the thick of it'. The 20th Brigade war diary includes comments that the Grenadiers were 'hard pressed' and that 'the situation is most critical and it is as much as we can do to hold on'. On 25 October, 21st Brigade reported that their line was broken and 20th Brigade recorded a further 200 casualties including Captain Gordon and Lieutenant Clancy of the Borders.

Just after midnight on 26 October, in pouring rain and pitch blackness, the Germans broke through the trenches between the Scots Guards and Borders and started attacking from behind. A gallant night attack to recover lost positions incurred heavy losses including the death of Major Hugh Fraser of the Scots Guards. Major the Viscount Dalrymple took over command and together with Captain Fox and 50 men stormed a house full of Germans at the bayonet, killing the commanding officer and taking 200 prisoners. With heavy losses and great heroism, 20th Brigade's line was restored. The brigade diary for 7 a.m. on 26 October records terrifying conditions:

The Germans began shelling the trenches, the fire increasing to such an extent that occupants of the line counted as many as sixty per minute on each small trench. The men gallantly held on till 10 a.m. in spite of the shells relatedly blowing in the trenches and burying five or six men who had to be dug out with a shovel – in some cases as much as three feet of earth being on top of the men. Many of course were suffocated before they could be extracted.

By 8 p.m. the brigade's position was considered so isolated that the decision was taken to fall back to the hollow west of Zandvoorte. The diary continues.

The men were almost completely worn out, many of them having been in the trenches for five days and nights without relief. They were constantly shelled throughout the day, finishing with a very severe night and day fighting, and yet their spirits and discipline were not at all upset.

The brigade had suffered some 2,000 casualties which was nearly half its total strength and was withdrawn into billets on the outskirts of Ypres in order to reorganise. Harold took the opportunity to write to Dertha about the fighting.

27 Oct 1914

My own darling one,
Just a line before the post goes to say that we have just finished a battle in which our inferior strength had to hold back a superior force. Though we had to leave our positions last night we did what we had to do, but we have had an awful lot of casualties both officers and men. You will see this all in the paper and my battalion has suffered severely (1) – but we have slain whole heaps of Germans. They principally came on in the night, but the daytime was most trying. They have a howitzer which we call 'black maria' which blows in the trenches and has a most demoralising effect (2). The Scots Guards are the worst sufferers (3). The Border Regiment has lost six officers killed and three wounded and the casualties in the battalions varied from about 200 in the Gordons to almost 300 in the Scots Guards. We took 200 prisoners one night. I never saw such a wicked looking lot and the dead lay in heaps. I am very much devastated about our poor brigade, but it has done well.

I am too distressed about Geordie. Hugh Fraser (4), Kinnaird (5) have been killed. Bolton (6) we think is a prisoner, so is Dalrymple (7). It is too dreadful.
From your most loving Harry

Notes

1. Presumably Harold is referring to the 1st Battalion Grenadier Guards as he does not mention them elsewhere in the letter. They lost nine officers and 301 men.
2. The 15cm *Schwere Feldhaubitze 13* fired a HE shell weighting 93 lbs.
3. Harold is using the initial casualty returns. The losses were far worse -the 2nd Battalion Scots Guards lost 17 officers and 511 men; the Border Regiment 17 officers and 431 men; the 2nd Gordon Highlanders three officers and 159 men.
4. Major The Hon Hugh Fraser, Scots Guards, son of the late Simon Fraser, 13th Baron Lovat. Killed leading a counterattack.
5. Captain The Hon Douglas Arthur Kinnaird, the Master of Kinnaird. His brother The Hon. Arthur Middleton Kinnaird, Scots Guards, was also killed during the war.
6. Lieutenant Colonel Richard Bolton, Commanding Officer 2[n] Battalion Scots Guards, was captured along with Major Charles Fox, Scots Guards.[8] Fox later escaped from Schwarmstedt POW camp and crossed the border into Holland.
7. Major the Viscount Dalrymple (later 12th Earl of Stair), Scots Guards, was captured and remained a prisoner until 1917 when he was repatriated for medical reasons due to degradation in his eyesight. He was awarded the DSO in 1919 and retired the same year at the rank of lieutenant colonel.

Included is a note in the Harold's hand which records the losses in that early fighting in which his men played such a key part:

7th Division holding 7,000 yds of trench. German trenches 60-600 yards away (opposite Scots Guards only 60).
25 October
6 p.m. Scots Guards and Border Regt attack. Borders fail. S. Guards seized German trench with rifles clogged with mud – further attacks stopped.
26 October
Germans reinforced about 2 a.m. – trenches untenable. Scots Guards compelled to withdraw – of seven officers and 300 men only one officer and 120 men returned.
2 ½ battalions took part in the attack – losses three officers and 780 men.[9]
Germans opposite Scots Guards behaved well to wounded – but those opposite Borderers shot wounded whenever they moved.
In front of 22nd Brigade they had an unofficial truce to carry out wounded.

Come 28 October, Harold's brigade could only muster the following (the nominal strength of a battalion being 30 officers and some 977 other ranks):

8   TNA WO 95/1657/3 2 Battalion Scots Guards
9   Harold is way off. The Scots Guards alone lost 17 officers and 379 ORs.

Battalion	Officers	ORs
1st Bn Grenadier Guards	20	670
2nd Bn Scots Guards	12	460
2nd Bn Gordon Highlanders	26	812
2nd Bn Border Regiment	12	536
Total	70 (58%)	2,478 (63%)

That same day, Dertha wrote to her father.

Commandant's House
Hythe

Dearest Father,

I have not been able to write to you all this time. I have been so busy with my wounded Belgians. I go on to work at 4pm and start giving the patients tea. I have charge of 10 beds. Then make beds and partially wash patients. Then about 6 o'clock get patients ready for 'Sister' to do the dressings, do the easier dressings myself and attend and go round with 'Sister'. At 7 give supper to patients. At 8 put patients to bed and eat four sandwiches myself. At 9 get ready for doctor's visit to more serious cases. At 10 receive new patients (if any empty beds). This is often very heavy work and I have to cut the clothes off in many cases. Two days ago there were five privates from Royal Irish came in, who had not had their clothes off for seven weeks, and their wounds untouched, except for the field dressing 6 days before. Lately, as all our beds were filled up, I have been able to get off at 10.30, instead of 12, which makes all the difference.

Thousands of wounded Belgians are landed at Folkestone every night and distributed through the country. At the place where I work, Bevan Home, Sandgate, Hythe (1), they have about 280 beds. If the Germans really do get to Calais, this place may be pretty lively.

I heard last from Harry on 15th, up to which time they had no serious fighting, but I gather they have been engaged lately, though there is no list of casualties in that brigade, with the exception of Lord Esme Lennox, who was shot through the lung. Talking about lungs I hear Colonel Trotter is dangerously wounded through both lungs (2). I am sending you a list of the battalions in Harry's (or rather General Capper's) division as it may interest you.

I don't know if you know about Harry's niece, who lives with us. She was engaged to a young Sanderson in 4th Dragoon Guards. He was dangerously wounded on 26th August at the battle of Mons and left lying unconscious on the field. His father, who is a director of the Suez Canal, was able to pull many strings in Germany, but there was no trace of him. The War Office returned him 'believed killed'. Yesterday a letter came from him announcing that he was a wounded prisoner in Germany. It makes me have more hopes of Geordie turning up and has cheered me a good deal.

I don't know anything about Bardie's movements, as no-one ever tells me, but I have two letters from acquaintances near Kettering asking me to stay there – so I suppose he is in that neighbourhood (3). When is he likely to go, and where?
Your affectionate daughter Dertha

Notes
1. The Bevan VAD Hospital was opened almost immediately upon the declaration of war. The premises in Sandgate had been used as a convalescent home, though for a long time they had been empty, and had fallen into a dilapidated condition. After six months, the hospital became an annexe to Shorncliffe Military Hospital. More than 12,100 patients passed through the Bevan, and there were 1,552 operations performed.
2. She meant Lieutenant Colonel Earle, commanding officer of 1st Battalion Grenadier Guards.
3. 2/1st Scottish Horse Yeomanry was formed as a Second-Line regiment in September 1914. It moved to Kettering, coming under orders of 2/1st Scottish Horse Mounted Brigade.

The 20th Brigade spent much needed time in billets but this was cut abruptly short with news on 28 October that the 27th German Reserve Division was to attack near Gheluvelt within hours. Harold was to order his men forward, the Grenadiers and Gordons into the line and the Scots Guards and Borders in support. The Reverend Kennedy wrote of the moment: 'An eye witness assured me that the Brigadier (Ruggles-Brise) gave the order in a voice which was broken with emotion, for he knew full well the desperate nature of the task he was setting his men.'[10]

There were no prepared positions or trenches to offer protection and the men were told they could withdraw at daybreak if there was no attack. The Scots Guards sustained twenty casualties from shell fire before even reaching their positions. At 5.15 a.m. on 29 October, a densely foggy morning, apart from the Grenadiers being heavily shelled by their own guns, no attack materialized, so Harold ordered them and the Borders back to Veldhoek to get their food. Respite was short lived as at 7.30 a.m. a tremendous artillery barrage heralded the German attack on the crossroads to the left of the Grenadiers. The morning was misty and before

10   Kennedy, Edmund John, *With the Immortal 7th Division* (London: Hodder & Stoughton, 1916), p.123.

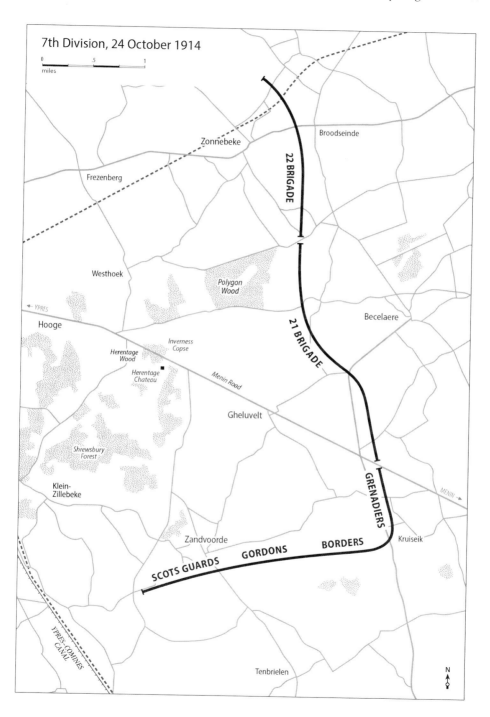

7th Division, 24 October 1914

0   .5   1
miles

Zonnebeke

Broodseinde

Frezenberg

22 BRIGADE

Westhoek

Polygon
Wood

← YPRES

Becelaere

Hooge

21 BRIGADE

Inverness
Copse

Herentage
Wood

Herentage
Chateau

Menin Road

Gheluvelt

Shrewsbury
Forest

Klein-
Zillebeke

GRENADIERS

MENIN →

Zandvoorde

GORDONS

BORDERS

Kruiseik

SCOTS GUARDS

YPRES-COMINES
CANAL

Tenbrielen

N

the Guardsmen knew what was happening, they were rushed by overwhelming enemy numbers. One officer said afterwards that the attacking force reminded him of 'a crowd coming on the ground after a football game'.[11] Major Stucley led a counterattack by the King's company despite being outnumbered by ten to one. As he dashed forward at the head of his men, he fell shot through the head. Captain Lord Richard Wellesley was killed in the same way.

The Gordon Highlanders moved to support the overwhelmed Grenadiers who were engaged in close quarter fighting. A company of Gordons under Captain Burnett linked up with Captain Rasch and the remaining Grenadiers and began to advance. As they neared a wood, despite coming under enfilade fire from a German machine gun, they pressed on through it and gained the northern side of the brickfields. From there they made it to the ditch on the south side of the Menin Road where they were joined by two platoons of Gloucesters. They remained in that ditch until the order came to retire. The Gordons held their trenches and fought all day, one platoon accounting for slaughtering 240 Germans. The Scots Guards, supported by the Queens, fought tirelessly and eventually recovered the position held by the Grenadiers that morning.

As evening approached, 20th Brigade held the same ground which it had occupied that morning. There can be no doubt that the Germans were misled by the reckless audacity of the Grenadiers and Gordons into thinking that these continual counterattacks were indicative of large reserves. Had they known that there were no reserves at all, and what lay between them and Ypres was the remains of a battalion with hardly an officer or NCO left alive, the result of the battle would have been very different and at nightfall they were withdrawn. Of the 20 officers and 670 men of the Grenadiers who had started the day, four officers and 250 men were left. Colonel Earle, the commanding officer, who had been severely wounded during the engagement, had to be left on the battlefield such was the intensity of the fighting.[12] The RAMC doctor who was dressing his wounds was shot dead. The Scots Guards sustained 70 casualties and the Gordons 100. The brigade diary records their losses as 'grievous'.

30 October saw a number of movements for Harold's battalions in the Zandvoorde area including the despatch of the Gordons to support Brigadier General Bulfin's 2nd Brigade[13] in woods to the southwest of the village. It was to be a day of heavy shelling and repeated attempts to break through the lines. 20th

---

11   Ponsonby, Vol.1, p.125.
12   He was taken prisoner and survived the war.
13   During Ypres fighting of late October 1914, Brigadier-General Edward Bulfin organized an impromptu force of six battalions (known as 'Bulfin's force') and led a counterattack to stem the German advance. In December, the wounded and convalescing Bulfin was promoted to command the newly formed 28th (Regular) Division.

brigade was placed in reserve to the other two brigades and withdrew to Veldhoek. Now sooner had it settled own for the night that it was ordered to a new defensive position which it reached at 3 a.m. after a long and circuitous night march. The idea was that from this position, it could provide rapid support with its three remaining battalions.

Daybreak on 31 October brought with it terrific German shell fire causing 21st and 22nd Brigades to retire at noon. The Scots Guards and Borders held their positions and the Grenadiers were personally led up to the line by Harold to stem the German advance and, despite shell fire, managed to occupy the trenches that 21st Brigade had vacated. The fifty or so Grenadiers, all that were left of the 1,000-strong battalion that had marched out of Ypres 15 days ago, now confronted thousands of advancing Germans and succeeded, in the words of the brigade diary, in 'mowing down' the Germans at a range of 300 yards. The right flank of the Grenadiers was exposed and the Germans poured through, presenting an even greater threat to the Grenadiers. The Brigade Staff Captain, Captain Sergison-Brooke,[14] made a daring reconnaissance, secured a loose horse and galloped off to find Major General Capper who sent urgent reinforcements. Incredibly the Grenadiers held their trench and were still repelling attacks until withdrawn at 6 p.m. 20th Brigade now took up positions to the east of Herenthage Woods (also referred to as Chateau Herenthage Woods) on the Menin Road. Shelling remained intense but 7th Division and 20th Brigade hung on despite overwhelming odds. In the words of the war diary: 'The German infantry can neither shoot nor make any use of the ground over which they manoeuvre. Had they been of any use at all they must have wiped us out of existence by sheer weight of numbers and advanced into Ypres.'

The brigade diary records the fighting strength as of 1 November:

Battalion	Officers	ORs
1st Bn Grenadier Guards	5	200
2nd Bn Scots Guards	5	250
2nd Bn Gordon Highlanders	3	200
2nd Bn Border Regiment	5	270
Total	18 (15%)	920 (23%)

---

14   Later Lieutenant General Sir Bertram Sergison-Brooke, KCB, KCVO, CMG, DSO (1880 – 1967)

Harold's brigade HQ in Herenthage Chateau was heavily shelled, one shell stripping off the roof. Such was the damage that Harold and his staff moved to a dug-out in Herenthage Wood where the Grenadier Guards and French cavalry detachment were in position. At 9.40 a.m. the enemy were again massing in front of the woods and shells rained down. The experience of being shelled in a wood is terrifying as the sound of an explosion is contained and amplified by the trees and echoes. Jagged branches, sections of trunks, debris and even entire trees fly in all directions and the floor of the wood is thrown up in a thicket of tree roots, torn earth and vegetation. Visibility is greatly reduced, the mental strain on those in the wood is horrendous and communication becomes extremely difficult. Despite these horrors the German attacks were repelled and the brigade prepared a second line of trenches and improved the existing dug-outs.

On 2 November, the Germans launched another attack. This time it was the Borders who bore the brunt of their offensive. Subjected to enfilade machine gun fire, they stubbornly held on to their trenches until relieved by the Grenadiers that evening. It was during this period, when German gunners were searching the ground in Herenthage Woods behind the forward trenches, that Harold sustained dreadful wounds to both arms and his shoulder blade and was stretchered back half dead, leaving Major Cator[15] in command. In hindsight maybe he was lucky for his Irish Guards contemporary, Brigadier-General Charles FitzClarence VC, was killed outright nine days later when leading the 1st Guards Brigade in a counterattack at Veldhoek.

The evacuation of the severely wounded from the front line was a hazardous and remarkable process in which Harold would have moved along the 'evacuation chain' which, depending on how injuries were assessed, would typically include a Regimental Aid Post (RAP), an advanced dressing station (ADS), a casualty clearing station (CCS), a Base Hospital and then a return to facilities in Britain. News must have reached Dertha very quickly for she wrote to her father from Boulogne where Harold was in hospital.

7th Nov 1914
Postcard
Hotel Folkestone, Boulogne-sur-Mer (1)

Dearest Father,
Not seen H as he is asleep. Shrapnel wound, left shoulder and arms. Right arm fractured – cannot move from here for 10 days or fortnight then home.
Dertha

15   Later Major General Albemarle Cator CB DSO (1877 – 1932)

Note

1.   Harold was undergoing treatment at No.11 General Field Hospital in Boulogne. Such hospitals with their large facilities often utilised large seaside hotels.

11th Nov 1914
Hotel Folkestone
Boulogne-Sur-Mer

Dearest Father,

Harry is getting on slowly but the doctors are satisfied. He is under the care of Malyn the London surgeon, so he is in good hands. What they call a deepish hole, means his left shoulder is pretty much torn open. Another piece of shell has gone through the top of his right arm, fracturing his bone and came out on the other side. His temperature remained at 101-102 till this morning when it came down. I hope it will remain so. He gets hardly any sleep and can rest in no position. Otherwise his condition is good for such a wound. He is now in a little room all by himself. The surgeon and sister-in-charge come to dress him in the morning and evening – Otherwise I do practically everything for him myself. They have no time for the small attentions that he needs all day. He will be some time before they move him, I think. I am glad his servant Holmes has come home, as, when he is convalescent, he will need a great deal of help for a long time. Your affectionate Dertha

For Dertha's family, the bad news was unrelenting.

27th Nov 1914

My Dear Harry,

I am glad to hear that you are on the mend, but I fear you must have suffered much – lucky you stopped the shell with your wings instead of your body and very lucky for you have always led a steady and active life and are always in the pink of condition as now with severe wounds you will find the benefit.

Hamish left Invergordon with 160 men on early morning of the 8th. He arrived on 22nd at Bone near Hazebrouck. The Camerons have lost 48 officers and 1400 men – you heard of course of the shell that smothered HQ staff – 30 deaths.

Then today I received Geordie's sword. Who sent it I have no idea – carefully packed and posted in England. There are about 200 officer prisoners about whom nothing is known – they cannot all be dead. Discoveries are daily cropping up so I am still hoping for good news, but as time goes on my hope gets rather slight. I know he was carried

bandaged into a village which was shelled and had to be evacuated and he is said to have been placed in a quarry for safety.
I am Yours Sincerely
Atholl

Protective of Harold, Dertha was not afraid to asserted herself when it came to his care.

8th December 1914
No 11 General Hospital, Boulogne

Dear Lady Dorothea,
I fear my manner of departure was rather abrupt yesterday and must ask you to excuse me. I was so upset to hear that things weren't going on quite satisfactorily with your patient that I feared I might be betrayed into an expression of opinion which was not only unprofessional but unfair to those who are now attending him ; and we on this side are certainly experiencing the criticism of professional brethren at home who are not cognisant of the conditions under which the work has to be done.
W.D. Waugh, MD, RAMC (1)

Note
1. William Grant Waugh studied law before becoming a medical student at Edinburgh University. He served with the Royal Army Medical Corps as surgeon, attaining the rank of colonel. In the Army List, he is shown as a Temporary Captain in 1915.

By 14 November Harold had been moved to London:

14th Dec 1914
Wilton Crescent

Dearest Father,
Harry is very much better. The fever seems to be leaving him and he is getting very hungry and eating solids again. If you chance to come to London this week he could see you. It has been an anxious time but if there are no further complications he should get ahead.

There will be some nice amusement in store for him when his wounds are allowed to heal as they want to pick out bits of bone from his right arm and graft them on his shoulder.
Your affectionate Dertha

It was to be a long and painful recovery. By February 1915, his left arm had still not healed although his right one was being massaged and exercised every day and he could lift it quite high. On 2 February 1915, the *London Gazette* carried the news that Harold had reverted to the half-pay list. Given the cause of Harold's wounds and unavailability for service, the sense of injustice must have been profound. To make matters even worse he was reverting to half pay in his substantive rank of colonel. On 7 April Harold received a letter from a soldier (either of rank, a friend or both) who had suffered a similar fate. The same correspondent wrote again on 11 April and the address of 'Sunlaws' Roxburgh indicates the writer was Brigadier-General Robert Scott-Kerr who commanded the 4th (Guards) Brigade in the BEF and was severely wounded on 1 September 1914 during the Retreat from Mons. So severe were his injuries that he never again held a field command:

7 April 1915
Roxburgh

My Dear Ruggles,
Many thanks for yours. I enclose the answer from the WO to my letter about being put on half pay. Knowing the line they take may be of use in your interview – as far as I am concerned I consider this letter the ultimatum as far as the WO goes so I intend now to make it a parliamentary job and to do so by trying to get a radical to take it up. Walter Long (1) or any other unionist will make it a party business and try to work it not with a view so much of getting what we want as to annoying the government, so I propose when I go to London, where my correspondence is, to state the case to Ivor Herbert(2). He will I think be sympathetic and may get what we want without making a fuss. I have fled here from my Missus and her measles but the doctors won't do my job till the 20 days infectious period is over. Have just been over to see Roxburghe (3). He is a lot better in health but his leg is quite useless still and he suffers a lot. I am glad to say they are going to let my wife go to Hastings on Saturday. She has had a rotten time shut up by herself in London. I don't think I can stand being all alone here much longer and shall probably join her there next week. It's beastly weather, cold, gales and showers of rain and hail. I've tried the fishing but it's too cold and I only catch enough for my dinner and breakfast with difficulty. I'm glad to see in the papers today Ma Jeffreys (4) and several 2nd Battalion officers mentioned at last. The Russians seem plugging away successfully but it is slow work and I wonder when we will hear again from the Dardanelles. My very best to Lady Dertha and hoping to see you again 'ere long – send the WO letter back.
Yours Ever,
Robert (5)

Notes

1. Walter Long, first Viscount Long (1854-1924). , With the formation of the first coalition government in 1915, Long became president of the Local Government Board.
2. Major General Ivor Herbert, 1st Baron Treowen, CB, CMG, KStJ (1851-1933). A former Grenadier, he was a Liberal MP for South Monmouthshire.
3. Henry Innes-Ker, 8th Duke of Roxburghe, was severely wounded in 1915.
4. Later General Lord Jeffreys, 1st Baron Jeffreys, KCB, KCVO, CMG, DL (1878-1960). He saw service at Mons with the 2nd Battalion and was promoted to command it in June 1915. He remained with the battalion until January 1916, when he was promoted to command the 58th Infantry Brigade in the 19th (Western) Division.
5. Brigadier General Robert Scott Kerr CB CMG DSO MVO, formerly Grenadier Guards. On the outbreak of war, he took command of 4th (Guards) Brigade in the BEF. He was wounded on 1 September in a rearguard action during the Retreat from Mons and returned to England. The injuries proved so severe that he never again held a field command; he commanded a brigade in the Home Forces for the remainder of the war, before retiring in 1919.

11th April 1915
Sunlaws,
Roxburgh

Dear Ruggles,

Thanks for yours. They are d–d swine. I enclose a draft of my proposed letter to Ivor Herbert . Will you comment on it and return it?

I am staying on here a bit longer than I intended because the doctors are unwilling to do my job till all the chance of infection is over. I think I told you my Missus got measles didn't I, hence my flight into Scotland. Will go back about the end of the week. Send a line of approval or otherwise.

Yours Ever,
Robert

The 1st Viscount Long, a British Unionist politician, took up Harold's cause.

27 April 1915
25, Victoria Street,
Westminster SW

My dear Ruggles-Brise,

I think we may drop formalities. I am very much obliged to you for your letter, the more so as I was really very much afraid that I had bungled your case. Do write me quite frankly; don't hesitate to criticise or find fault if

I make mistakes: these matters are so technical that it is very difficult for an outsider to deal with them satisfactorily, particularly when you have to face the War Office who take advantage of every subtlety.

I sent an abstract of the case to the Prime Minister, and I am going to press Tennant. I don't mean to leave the matter where it is; but do not let me do anything through my ignorance which would make your position worse than it is now.

Yours sincerely,

Walter Hume Long, 1st Viscount Long

It may have been the Viscount's efforts that yielded fruit and Harold wrote to Dertha on 10 October with good news.

I hear that I am to be given £800 as a wound gratuity. I have been treated very generously after all. The WO are extraordinary. They have now given me 6 months full pay from Nov 2 1914 instead of 3 months half pay and 3 months full pay.

The work of 7th Division in 1914 is a remarkable story which owes much to the outstanding leadership of General Capper and his Brigadier-Generals. Lieutenant General Sir Henry Rawlinson (IV Corps) issued the following order to 7th Division in December 1914.

'I desire to place on record my own high appreciation of the endurance and fine soldierly qualities exhibited by all ranks of 7th Division from the time of their landing in Belgium. You have been called to take a conspicuous part in one of the severest struggles in the history of war, and you have had the honour and distinction of contributing in no small measure to the success of our arms and the defeat of the enemy's plans. The task which fell to your share inevitably involved heavy losses, but you have at any rate the satisfaction of knowing that the losses you have inflicted on the enemy have been heavier. The 7th Division have gained for themselves a reputation for stubborn valour and endurance in defence and I am certain that you will only add to your laurels when the opportunity of advancing to the attack is given you.'

On 18 December 1914, Major-General Capper forwarded a despatch to IV Corps headquarters concerning the commendable conduct of 20th Brigade:

This brigade had, eventually, the most difficult task to perform as it had to hold the exposed position of Kruisek Hill. It was impossible to abandon this point without prejudicing not only the rest of the line, but also the pivot of all contemplated offensive action. In spite, therefore, of its natural unfavourable situation, Kruisek Hill had to be held. The 20th Brigade did this itself, under constant violent artillery fire by day and often by night. The defence was by no means passive, but counter attacks were frequently and successfully made. Later on in the fighting the brigade showed the same tenacity in defence and on one critical occasion by its forward action was mainly instrumental in restoring the fight. The losses of this brigade were very heavy.

20th Brigade's losses during First Ypres (19 October-22 November) were indeed terrible:

Battalion	killed	missing	wounded	total
1st Bn Grenadiers Guards	89	315	291	695
2nd Bn Scots Guards	47	537	212	796
2nd Bn The Border Regiment	88	253	270	611
2nd Bn Gordon Highlanders	95	163	310	568
Total	319	1,268	1,083	2,670

These were grievous irreplaceable losses for the battalions of 20th Brigade consisted of seasoned regular soldiers. Their replacements had neither the experience nor level of training to replicate these dedicated professional soldiers who had given their lives so unstintingly in defiance of overwhelming odds. If the War Office and its political paymasters had agreed to the School of Musketry's request for infantry battalions to have six rather than two machine guns, would it have made a difference? The Grenadier experience suggests that the answer is yes for the two Vickers Mk I machine guns of the 1st Battalion over the course of seven days fired 56,000 rounds. Multiply that by three – 168,000 – and then by four battalions and the result would have been nearly half a million additional rounds directed at bunched German infantry.

Lord Ernest Hamilton MP[16] included this tribute in *The First Seven Division*:

'The desperate fighting of this period at and around Kruisek will always be associated with the 20th Brigade … The gradual annihilation of this

16   *The First Seven Divisions* by Lord Ernest Hamilton, Hurst and Blackett, London, 1916

splendid brigade - possibly the finest in the whole Army - forms a story which is no less stirring than it is tragic. The tragedy is obvious, but it is relieved by the thought of the superb devotion of each of the battalions that formed the command of General Ruggles-Brise. Each battalion, in its own allotted sphere, fought to a finish. Each battalion in its turn furnished an example of unflinching heroism which is an epic in itself. They not only fought till there were no more left to fight, but they fought up to the very end with success. It must have been a consolation to their gallant brigadier, when in the end he was carried off with bullets through both arms, to feel that he had survived long enough to share in a glory which will never be excelled … The 7th Division's performance, during its three weeks east of Ypres, will go down to history as one of the most remarkable achievements in the records of war….'

By way of summary, celebrated author Sir Arthur Conan-Doyle paid tribute to Harold's brigade during the desperate fighting of autumn of 1914:

The story from this time onwards is one of incessant and desperate attacks by day and often by night. At first the (7th) division was holding the position alone, with the help of their attendant cavalry, and their instructions were to hold on to the last man until help could reach them. In the case of some units these instructions were literally fulfilled. One great advantage lay with the British. They were first-class trained soldiers, the flower of the Army, while their opponents, however numerous, were of the newly-raised reserve corps, which showed no lack of bravery, but contained a large proportion of youths and elderly men in the ranks…But though the ascendancy of the British infantry was so great that they could afford to disregard the inequality of numbers, it was very different with the artillery. The German gunners were as good as ever, and their guns as powerful as they were numerous. The British had no howitzer batteries at all with this division, while the Germans had many. It was the batteries which caused the terrific losses. It may be that the 7th Division, having had no previous experience in the campaign, had sited their trenches with less cunning than would have been shown by troops who had already faced the problem of how best to avoid high explosives. Either by sight or by aeroplane report the Germans got the absolute range of some portions of the British position, pitching their heavy shells exactly into the trenches, and either blowing the inmates to pieces or else burying them alive, so that in a little time the straight line of the trench was entirely lost, and became a series of ragged pits and mounds. The head-cover for shrapnel was useless before such missiles, and there was nothing for it but either to evacuate the line or to hang on and suffer. The 7th Division hung on and suffered, but no soldiers can ever have been exposed to a more deadly ordeal. When they were at last relieved by the arrival of reinforcements and the consequent contraction of the line, they were at the last pitch of exhaustion, indomitable in spirit, but so reduced by their losses and by the terrific nervous strain that they could hardly have held out much longer.[17]

On the home front, the horrors of war were never far away and the German U-boat campaign meant that civilians were vulnerable. On Friday 7 May 1915 the Cunard liner RMS *Lusitania* was torpedoed and sank in 18 minutes eleven miles off the Old Head of Kinsale with the loss of 1,198 lives. Dertha wrote to her father on 31 May with sad news.

> My late housemaid Hettie Pirrie, the daughter of a Perth coach-builder and who was probably coming back to us from Canada, was drowned on the Lusitania. We were corresponding about her coming back and she was drowned on the way home.

Meantime, Harold had continued his recuperation and on 6 July was passed fit for light duty and appointed Brigadier General on the General Staff at Aldershot:

13 August 1915
The Officers Club, Aldershot

My own darling one,
Our review by Lord Kitchener went off very well (1). Monty came down with him (2). You know his son was wounded in E Africa but is now out of danger. The new army looked very well on parade, so long as they stand still and the mass of men was really quite impressive.

We have heard no news from abroad. Read in yesterday's Times of the retaking of the trenches at Hooge (3). This is the way we have to fight the brutes. Hunter-Weston (4) is back from the Dardanelles, looking rather bad, but not seriously ill.
Ever your most loving
Harry

Notes
1. The 24th Division had moved to Aldershot for final training during June. Kitchener inspected the Division at Chobham ranges on 19 August and next

---

17 Conan-Doyle, Arthur:'The British campaign in France', *The Strand Magazine*, September 1916, p.331.

day it was the turn of King George V. Orders were received to move to France and the first units departed one week later.

2. Major-General Robert Montgomery, CB, CVO (1848-1931) commanded 22nd Division of the Third New Army and subsequently assumed post of Inspector-General of Recruiting in autumn of 1915.

3. 'Yesterday's action at Hooge was a really great success ... Among the litter of broken trenches and dead bodies they found living men not willing to surrender, and in the pale light of yesterday's dawn these British battalions fought with bayonets, butt-ends, and even with their fists, until after a few minutes no German was left alive unless he flung up his hands.'[18]

4. Major General Aylmer Hunter-Weston ('Hunter-Bunter') who commanded 29th Division at Gallipoli and had been relieved of his command on 23rd July. Records suggest the reason for his relief was enteric fever or sunstroke whilst some suggest a breakdown. He went on to command VIII Corps at the Somme and for the rest of the war.

Further letters to Dertha included news of a Royal visit, Bardie and continuing problems with Harold's wounds.

17th August 1915
The Officers Club, Aldershot

My own darling wee one,
The King and Queen arrived yesterday. Both knew all about me and asked about my mum. They are both very nice. The Queen came and saw some entrenchments and jumped over the ditches like a two year old.

19th August 1915
Aldershot

This weekend I cannot possibly get away. Sir AH (1) would make a real muddle of things. I had to dine with His Majesty at the Pavilion (2) last night. I sat next to the King who had just heard from Bardie that he was off to the Dardanelles (3).

21st August 1915
Aldershot

Bardie has done magnificently. It really is a great work to raise and get out in command of so many men.

18 *The Times* 19 August 1915.

HM has been very nice and continually asking about my arm. I think we gave him a good show. Sir AH is rather useless on these occasions so I had to take command.

The arm is going on alright. I do not think they are as gentle with it as Blackett was. I have still a sort of plug in the hole and it suppurates a lot.

Notes

1. General Sir Archibald Hunter whom Harold had first met when he was in Gibraltar
2. Prince Albert had been quick off the mark to site a shelter on a small hill overlooking Long Valley and Ceasar's Camp for the Queen's stay when she reviewed her troops. Two years later, a Royal Pavilion took shape which could accommodate the Royal family and their guests.
3. On 17 August 1915, 1/1st Scottish Horse Yeomanry sailed on *Transylvania* from Devonport. Went via Malta and re-equipped as infantry for service at Gallipoli. On 2 September 1915, they landed at Suvla Bay, where brigade came under orders of 2nd Mounted Division. Evacuated from Gallipoli in December, they moved to Egypt and were absorbed into 1st Dismounted Brigade, which was under orders of 52nd (Lowland) Division on Suez Canal defences.

On 14 September Harold received a letter from the CIGS.

From Sir Archibald Murray, War office, Whitehall
'Private'

My Dear Ruggles,
I want to get you a Division. Are you practically fit now or is it 'light duties' only?
Yours ever,
Archibald Murray[19]

Seven days later, Harold was able to write to Dertha with some good news:

21st Sept 1915

I went up before my medical board and I think they passed me fit for general service but that does not mean I shall go abroad. They thought that I had made a wonderful recovery. Murray is not coming down now, so I shan't hear about a Division. I am afraid it is too good to be true.

---

19   General Sir Archibald Murray (1860-1945): CIGS September 1915-December 1915; Commander-in-Chief of Mediterranean Expeditionary Force (MEF) January-March 1916 and MEF (Egyptian Expeditionary Force), March 1916-June 1917.

9

The Fighting Fortieth

Harold was passed fit for general service on 25 September 1915 and promoted temporary Major General commanding 40th (Bantam) Division. Dertha wrote to her father with the news.

26 Sept 1915

> Harry has been given the 40th Division in the New Army. Of all queer things it is the Bantam Division – that is men under 5'3'. They are odd to look at, but mostly sturdy little men. I saw a Welsh brigade of them and they looked as if they were meant to be that size. They will take some time to collect together.

The 40th Division was formed at Aldershot Command[1] between September and December 1915 at a time when recruitment was proving difficult for compulsory service only received Royal Assent in January 1916. In response to the recruitment challenge, the War Office lowered the height limit for an infantry soldier and a 'Bantam Division', a mix of English, Welsh and Scots recruits, was duly formed with the required minimum height fixed between 4 feet 11 inches and 5 feet. Fit short and stocky men were to prove first rate soldiers but numbers were still insufficient so recruitment was extended to 'underfed badly grown men of poor stamina or boys of 14 to 16 who in their zeal had stated false ages'.[2] This resulted in a constant process of weeding out with batches of hundreds of 'immatures' being sent away very week – the wags called it 'Immatures, Prematures and

---

1   They were initially quartered in barracks in Aldershot but in late December 1915 moved 'by march' to Blackdown, Deepcut, Pirbright and Woking.
2   NAM 8002-40: Ruggles-Brise, some records of 40th Divisions prior to arriving in France, pp.1–2.

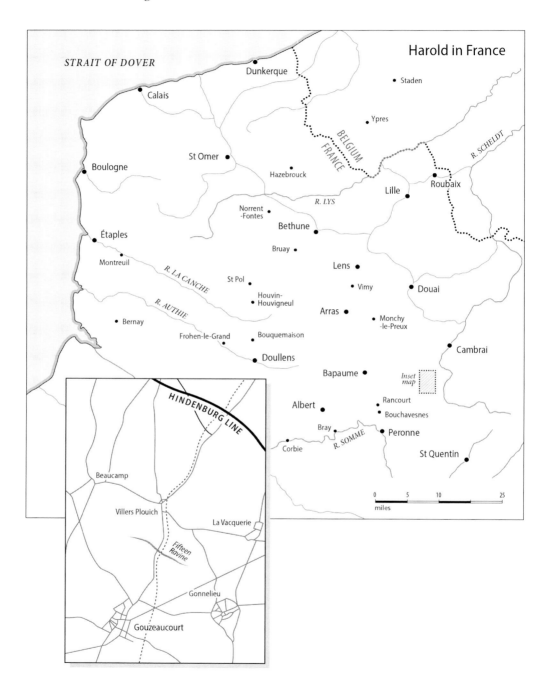

Harold in France

Caricatures'.[3] As a consequence, 'the battalion staffs were more occupied with making out nominal rolls of men who were joining and of men who were leaving that with the more important work of welding a battalion and training it for the fight'.[4] The weeding out took months and reduced the strength of one battalion by eighty per cent.

Harold's arm, however, was still causing him some difficulty as described by Dertha in a letter to her father.

6 Oct 1915

Harry was passed sound the fortnight his arm was healed, but it has now broken out again. They found out that the main part of the bone is separated from the flesh and it may go on being troublesome for a very long time and perhaps may never get quite right. However possibly it may be a blessing in disguise.

Eight days later Dertha wrote again to her father but this time having been eye-witness to a Zeppelin raid.

14 Oct 1915

A zeppelin came over us last night. It came from the north and had nothing to do with the London one. It dropped bombs over the artillery camp at Otterpool (1), three miles off. It killed 14 men and I don't know how many injured and a large number of horses. It then came back close to this house and over the main street and went back over the sea – all the little guns here lost their heads and went on popping for ages. There is one at the bottom of our garden just over the wall. It was just about 10 o'clock and as it happened I was coming back from the hospital on the front seat of the motor bus and I had a splendid view of it as it went back over the sea. It was a splotch of light in the cloudy sky, very high up, and then it disappeared. I thought at first that the moon had gone mad – but there was no moon. It made a queer turn before it disappeared into the clouds. It was rather a misty night. Motor ambulances were running about all night; they probably took people to our hospital. They tell me that the camp brought it on themselves as they were a blaze of light, though they had been repeatedly warned.

3   Ibid.
4   Ibid.

Note
1. Situated to the west of Shorncliffe near Folkestone 'Otterpool' camp was home to the 5th Brigade Second Canadian Division Artillery. 14 men were killed and 13 wounded.

On Boxing Day Harold wrote to his sister Florence.

26 Dec 1915
Blackdown House, Farnborough, Hants

My Dearest Flory,
Thank you very much for your letter and post card to Ralph. The boy has done splendidly (1). I thought from his own account that he had done a gallant act. Archie and Mable must be a proud pair of parents. I expect that Evy (2) will be next but I am very glad that he is off the Gallipoli Peninsula. Haig is TAB's and my old friend. He has done very well during the war and in time will command a larger British army than any other British General has. My Division is getting on slowly. I am weeding out all the immature youths and little boys. And I have been promised that some more seasoned material will be sent to me.

My staff share this house with me and I have sent them all away on Christmas leave and get Dertha staying here. Holmes makes a capital lady maid for her. I think she will go to London for a short time in January. The best of New Year's to you from us both.
Yours affectionately,
Harold
My Division has moved from Aldershot to Blackdown – Pirbright about six miles from Aldershot. My arms aren't quite healed up yet. But both are wonderfully well. No rheumatics pain of any kind.

Notes
1. Harold's nephew Ralph (Harold Ralph Ruggles-Brise) had been awarded the Military Cross for gallantry during tunnelling operations near Hooge in Belgium (indeed not far from Herenthage Woods).
2. 'Evy', Ralph's brother (Evelyn Coope Ruggles-Brise), was headed for Gallipoli as a captain in the Norfolk Yeomanry.

On the last day of 1915, Dertha wrote to her father with a typically frank assessment of life in 40th Division's camp.

31 Dec 1915
Blackdown House, Farnborough, Hants

Dearest Father,
The new huts are not yet finished and the men are packed like sardines and Harry is afraid of disease for them. Also their predecessors the Irish Brigade never cleaned anything and the accumulated filth is beyond anything. The battalions are spending most of their time digging holes to bury refuse.

By the close of February 1916, following an inspection by Lord French that revealed the Division was in no fit state to go overseas, Harold was finally given four battalions from another division to bring it up to scratch. Prior to the arrival of the 13th East Surrey Regiment, 14th Argyll and Sutherland Highlanders, and the 20th and 21st Middlesex Regiment, Harold ordered his brigade commanders to convert their existing four weak battalions into two strong ones. This restructuring was completed within three days and a new sense of urgency percolated down through the division. Training intensified and equipment arrived along with machine gunners, field ambulances and a variety of other units needed to make up a full fighting division.

French was back the next month for another inspection of a portion of the division. The troops were drawn up in the open spaces alongside the Blackdown–Jolly Farmers Road and presented 'a brave spectacle. The goats of the Welsh battalion with their brilliant trappings caused some trouble with the horses of the inspecting Field Marshal and his staffs as they rode past, and it was found wiser to avoid the goats'.[5] Around this time, a divisional band was formed with the musicians all coming from Nottingham and the instruments donate by the Players tobacco family.

In early May, the fully turned out 40th Division was inspected on Laffan's Plain by the King who remarked favourably on the turn-out and bearing of the men. Indeed, he stated that it was the best parade he had witnessed at Aldershot since the beginning of the war.[6] By the end of May 1916, The Division was ready for embarkation to France. Gone were the days when a six-mile route march had resulted in numerous casualties; now 12 to 15 miles could be undertaken by every man carrying a full pack, rifle and equipment. Momentarily, it was thought Harold and his men might be bound for Ireland because of the rebellion in Dublin

5   Ibid.
6   Ibid.

but France was quickly confirmed as their destination and on the 28 May, the advance party left Blackdown for Lillers.

Harold's three infantry brigades were Brigadier-General Henry Cunliffe-Owen's 119th (19th Royal Welch Fusiliers, 12th South Wales Borderers and 17th and 18th Welch Regiments),[7] Brigadier-General the Hon Charles Heathcote-Drummond-Willoughby's 120th (11th King's Own Royal Lancaster Regiment, 13th East Surrey Regiment, 14th Highland Light Infantry and 14th Argyll and Sutherland Highlanders) and Brigadier-General John Campbell's 121st (12th Suffolk Regiment, 13th Yorkshire Regiment and the 20th and 21st Middlesex Regiments). The Division was said to be half English, one third Welsh and one sixth Scottish. To this was added three field companies of engineers, a signal company, a cyclist company, a cavalry squadron (A Squadron 1st Wiltshire Yeomanry), three Machine Gun companies, a pioneer battalion (12th Yorkshire Regiment -the Teesside Pioneers), four companies of the Army Service Corps, three field ambulances, field artillery, a sanitary section and a mobile veterinary section. Thus 40th division consisted of some 20,000 men, 6,000 horses, 64 guns and over 1,000 vehicles. It took from 29 May to 5 June to transport the Division to France, the majority travelling between Southampton and Le Havre.

The divisional artillery was commanded by Brigadier-General Hamilton Reed, VC[8], and consisted of three field artillery brigades (181st,185th and 188th) and one field howitzer brigade (178th). Theoretically this gave Harold the combined fire power of forty-eight 18-pdr field guns and sixteen 4.5 inch howitzers; in practice, these assets were often redistributed or broken up.

Key to the success of any divisional commander are his staff:

G.S.O.1 – Lieutenant Colonel H.A. Walker, DSO, Royal Fusiliers[9]; two tours of Somaliland; Nandi 1905-06.
G.S.O.2 – Major F.D. Finlay, Suffolk Regiment; NWF 1897-98 including Tirah Expedition.
G.S.O.3 – Captain G de C Glover, South Staffordshire Regiment[10].
A.A. and Q.M.G.- Lieutenant Colonel C.F. Moores, DSO, Army Service Corps; South Africa 1899-1901 Queen's Medal with nine clasps.

---

7   The 119th Brigade had four commanders in the space of six months: Brig Gen C.S. Pritchard 8 May 1916 to 16 August 1916; Brig Gen H. Cunliffe-Owen 16 August 1916 to 16 November 1916; Brig Gen E.A. Pope 16 November 1916 to 20 November 1916; and the controversial Brig Gen F.P. Crozier from 20 November 1916 onwards.
8   For gallantry during the battle of Colenso (South Africa) on 15 December 1899.
9   Later Brigadier-General Henry Walker CB CMG DSO JP (1874-1953).
10   Later Major General Sir Guy de Courcy Glover KBE, CB, DSO, MC (1887-1967).

D.A.A. and Q.M.G. – Captain A.H. Bathurst, Manchester Regiment; South Africa 1899-1902; Garrison Adjutant St. Helena (Boer POW camp).
D.A.A.Q.M.G. – Captain A.R. Gordon, Royal Irish Regiment.
A.D.M.S – Colonel A.J. Luther, RAMC; Nile expedition 1898 (Battle of Khartoum)
A.P.M. – Major A.R. Maxwell.

On the night of 5 June, as the last of Harold's men crossed the Channel to France, HMS *Hampshire* sank after striking a mine off Scapa Flow. All hands but twelve were lost. Field Marshal Lord Kitchener was amongst the fatalities. The 40th Division assembled ten miles west of Bethune with their headquarters at Norrent-Fontes and then later Bruay. The men still had much training to undertake including essential front-line experience. To achieve this, brigades would send their men out for patrolling, wiring, sniping and bombing training by more experienced and seasoned soldiers. This hardly constituted a safe environment and within three weeks the 40th had sustained 250 casualties including 47 fatalities.

Serving amongst Harold's men was the poet Isaac Rosenberg (11th King's Own Royal Lancasters) who wrote some of the finest war poems including 'Break of Day in the Trenches', 'Dead Man's Dump' and 'Returning We Hear the Larks'. Rosenberg was killed in action on 1 April 1918.

One of Harold's ADCs was Captain Stuart Grant, a man of particular administrative abilities. He was talent spotted by I Corps HQ and would have been a great loss to Harold. On 25 June Captain Grant wrote to Dertha testifying to Harold's energy.

25 June 1916

We did four hours walk around our line of trenches the other day. I must say I was very exhausted but the General seemed quite ready for lots more hours. He did not like his steel helmet very much but he kept it on all the time.
Yours Sincerely
Stuart Grant

Meantime, Dertha confirmed that the sound of the guns was never far away.

3 July 1916
Hythe

Dearest Father,
All this week we hear the guns in France banging away all day and
sometimes in the night. Harry's lot quiet at the present – round about
Ypres I think.

On 1 July 1916 the great Somme Offensive, 'the Big Push', had opened and
although 40th Division was not part of the action they were kept busy for they
were ordered to take over part of the notorious Loos Salient near Lens, a flat area
of pitheads, mining villages and slag heaps known as *crassiers*. The landscape was
generally one of devastation caused by the great Loos offensive of September–
October 1915. Enemy mining was a constant threat. The divisional lines ran
through an uninspiring landscape – the Gohelle – consisting of a chalk plain
dominated to the west by Vimy Ridge. The crassier heights, not least of all the
enormous parallel spoil heaps known as the Double Crassier, provided excellent
observation posts for both sides.

8 July 1916

All the fighting is taking place a long way from here and it seems to be
going very well. Up here the Boche is trying to annoy us with a few shells
now and then and his trench mortars. It is so annoying losing men by
chance shots, and those form our principal contribution to the casualty
list. I am living in the midst of luxury. Breakfast at 8, do a little office
work then down to inspect trenches. There are some 100 miles of them,
so it will take me some time to get around them, but it is good exercise
especially in this beastly wet weather. Get back to tea, then more papers
in the office, a good dinner and to bed early. Get up early and write to my
mum before breakfast.

14 July 1916

We are still working away at our fortifications, that brute of a Boche
mined under our trenches. I am half afraid that someday he will mine
under my bantams.

It was to fall to the men of the 18th Welch Regiment to undertake the first active
operation of any battalion in the Division, namely to carry out a trench raid on
enemy positions to glean intelligence and, hopefully, prisoners for interrogation.
These were brutal, difficult and highly dangerous operations. This particular raid

provided invaluable experience but was unproductive as recounted by Harold in a letter to Dertha.

20 July 1916

We had some excitement night before last, as the bantams raided the Boche trenches. I was rather anxious lest they should all get scuppered, but they did very well on the whole. Unfortunately the officer got wounded and the little men lost their heads and forgot to bring back a prisoner. The German front is mostly quiet. We pepper him up as much as we can with what ammunition we can afford. I have quite a nice Frenchman attached to me. I think he married an American. I had to interview the Maire of this place the other day and he could not speak a word of English. However, I got all smiles. I let him do all the talking and I said 'oui'. The bother is I have to ask him to dinner.

The raiding party had suffered three wounded and three missing. Meantime, 40th Division assisted with Royal Engineer Tunnelling Company offensive/defensive mining operations as part of the ongoing development of active service experience. Harold came in for particular praise from Captain Grant in another letter to Dertha.

23 July 1916

If he (the General) only knew it, his example has permeated through all ranks. I have seen many, many units out here but have never seen anything to equal the marching discipline of the 40th Division or their smartness in billets. There is no doubt to my humble civilian mind that the training of a Guardsman is to my mind the finest in the world and I am quite sure very few men could have done what the General has done to make this Division efficient as it undoubtedly is.

Routine trench warfare activity, mining, counter-mining, sniping and raids, was carried out during this period.[11] Harold was clearly pleased with the efforts of those under his command.

11   See Barrie, Alexander, *War Underground: The Tunnellers of the Great War* (Staplehurst: Spellmount: 2000), passim; Radley, Kenneth, *On the Dangerous Edge: British and Canadian Trench Raiding on the Western Front 1914-1918* (Warwick: Helion & Co., 2018), passim and Hesketh-Pritchard, Major H., *Sniping in France: Winning the Sniping War in the Trenches* (Barnsley: Pen & Sword, 2014), passim.

3 August 1916

The Division is carving a good name, but of course it has not been highly tested yet. This kind of war is a complicated game, fighting is going on 180ft. below the ground and 1200ft. up in the air. The rifle is the weapon that is least used, and all kind of bombs from one pound weight to 200lbs are in great demand. However, we are getting on and do not intend to let the Boche dominate us.

13th August 1916

We had a raid to try and get a prisoner. The little bantams – South Wales Borderers – got into the trenches alright and bagged a huge Hun. The officer was the only man who could carry the prisoner and was badly wounded. The little men were all so excited yesterday that they could not tell me what had happened (1).

Notes

1. The 12th South Wales Borderers undertook three raids. One was commanded by Captain Charles Pritchard, who, although wounded, had refused assistance and jumped into a trench and bagged a prisoner. Already weak from loss of blood, he was wounded a second time and handed the prisoner over to Second Lieutenant Charles Wood. He later died of wounds.[12] Had he survived, Pritchard would have been recommended for a DSO. Wood, who had returned to the enemy trenches to supervise the recovery of the wounded, was awarded an MC. There were nine other casualties, including four killed.

Harold's men had been holding positions very close to where Harold's nephew, Edward Archibald Ruggles-Brise, was wounded in September 1915. Harold's other nephew Harold Ralph Ruggles-Brise had by now also sustained wounds with 175th Tunnelling Company in Flanders and Harold took the opportunity to apply for his posting to the 40th Division. His plan came to fruition and Ralph joined as one of Harold's ADCs.

Harold wrote to Florence with something of a general update.

12   An outstanding rugby player, before the war Pritchard had won 14 caps for playing for Wales.

12 Sept 1916

My dearest Flory,
The French people are wonderful, but their crops are not heavy as the soil is poor and chalky and most fields are full of shell holes. I am still in the same place, in my comfortable chateau with plenty of little worries. There is nothing very exciting going on in my sector, but there seem to be a lot of Boches in front of me. I blow them up with my guns and if I do not kill them I give them a lot of work to do with their picks and shovels to keep their trenches going. There is splendid news from the south; we have given the Boche a nasty knock, but he wants one or two more.

September proved to be a slightly busier month which included a number of gas alerts and the use of trench mortars to cut enemy barbed wire. On 8 October four raids were made on enemy trenches and Harold wrote to Dertha the next day, clearly pleased with his men.

9 Oct 1916

There is no fighting going on. What you see in the papers only refers to raids ie attempts of some 20 or 30 men to get into a Boche trench and pull out a prisoner. Lately we have done very well and my little lads have shown great gallantry and some of their performances have been mentioned in the communiques.

On 15 October one of Harold's battalions (20th Middlesex) was proud to provide two guards of honour when the French President visited Bethune. Sadly, only three days later, Harold was to lose a senior officer when Lieutenant Colonel Charles Wilkie of the 17th Welch was killed by a High Explosive Shell at the junction of South Street and St. James's Street whilst on a tour of the trenches. On 20 October Harold learned that the Division was to be relieved and moved to near St. Pol, closer to the fighting on the Somme. Harold described prevailing conditions to Dertha on 26 October.

26 Oct 1916

In our old part of the line we had dug ourselves in really well, guns, trench mortars and everything. And we were just beginning to snap our fingers at the Boche, and to give him a bit back – more than he was giving us. Then we had to take over another piece of the line, where everything was in a disgusting state, trenches with mud up to your knees, parapets all falling in and very little wire in front. So we had to begin all over again.

And, besides, we had to hold a very large portion of the front, with barely one bantam to every yard.

The 40th Division's march to Houvin-Houvigneul south of St. Pol and then south-westwards towards Frohen-le-Grand had been in mixed weather – gales, snow, rain and occasional dry days. In late October Harold established his headquarters at Bouquemaison, north of Doullens. Orders were then received transferring the Division to Lieutenant General Sir John Du Cane's XV Corps, a part of Rawlinson's Fourth Army, so it set off towards Abbeville for three weeks intensive training.

During November 120th Brigade was temporarily detached to reinforce another division for the final push (Battle of the Ancre, 13-18 November 1916) of the Somme offensive. Thus 40th Division earned its first battle honour but not under Harold's command.[13] That same month, an interesting appointment was made when Brigadier-General Frank Crozier took command of 119th Brigade. Crozier's previous active service experience had been during the Second Anglo-Boer War and with the Royal West African Frontier Force in the Southern Nigeria Protectorate. He had also commanded 9th (Service) Battalion of the 107th (Ulster) Brigade during the assault on Thiepval. Earlier in his career Crozier had been forced to resign over dishonoured cheques and took up farming in Canada, returning in 1912 to join the Ulster Volunteers and then the British Army.[14]

Now headquartered in Ailly-le-Haut-Clocher, Harold shared some humour with Dertha.

9 December 1916

Things don't look very happy on the Eastern Front, but I am told they are not so bad as they look. The French are very optimistic still, especially so is my French Count who lives in my mess with me. This is what he was heard to say to a French proprietor who did not want to have us in his house:

'Do you know who you are hesitating to receive into your House? I am the Count of Maillard, (1) the General is one of King George's greatest friends and his wife is the daughter of the actual King of Scotland.'

---

13   See Becke, Major A.F., *Order of Battle Divisions, Part 3 B, New Army Divisions (30-41); & 63rd (R.N.) Division* (London: HMSO, 1945), p.106.

14   Following the Great War, Crozier joined the Lithuanian Army as an advisor and attained the rank of major-general. He returned to Ireland and commanded the Auxiliary Division of the Royal Irish Constabulary. He was also the author of several postwar volumes of autobiography.

Not bad for a Frencher who really is not at all a bad sort. When he wants to be smart, he puts on a light blue tunic, red breaches with black stripe, khaki puttees, brown boots and black galoshes. He thinks he looks 'tout Anglais'.

Note
1. Georges, Comte de Maillard-Lacombe (1869-1944). Born in Angoulême, he married Madeleine Wlgrin de Taillefer, daughter of the Marquis Charles and Emma-Félicie Taillardat de La Maisonneuve of Perdechat. Their son Aldouin became Comte de Maillard Taillefer et du Saint-Empire.

At last, orders for Somme front arrived. Division transport was by rail and road and Divisional headquarters was established at Chipilly on 15 December.

13 Dec 1916

I am leaving this place tomorrow. I shall not be far from that nice place where I can buy the biscuits which we eat at home (1). I do not suppose that we shall be particularly comfortable but we have been hitherto much too luxurious.

For the next fortnight I expect I shall be battling with the mud and after that go into the line again but for quite a short period. I have been out for a long walk with Blythe (2), we went through an enormous wood and only saw one rabbit. The other day we dived into another large wood and found an old chateau. The proprietor who turned out to be Count St. Pol (3) showed us his house which was very bare. But he had some nice carvings and china. He invited us to come and shoot 'sanglier' in his wood. But I think it should take a lifetime to find one.

17 Dec 1916

I am now in a small chateau and my little men are in huts in the neighbourhood. The mud is appalling and it is difficult to get ahead as the roads are bad.

I shall be seeing a good deal of the French Army. They look first class fellows, all well developed and of a decent age. Of course they look rather slack in line of march, especially this transport, but I do not think there is much the matter with their infantry.

18th Dec 1916

We have had two days without rain and the bantams are beginning to get the better of the mud. I lunched with Du Cane (4) today and a French General. He talked a thousand miles an hour and I could not catch a word. I am afraid I shall have to retire beaten in my efforts to understand the Frenchers. I shall never be able to do it properly and shall have to figure as a regular old insular Britisher. I notice that they never make the least effort to talk English, so I am doing the same as they do.

The French have again done splendidly. I think they have got their back up and won't listen to the Boche proposals for peace.

I have sent off young Ralph to learn soldiering under John Campbell (5). He is too good for an ADC and I shall send him to a staff school where he can complete his education; and afterwards he will be eligible for a proper staff appointment.

Notes
1.   Apart from 'Biscuits roses de Reims', it is hard to know what biscuits Harold had in mind!
2.   Either Captain P.A. Blythe MC, Manchester Regiment or Captain W.A. Blythe, RA
3.   Comte de Saint-Pol. Possibly Chateau de Ribeaucourt.
4.   Lieutenant-General Sir John Du Cane commander of XV Corps of which 40th Division was part.
5.   Commanding 121st Brigade

According to the 40th Division's postwar historian:

Now began three months in the most God-forsaken and miserable area of France barring the Ypres Salient. The entire countryside was a churned up yeasty mass of mud, as a result of the vile weather and of the battle which even yet had not petered out. The weather was awful. Constant rain was varied by intensely cold spells of weather and some very heavy snowfalls. Mud and dirt were everywhere ... no pen can do justice to the front region - 'line' it could not be called. It just beggars description. It consisted of a mass of shell holes; of a general sea of mud; of lesser lakes and lagoons of icy water. Trenches did not exist, except for short lengths on higher ground; of communication trenches here were none; men had to do the best they could to improve such shell holes 'as were least full of water and other more unpleasant relics of battle. Villages there were in profusion, at least on the map; but in reality, they were flattened brickwork.[15]

In these conditions, supplies to the forward battalions became a nightmare. Ammunition, water, rations and clothing had to be taken up on pack animals as the use of vehicles had become impracticable on account of the mud. Although the total journey from the mule park to the front line was only a few miles, the return journey lasted anything from 12 to 15 hours as the mule trains fought their way through mud, which at times almost came up to the arm-pit.

22 Dec 1916

I am deeply sorry to learn how ill your father is, and I cannot keep thinking of him suffering from the dreadful disease (1).

I go and live in a dug out on the 22nd, really quite a comfortable one and rather different to the one I inhabited two years ago. It was built for a French Corps Commander. I have a little room to myself with a little apartment for my beddy and a 'funk hole' about 30 ft down leading out of it. The Boche do not shell the place very much, but occasionally send five or six somewhere near. We have been having rain again and the whole country is a quagmire. The conditions in the trenches are severe and I shall be thinking of my little bantams suffering in the cold and the mud. I am tremendously struck with the appearance of the French infantry. They are big well grown men all looking well over 25 and no weeds. I passed a regiment of them today. Of course they straggle all over the roads and fall out when they like, but they look splendid. I am afraid you will have a sad Xmas and New Year, but I am always thinking of you. Have just seen Mr Wilson's note on peace (2). I do not think it will come to much.

26 Dec 1916

I go up to my dug out on Wednesday and paddle about in the mud for three weeks and then go back into comfortable quarters again. I went up and saw my old battalion yesterday (3). There are only 5 or 6 of the old lot left.

Our Xmas day went off quietly, we had a turkey (bought for 30 francs) and plum pudding for dinner and some carol singers from the

15 Whitton, Lieutenant Colonel F.E., *History of The 40th Division* (Uckfield: Naval & Military Press reprint of 1926 edition), p.42.

Yorkshiremen. I gave them some mulled claret and the result was they went on singing for so long that they kept me awake.

Notes
1.   The Duke had been suffering from heart problems and Alzheimer's.
2.   On 18 December 1916, US President Woodrow Wilson dispatched a long note to all the belligerents. The last paragraph read: 'The President is not proposing peace; he is not even offering mediation. He is merely proposing that soundings be taken in order that we may learn, the neutral nations with the belligerent, how near the haven of peace may be for which all mankind longs with an intense and increasing longing. He believes that the spirit in which he speaks and the objects which he seeks will be understood by all concerned, and he confidently hopes for a response which will bring a new light into the affairs of the world'.
3.   Presumably a reference to 2nd Battalion Grenadier Guards who would either have been in the line at Combles or at Rest Camp 15.

10

'The Tide Has Turned'[1]

The Asquith Coalition Government collapsed in November 1916, after which War Minister David Lloyd George, in a political alliance with the Conservative Party, assumed leadership of a new coalition. Talk was now of victory starting in April when French General Robert Nivelle's massive offensive, supported by a BEF push at Arras, would shatter the formidable German defences and commence a war of movement.[2] Unfortunately, the grand scheme, enthusiastically backed by the prime minister despite the reservations of his generals, failed to achieve the desired results and the world-wide conflict dragged on.

Writing to Dertha from the Somme front, Harold described his current accommodation, clean and comfortable as it turned out, and the difficulties experienced in getting about.

2 Jan 1917

My own darling one,
Just a line to say I am … in my dugout. I am still very busy. The mud is so bad that one cannot get about quickly and there are not many decent tracks to use – the one thing to avoid is any cart path or disused road as they are all knee deep in mud.

I do not think I told you that in my dugout I have electric light which is splendid when it does not go out and I really much prefer living as I am to being in a dirty French house. Holmes keeps the place nice and clean and spends the day collecting wood for my fire. Most of it comes from an old Boche entanglement on the top of the hill. I am quite pleased with

---

1   Lloyd George Guildhall speech, 27 April 1917.
2   See Murphy, David, *Breaking Point of the French Army: The Nivelle Offensive of 1917* (Barnsley: Pen & Sword, 2015), passim.

the London Gazette – all the people I wanted to get something and as for myself I did not expect one.

5 Jan 1917

My own darling wee one,
Still up to my eyes in work but am still thinking of my darling mum in all her worries and changing her house and other things. I am living in a dugout about 15 miles SSE of the place where I expected to be. My quarters are most comfortable having been built by a French Corps. I have got a sitting room with a recess behind for on the top of a hill and below there is an underground chamber about 35 feet down to which to enter if the Boche makes himself unpleasant. My upper room has about 8 feet of chalk on it and my sitting room has calico windows and a stove which will smoke in spite of Holme's efforts.

My Brigadier has also two comfortable places built by the French but everything else is uncomfortable. In places the soil is deep brown with no stones and the mud is appalling. The roads in places are half up to one's knees in mud and rain. The trenches just slide in. I am about three miles from the front trenches. An occasional shell comes over but never does any harm. The men are at present very uncomfortable having to live in the open and in the mud and they are suffering a good deal. We are all working as hard as we can to better their conditions, but it is a slow process and it is so difficult to get anything up to them. The whole area is crowded with French artillery. Post going …

The New Year commenced with increased German bombardment of 40th Division's front. The exceptionally severe winter weather, however, precluded any major operations. The Casualty Clearing Stations started filling up with cases of pneumonia. One company commander recalled how the risk of casualties from trench feet could.

'decimate a battalion. I had given instructions to platoon commanders as to the necessity of maintaining circulation by every possible means; tight puttees were discarded and replaced by sandbags tied round the legs, and even then boots had to be removed so that the feet could be rubbed and a change of socks put on. By a lucky chance, on the evening before we left for the front line, I received from Queen Mary's Needlework Guild[3]

---

3   In 1914 the London Needlework Guild was renamed the Queen Mary's Needlework Guild. Its aim was to provide comforts for the troops and an opportunity for upper class

a bale of socks, hand-knitted and of much better quality than the normal issue. And I distributed a pair to every man in the company, and our casualties from trench feet were very few. Such were the conditions in the front line during the severe winter of 1917. Each night I visited the front-line posts … I found the NCOs and men, not only without complaint, but cheerful and alert with their Lewis guns kept ready for action. No company commander could have asked for greater reward'.[4]

13 Jan 1917

My Dear Duke,

I am so sorry to hear that you are so ill. Dertha will tell you where I have eventually landed in a muddy country pitted with shell holes. There are no signs of any villages left, only a few stumps of fruit trees. There is scarcely any green grass and the whole country looks like a large ploughed field with white chalk trenches. Where there is no chalk the soil consists of a deep loam without any stones and if there is any wheeled traffic it soon turns it into mud in which you have to walk up to your middle. Consequently when off the chalk all trenches simply cease to exist after heavy rain (and we have it every day) and the men have to stand in the mud. So the poor infantry have a bad time of it … The worst part of it is that they get trench foot and are a long time in hospital. I think my kilted battalion suffered most of all. You know that they are recruited from the commercial classes in Scotland. I saw them come out of the trenches and though they are fine beings physically I have never seen men looking so miserable. They were soaked to the skin and covered with mud and when they got back some of them weighed their kilts and found they were 30lbs. The C.O. told me the kilts were not a serviceable dress but then he was an Englishman!

At the beginning of February, now out of the line in reserve, the Division's Headquarters were at Corbie , 8 miles due East of Amiens. Illness caused by the bitter conditions was a particular worry and acute pneumonia wards had been set up in 48th Casualty Clearing Station. On 3 February Harold found time to write to his sister.

women to contribute to the war effort.. Sewing groups were set up all over the country, the members both buying and making items and fundraising for materials and for donations to the Red Cross. During this period, there were 430 branches in the country.

4   Captain E.E.A Whitworth unpublished memoir, Royal Regiment of Wales Museum, Brecon.

My Dearest Flora,

I am quite ashamed of myself for not answering your letter before, but I have been very busy. I had to take my division into a nasty bit of the line and I found so much to do that I had not a moment for myself. I was living in a sumptuous dug out (made by the French) with electric light and a stove.

However I got all my little men out alright and we are now resting. I am occupying a chateau (1), the house of a factory owner, and it is difficult to keep warm. There is a scarcity of coal and problems with wood but we are jogging along quite happily.

Ralph as I expect you know has a flair for staff work and has gone to Corps HQ to finish his education. Bobbins (2) is with me now, he does splendidly, looks after everyone and everything and sees that we are not starved.

Write a line to Dertha and say you are going to Guildford. You know that we have been turned out of our nice house. Dertha has taken a little cottage higher up the hill (3). I should like to think you were with her as she wants a good rest after all the worry and anxiety of her Father's death (4). My arms are splendid. It got a bit rheumatic like …

Notes
1. Possibly Chateau Chantraine in Corbie.
2. Bobbins was his soldier servant.
3. Dertha had to vacate the Commandant's House at Hythe and was now living in Bourtree, a house on a hill which overlooked Hythe Church.
4. Dertha's father, the Duke, had died on 20 January. The 7th Duke had several issues mostly relating to his heart and towards the end of his life dementia

On 12 February, 40th Division returned to the line in the Rancourt sector with much patrolling to establish whether the Germans opposite their positions were, in fact, withdrawing. Indeed they appeared to be staying put – at least for a while. At the end of the month, the Division cooperated with XIV Corps in a successful attack against a portion of the German position. March brought attacks on Harold's trenches including the use of lachrymatory shells (tear gas) and to the consternation of all, two inches of snow fell on 9 March, a forestate of the inclement weather which was to last a month. The long-awaited German withdrawal opposite 40th Division commenced on 17 March and, switching from the defensive to the offensive, the Division pressed forward with the 13th East Surrey Regiment entering Peronne unopposed. At the end of the month, the Division headed out of the line to work on railways and to repair roads. This was an urgent matter as any advance required the infrastructure over which vital supplies could be delivered to the forward units in contact with the enemy. Matters were exacerbated as the withdrawing German Army had done all it could to lay waste to land and booby trap buildings. The conditions Harold's soldiers lived in while carrying out 'these monotonous duties' were desperate, often living in cellars or draughty tents. One battalion refused to parade for four days in March until some particularly brutal instructors were posted elsewhere.[5] Brigadier General Crozier was instructed to form a 'flying column' based around a battalion of 119th Brigade but kept on a short rein by Corps HQ, it never flew and was disbanded after three days.

On 2 April Harold wrote to Dertha enclosing a small flower.

My own dear one,
Just a line in answer to your letter about the money. I am sorry to hear that you have caught another chill. Is my mum looking after herself properly? I went up to Sailly-Saillisel (1) yesterday afternoon. I never saw such a dreadful place in my life. There is no sign of any village, scarcely a brick to be seen. Nothing but shell holes full of water and deep mud. The only living thing in the place was a bunch of snowdrops otherwise there is not a blade of grass. I send you a little flower to show you that I am always thinking of my darling mum.
Ever your most loving Harry

Note
1.   Sailly–Saillisel is a village situated on either side of the Bapaume–Peronne road. An objective of French attacks, it was captured on 18 October. Harold's grim description matches contemporary accounts.

The first three weeks of April saw the division advance cautiously with XV Corps and engaging with the German rearguard. By 20 April Harold held a section of front between Gouzeaucourt and Gouzeaucourt Wood some eight miles from Cambrai. On 21 April, 8th Division was tasked to attack the villages of Villers-Guislain and Gonnelieu while the 40th was to make good the 'Fifteen Ravine' spur to the northeast of the village and then continue until it was in touch with the 20th (Light) Division on the left. At 4.15 a.m., Harold's Division attacked across ' open and undulating (terrain), intersected by numerous so-called ravines…There was little or no cultivation, but the grass was thick and high. The villages were mostly standing, as the enemy was using them as strongpoints, while the ground was fairly free from shell holes … All cross-roads had been cratered … Taken as a whole it was good fighting country, with natural cover and good observation'.[6]

5   Mitchinson, K.W., *Villers–Plouich* (Leo Cooper, Pen & Sword, Barnsley, 1999), passim.
6   Whitton, p.60.

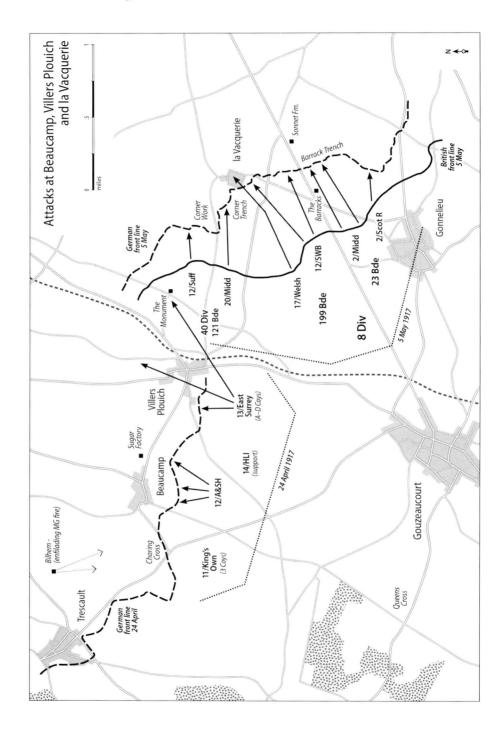

Attacks at Beaucamp, Villers Plouich and la Vacquerie

Fifteen Ravine was some ten feet deep and stiff resistance was encountered before the position was taken by the South Wales Borderers. Divisional casualties were relatively light although the Borderers had 25 men killed, over 50 wounded and five later dying of their wounds. 119th Brigade suffered 157 casualties as well as taking 40 prisoners and the 19th Royal Welch Fusiliers some 50 casualties. Harold's attack, carried out with steadiness and precision, had been supported by very accurate and well-timed artillery fire but a harder task lay ahead – the attack on the defended villages of Villers-Plouich and Beaucamp and the high ground beyond them.

The divisional plan was as follows. The 119th Brigade on the right was to take the line of low spurs just beyond Gonnelieu and Villers-Plouich. All positions once gained were to be consolidated. On the left, 120th Brigade's objective was a line north of Villers-Plouich and Beaucamp after first capturing the two villages. The 121st Brigade was to hold two battalions and a machine gun section in readiness to support either brigade as required. Just before midnight of 23/24 April, the 18th Welch of 119th Brigade advanced and by 2 a.m. had occupied and consolidated on its objective. The 17th Welch hit a strong belt of wire but found a gap made by the barrage and by 9.40 a.m. all the battalion's objectives had been reached and were being consolidated. For the 119th Brigade, it had been a smart and well-managed attack with casualties limited to eight officers and 79 ORs.

At 2 a.m. on 24 April, 120th Brigade's battalions moved forward to their start lines, the 13th East Surreys supported by the Highland Light Infantry to Villiers Plouich and the 14th Argyll and Sutherland Highlanders to Beaucamp. At 4.15 a.m., the Surreys crept forward in four waves and within seven minutes had entered the German trench system. By 5.30 a.m., they were in Villers-Plouich where they divided into three groups to take out the German strongpoints. An hour later the covering barrage shut down and they began to consolidate around the village. However, ten minutes later heavy artillery fire crashed down on them and they withdrew to the entrances to the village where the Highland Light Infantry had arrived to reinforce them. Strong posts were established and in spite of heavy enemy artillery fire continuing throughout the day, the line held. By dusk, the commanding officer of the Highlanders had established all round defence and it was time to count the cost. The East Surreys had incurred 200 casualties, including 29 killed. On the credit side, four German officers and 300 ORs had been captured along with ten machine guns and some 500 rifles. The courage of the East Surreys was recognised with the award of a battalion VC,[7] a DCM and five MMs.

---

7   Corporal Edward Foster citation: 'For most conspicuous bravery and initiative. During an attack the advance was held up in a portion of a village by two enemy machine guns which

The 14th Argyll and Sutherland Highlanders had crossed their start line at 3.45 a.m. to begin their assault on Beaucamp. They too hit a thick belt of wire and their progress was further impeded by enemy machine guns enfilading them. Having dealt with the guns, they reached the centre of the village at 4.40 a.m. where, contrary to expectations, practically no resistance was encountered. Then as the two lead companies deployed to the left and right, sustained machine gun fire came in from the direction of Bilhem. Every available Lewis gun was brought into action but by 6.30 a.m. the situation was serious. All three company commanders had been hit (D Company was being commanded by Corporal Johnston) and it was evident that progress was impossible. When the two supporting companies attempted to pass through, three officers were killed and two wounded. In the half light of dawn, the battalion withdrew back through the village and waited until daylight. At 9 a.m., they managed to get a message back to the gunners indicating the position of the enemy machine guns and the effect was marked.

Harold alerted 119th Brigade to stand by to attack Beaucamp but when the Argylls sent patrols into the village at 11 a.m., it transpired that the Germans had reoccupied it soon after the withdrawal and they were still covered by the machine guns firing in enfilade from Bilhem. Around 2 p.m., a further attempt was made to gain a foothold in the village but with no success. By now it was clear that until the enemy guns at Bilhem had been silenced, Beaucamp could not be taken. Corps HQ directed the 20th Division to attack Bilhem and if successful, the 11th King's Own Regiment would relieve the Argylls during the night and attack Beaucamp. All went to plan. The 60th Brigade seized Bilhem and when the King's Own entered the village, there was no reception by intense machine gun fire. The task allotted to 40th Division had now been successfully completed. The fighting had been severe, especially on the left, and total casualties amounted to 664, including 133 killed. Harold wrote to Dertha about the success.

26th April 1917

We have just fought a battle on our own – but during the fight you must not think that I am running risks. I sit in my hut and direct operations by telephone. We had to take two villages on a front of 3,000 yards and we took them both, though one was not captured till the following

were entrenched and strongly covered by wire entanglements. Corporal Foster, who was in charge of two Lewis guns, succeeded in entering the trench and engaging the enemy guns. One of the Lewis guns was lost, but Corporal Foster with reckless courage, rushed forward and bombed the enemy, thereby recovering the gun. Then getting his two guns into action, he killed the enemy gun team and captured their guns, thereby enabling the advance to continue successfully.'

morning, we got over 380 prisoners and 10 machine guns and everyone did very well and we have been congratulated by all the swells from the C in C downwards. The bantams did very well indeed, the little Welsh men especially. We had in front of us one of the newly formed Boche divisions, consisting of about fifty per cent of youths of 18 years old. The bantams quickly cleared them out of the trenches. Most of our losses(1) were caused by the artillery fire afterwards. I think everyone is quite pleased with us.

I have got a nice little garden at my front door and have some canariensis and sweet peas.

Note
1. Harold did not mention the terrible losses sustained by the Argyll and Sutherland Highlanders. In all, 72 ORs were killed and 160 wounded including seven officers.

Beyond 40th Division's front lay the enemy-occupied village of La Vacquerie, just off the Cambrai road. XV Corps decided to mount a two divisional raid over a wide front. 40th Division's objectives were La Vacquarie and the German trenches to the northwest of it. Zero hour was fixed for 11 p.m. on 5 May, and withdrawal was to take place at 1 a.m. the next morning. Harold allocated La Vacquarie to Crozier's 119th Brigade and the trenches to Campbell's 121st Brigade. The mission was to inflict loss on the enemy; to damage his defences; and , above all, to obtain identification of enemy units. The raid was to be short, sharp and destructive. Four trench mortars were in support as well as the Divisional artillery. Once on the objective, the brigade's assaulting waves were to go firm and act as a covering party while 'moppers up' destroyed dug-outs and generally cleaned gup. They would be assisted by a company of Royal Engineers who would set about destroying cellars and hardened defences. If the concept seemed simple, the planning and execution were complicated.

The assault duly went in at 11p.m. on 5 May with Harold's 'Rhondda Bantams' (17th Battalion Welch Regiment) on the left, supported by the Suffolk and Middlesex battalions, and the South Wales Borderers on their right. The moon was nearly full but the night was cloudy and rain began to fall. The Borderers met little opposition until La Vacquarie was reached when they came under heavy machine gun from the northwest. Numerous enemy flares and rockets illuminated the village; at least two enemy spigot mortars firing requisitioned aerial flechettes were also employed. Uncut wire straddled the village, making progress extremely slow in the pitch dark and often the 'moppers up' found themselves in the actual battle with the assaulting troops. The same went for the sappers. The retirement went unmolested and the brigade returned with eight prisoners. Although the sappers had managed to blow up several houses and destroy two dugouts, the raid fell short of expectation. The casualties sustained by the brigade were four officers and 101 ORs, including ten missing.

The 121st Brigade set off with the 20th Middlesex on the right and the 12th Suffolks on the left to take the trenches to the northwest of the village. The Middlesex soon came under heavy artillery fire and by twenty minutes past midnight, after losing three officers and two platoon sergeants, the decision was made not to press on any further and the battalion was back on its original position by 2.30 a.m. The Suffolks had managed to find a gap in the wire cut by the Divisional artillery but once through they came across a second belt of intact wire covered by fire from an enemy trench. The battalion had disturbed a hornets' nest and after destroying two dug-outs from which the enemy refused to emerge, it withdrew in some confusion. Although 40th Division had incurred 257 casualties, including 31 killed, a costly but valuable lesson had been learnt, namely that the German defensive organization now bedded down on the new Hinderburg Line, was back in working order.

There then followed a period of comparative quiet with XV Corps adopting a generally defensive posture. During the rest of the month, three much smaller raids were mounted by the Division with varying degrees of success.

23 May 1917

My own dear wee one,
I have been busy lately. We have been shifting up and down the line a good deal and now we are told we are going to be stationary for a bit.
So far as the Boche goes we are having a quieter time. He does not shell so much though we worry them a good deal. I think he expected to make peace with Russia but the news lately has been very good and I think that everything will turn out alright though events may lengthen the war. We also hear much better news about the submarines and that we really are destroying a good number. Everyone too is much pleased with the Italians as they have done better than they themselves expected.
So we are all in good spirits. The mud is disappearing and the country is quite green and the shell holes are disappearing.
H
(Lots of old pals gone except Kirk (1) who is coming to dinner and sleep on Sat)

Note
1.   Captain H.C.B. Kirkpatrick, CB, MC, Kings Own Scottish Borderers. He had been one of Harold's instructors at Hythe.

Three days later Dertha wrote to Harold having been eye-witness to a deadly German Gotha bomber raid on Hythe and Folkestone.

26 May, 1917
Bourtree

My Dearest,

I am writing at Charing Cross. I am not sure whether you will hear about it but we had a German raid (1) on a biggish scale at Hythe and Folkestone yesterday – about 6.15 p.m. I was in the kitchen talking to old Grace. Suddenly we heard a tremendous roar and we simultaneously stopped speaking. Then I heard two huge bangs behind the house. I said. 'That's bombs!' and I seized a pair of field glasses in the hall and rushed upstairs to my bedroom window which has a view all round the country. I suppose it was a foolish thing to do but I wouldn't have missed what I saw for anything. There were 24 German aeroplanes spread out dropping bombs all round. As you know we are on the top of the hill just behind the church. The sky was very clear and pink before sunset and everything sharply outlined. The aeroplanes had white transparent wings – beautiful things. I saw them drop four or five bombs near the aerodrome beyond the ranges, missing the sheds. Two in the town just below us. Three or four in the sea, two on the beach, two on the cricket ground, two in the churchyard. One on the allotment ground near our corner – then I remembered that Dulcie was in the bottom of the garden near where they were falling and I shouted to her to come in. She ran up and said 'Whatever is happening? Are they practising big guns round the house!' She could not see the aeroplanes on account of the trees. When she found out she wanted to run out into the road to have a better view but I stopped her. Then the aeroplanes took a turn to Shorncliffe and Folkestone dropping bombs all the way and I lost sight of them as the trees on the other side hid them. All the time the noise was deafening and I could hear Zeppelins (2) but could not see them.

None of our aeroplanes were able to get up till long after they had gone. When the noise died away I went with Dulcie (who was more excited than frightened) down our road coming onto the churchyard. There I found the only unpleasant sight that I saw – the poor old white bearded Verger had run out of the church and been caught by a bomb – the Vicar's wife with a long gash on her face was attending to him and a nurse and doctor had just come up (3). The report came down that his legs were badly shattered and there is not much hope of recovering at his age. The gravestones hurled about. Then I went below the church and a young Canadian soldier who had been sent up with a stretcher dropped in a faint at my feet. I was passing an open door and told his pal to bring him in and that was the only casualty that I attended to. When he came to he explained that he had been invalided from the front and had run too fast up the hill which may or may not have been.

Then I went down to see Marion and her mother and sisters in the town as I had seen a bomb fall close to their house. They and many others had a wonderful escape. They were all playing lawn tennis on the cricket ground. The aeroplanes appeared and dropped two bombs among them without touching anyone. Someone shouted to run to the cellars in the Imperial Hotel! Everyone rushed towards it and the girls dragged their mother through two fields until they got there. A Mrs Steele, whom I know, fell in a faint on the cricket ground. A little girl of 17, a stranger to her, a daughter of General Atkinson (4), ran back and attended to her, which was a very plucky thing to do as the aeroplanes were still overhead.

Meanwhile Lucy, my housemaid, had been spending the evening with her people at Elham. She was entertained by the sight of five Zeppelins who dropped many bombs over the aeroplane works at Capel and behind Shorncliffe. A whole army of British aeroplanes came and buzzed around them like a swarm of bees until they were all lost in the distance and the smoke. I hope they bagged one.

What struck me most about the whole affair is the extraordinarily small amount of damage they did. I saw over 20 bombs drop about Hythe and they killed one old woman and probably the old man whom I saw. Where bombs dropped on a roof they made a round hole. They struck two empty houses that way. They were of course trying for the aerodrome and then for the church and made extraordinarily bad shots of both. Coming up on the train this morning they said a bomb fell on the large draper's shop in Folkestone and killed five assistants. I had shopped there that afternoon. Also on the station, killing a man and two children in a house. Probably considerable damage where the Zeps were. Also at Ashford they tried for the SE Railway Works and killed one girl.

That is all that I heard and I must get back into the train.

Notes

1. *Unternehmen Türkencruz* (Operation Turk's Cross)[8]opened at 2 p.m. on Friday 25 May when twelve Gotha G.IV bombers took off from airfields in occupied Belgium. Their mission was to bomb London. Two turned back after experiencing mechanical difficulties over the North Sea and, after finding London covered in thick cloud, the remaining 10 headed for their secondary targets at the Channel port of Folkestone and the nearby Shorncliffe Army Camp. At

8 See White, C.M., *Gotha Summer: The German daytime air raids on England, May to August 1917* (London: Robert Hale, 1986), passim.

Shorncliff and Cheriton, 17 Canadian soldiers were killed and 93 wounded. At Folkestone a soldier and 15 men, 31 women and 25 children were killed, 8 soldiers, 23 men, 48 women and 12 children were wounded, most of the casualties occurring in Tontine Street, which was full of shoppers. As the formation flew out to sea under anti-aircraft gun fire, they were pursued by 33 RFC and 37 RNAS aircraft. A captured German airman later said that a Gotha had been shot down off the Belgian coast, one crashed in Belgium and one landed damaged at St Denis Westrem.

2.   Dertha's reference to Zeppelins appears to be an error as the raid was entirely carried out by Gotha bombers.

3.   Over Hythe, the bombers dropped 19 bombs including 7 on the beach and one on the golf course. Two houses were hit and there were two fatalities including Daniel Stringer Lith, the Verger of St. Leonard's Parish Church who was hit by a bomb splinter when a bomb exploded in the churchyard as he was chatting to the Vicar, the Rev Herbert Dale. The shrapnel also hit the vicar who was miraculously saved when it ricocheted off a tin box in his jacket. Lith died of his wounds in Folkestone hospital that night. The Vicar's wife, Mrs Herbert Dale, was also injured.

4.   Major General Sir Edwin Henry de Vere Atkinson, later Chief Engineer.

With the exception of a mighty storm in June which reduced the sunken lanes to raging torrents and the ravines to impassable bogs, June passed as a 'quiet month' with a routine for battalions of four days in the front trenches, four in support, four in reserve and four at rest. When in the front line, active, asserting patrolling was the order of the day or rather night.

20 June 1917
HQ 40th Div

My Dear Aunt Dertha,

I thought a description of a dinner party given by Uncle Harry to celebrate his Birthday honour (1) would interest you. It was attended by the senior members of his staff, Bobbins and myself.

Some foraging in Amiens by Bobbins produced all sorts of eatables, strawberries, to say nothing of champagne and a bottle of Waterloo port provided by the liaison officer. If further proof was needed, which I know it is not, and I don't say it because I am a nephew — the dinner was one long tribute to the immense popularity of the General and the esteem in which he is held throughout the Division.

RRB

Note

1.   There was no honour for Harold in the King's 1917 Birthday List. Harold's name was published in *The London Gazette* for 1 June and in Haig's despatch of 9 April 1917.

Early July was relatively quiet. However, on the 13th 40th Division headquarters was shelled for 45 minutes by an 8-inch high velocity gun. Raids against an alert enemy achieved little. Indeed, five launched over a period of one week proved entirely unsuccessful. Conversely, the Germans executed a carefully planned raid on 26 July during which they seized 25 members of 13th Yorkshires before hustling them across no man's land and captivity. August proved more fruitful and on 13 August, 119th Brigade captured a member of 6th Bavarian Infantry Regiment who proved of great value to intelligence.

Harold proceeded to England on 24 August and Major General John Ponsonby, former Coldstream Guards, assumed command of 40th Division which was in fine fettle and a tribute to Harold's care and leadership. A moving personal tribute was composed by Captain Eric Whitworth of 12th South Wales Borderers.

> Such was our Divisional General (Ruggles-Brise), a man of justice, a soldier who inspired in all ranks a feeling of confidence and loyalty and not merely a picturesque figurehead, unknown and misunderstood. A man whose personality breathed kindness but never weakness, and lastly a soldier who, whilst he showed us that he understood our difficulties, made us feel that they were there to be overcome at all costs.[9]

Over two months after Harold left 40th Division it was engaged in very heavy fighting for Bourlon village and the 600-acre Bourlon Wood. A first day objective in the Cambrai tank offensive (20 November–6 December 1917), the Division, on assuming responsibility for the sector, attacked on 23 November and succeeded in capturing the wood but not the nearby village. The fighting was brutal and bloody, the Division sustaining over 3,000 casualties of which a 192 were officers. The sacrifice did not go unnoticed – seven DSOs, 44 MCs (two bars and a second bar were also given), and 27 DCMs were awarded. After the fighting Harold received a tribute from John Ponsonby.

> Dear Ruggles,
> I know that you will be glad to hear that your old division went like Hell on the 23rd and took Bourlon Wood. There was no stopping the little men and they fought well and all out for three days.
>   The Commander-in-Chief came himself to congratulate the Division personally. Charles and the rest of the staff were invaluable and in fact everybody played up for all they were worth. I send you Byng's letter as I thought you might like to see it.

9   Emden, Richard van, *The Soldier's War: The Great War Through Veterans' Eyes* (London: Bloomsbury, 2010), p.356.

I have always felt that it was owing to your great interest in the Division and the good spirit you put into all ranks that any credit is due, and I am therefore glad to say your work with the Division has brought its reward and we all feel we owe a lot to our old Divisional Commander.

Yours,

John Ponsonby

Our casualties were, I regret, rather high.

Two of Harold's former battalion commanders died during the fighting: Lieutenant-Colonel Clinton Battye DSO of the Highland Light Infantry and Lieutenant-Colonel William Kennedy MC of the 18th Welsh (he was from the Highland Light Infantry). To reflect the sacrifice of 40th Division at Bourlon Wood, General Sir Douglas Haig allowed an acorn to be added to their cockerel divisional emblem. Enemy prisoners numbered 700 and 42 machine guns had been captured.

Harold received two further letters about Bourlon, the first from Dertha and the second from Brigadier-General John Campbell.

6th Dec 1917,
Bourtree

My Dearest,

I am so glad your Division did well at Bourlon but I know how sorry my Man is not to be with them. I am anxious just now about many things. I have just got a coded message from Hamish from his new place Freiburg (1)," treatment worst yet", which means a great deal and he says he has given up all idea of going to Holland.

Loving Dee

15th December 1917

Dear General,

Many thanks for your letter of 12th inst. It was awfully nice of you to write as you did but I really do not deserve so much praise. I am sure anyone who was in my place would have acted as I did and I cannot feel grateful enough to my brigade for the splendid way in which they behaved – they really did magnificently, officers and men, for their task was a very difficult and trying one. You will I know be pleased to hear that General Pulteney wrote an exceedingly nice letter withdrawing what he had said about the Yorkshire Regiment and congratulating them on their fine behaviour. The Battalion is delighted and it has bucked them up tremendously. In fact all Battalions have their tails well up now. Again with many thanks for your letter and congratulations and with kindest regards to Lady Dorothea.

Yours ever,

John Campbell

Note

1.   The officers' POW camp was located in the old university building in Freiburg-im-Breisgau (Baden-Wurttemberg).

Harold had been on an extraordinary odyssey from the September day in 1915 when the 40th Division was first constituted in Aldershot to 24 June 1917 when he said farewell to it on the banks of the Somme. In the beginning, no one believed that the Bantams would ever deliver victory on the battlefield. At times Harold himself had doubts when the winnowing process removed the chaff of medically unfit and underaged recruits to the extent that most of the bantam battalions were reduced to less than half their strength. Through sheer persistence, he persuaded the War Office to dispatch four battalions of trained men and, as if a wand had been waved, this infusion transformed the sinews of 40th Division. Meticulous attention to the training of all ranks now ensured the men could march and shoot as fully fledged infanteers.

Once in France, Harold's main concern was to combine all arms into a cohesive fighting force seamlessly working together in both the offensive and defensive roles. To do this he needed to join in the fight. Instead, 40th Division, considered 'poor' material up the chain of command, spent the next six months doing relatively little beyond participation in position warfare whilst the Arras and Third Ypres offensives raged on. The esprit de corps he instilled into it before leaving England began to ebb away. With the assistance of capable brigade commanders, discipline and morale were maintained across the Division and the men's health carefully monitored at battalion level for illness and disease had a debilitating effect on troop numbers.

Out of the line, Harold put his troops through intensive training, especially with Lewis guns and Mills grenades which had become the weapons of choice in trench warfare. Command and control depended on the transmission of up to date and accurate information, a principle of war which Harold had seen so poorly executed in South Africa. He therefore took the greatest interest in making sure good communications were in place between battalions and brigades. He also was a great believer in personal communication and recognised brigade staff and battalion commanders, indeed many company commanders, by name.

Under Harold's leadership, the 40th Division was not found wanting: 'Its history properly ends on the Escaut in November 1918. It came into being to fight.

It fought well. And, after the fighting was over, the tale was done. To the 40th Division England, Scotland, Ireland and Wales contributed units and personnel. Each country may well be proud of those of its sons who made the Fighting Fortieth what it was'.[10]

10   Whitton, p.310.

11

The Home Front and Back to the Cauldron

On 6 September Harold took command of 73rd Division, Home Forces. Three home defence divisions had been formed in 1916, the 73rd first assembling in Blackpool in November of that year, for there was a very real fear that Britain could be invaded if the German submarine campaign succeeded. Over 300,000 men were under arms on the home front. In January 1917 the 73rd was assigned to the Southern Army of Home Forces and was based in Essex and Hertfordshire with Headquarters (conveniently for Harold) at Boreham House, Chelmsford, not far from Spains Hall. As per the usual organisation, Harold's new formation consisted of the three brigades plus cyclist battalions, artillery, engineers and transport. Home Forces had two key roles, namely training men for overseas service and home defence. The three Home Service divisions were broken up in early 1918 and the 73rd was officially disbanded by 18 April 1918. Doubtless 73rd Division benefitted greatly from Harold's experience and leadership but sadly little is known of his efforts and, being based at home, neither he nor Dertha's correspondence has shown much light on events up to this point.

It was not long before Harold was again on the move and he penned a quick note to Dertha.

3 January 1918

I have just had a cryptic message on the telephone 'am I ready for France?' I said 'Now! I do not know what it is all about ...'

20 January 1918
c/o GHQ France

My own dear wee one,
I sleep, and Holmes does too, in a French billet in a barn opposite the one occupied by Adjutant General Lucky Whitbread (Coldstream) (1).

I dined with Sir D Haig the other night, had a very pleasant dinner, met Gen Kiggell (2) and Sassoon of Hythe (3). I dined last night with Whitbread to celebrate his birthday and had some champagne.

There is no-one at GHQ that I know well except Kirkpatrick of Hythe (4). He has done very well with an MC and DSO and is now on the General's staff. There is one guardsman, Beckwith-Smith of the Coldstream Guards (5) whom I know. The Brigadier General with whom I work is one Wigram (6), brother of the King's secretary who was educated at Winchester.

I spend all my time running around telegraph and post offices. I shall hop to Boulogne, St Omer, Abbeville, Étaples and tomorrow I am off to Rouen and the next day to Le Havre. My idea is to finish off the lines of communication first and then to visit armies and Corps where I expect I shall have the most trouble.

I think I expect to finish in about a week's time unless the authorities here want me to go deeper into the question than I propose to.

Notes
1. The only Coldstream Whitbread is Robert, who was wounded when serving with the 3rd Battalion in France. He joined the Coldstreams in 1900 from the Durham Light Infantry.
2. Lieutenant General Sir Launcelot Kiggell, KCB, KCMG (1862 – 1954) was Chief of the General Staff for the British Armies in France under Haig from late 1915 to 1918.
3. Major Sir Philip Sassoon Bt., MP for Hythe and a second lieutenant in the East Kent Yeomanry, spent most of the war working as a secretary and general fixer for Haig.
4. Major Hugh Kirkpatrick, DSO, MC, King's Own Scottish Borderers. He had been on Harold's staff at Hythe. Killed in October 1918.
5. Later Major General Merton Beckwith-Smith, DSO, MC (1890-1942). He would have been a young staff officer.
6. General Sir Kenneth Wigram, GCB, CSI, CBE, DSO (1875-1949). His brother Clive, Clive Wigram, 1st Baron Wigram, GCB, GCVO, CSI, PC, FZS (1873-1960) was Private Secretary to the Sovereign from 1931 to 1936.

Wigram was Head of Operations (B) Section at GHQ France but apart from Harold's letters, it is not clear as to the task he had been given.

25 Jan 1918
GHG, France

My own dear wee one,
I have been on the road since I last wrote, have motored all the way round the lines of communications and am starting to go round the armies. The

whole project. is a complicated job and I am afraid I shall be longer than expected and shall not finish for another week.

Have met a great many people but so far no-one very interesting. Wallace, Black Watch,(1) is on staff here and remembers you visiting him in hospital. I have also Lindsay (2), Kirkpatrick and Hartt (3).

Notes
1. Lieutenant Colonel Robert Wallace of that Ilk. Seriously wounded with gunshot wound to the thigh; mentioned in despatches four times. Became Chief of Clan Wallace in 1948.
2. Lindsay is not shown on Q1 1918 Staff List
3. There was a Royal Sussex officer of this name. Not shown on Q1 1918 Staff List

Dertha wrote with more news of activity in the skies above Hythe.

30 Jan 1918
Bourtree

My Dearest,

Had such a night. As I told you we heard nothing of the raid on Tuesday night (1) but last night at 12.30 when we were all sound asleep we were woken up with the worst banging I have heard yet. I suppose they have increased their guns. Everything was rattling. I rolled myself up and ran down into the kitchen. The Boches were flying low over the houses and apparently they went round and round for over half an hour before they got away. I think there was considerable shooting from the sea as well as the land.

However, if one doesn't lose one's sense of proportion there is nothing much to trouble about.

Loving Dee

I expect a lot of people will decamp today. I hope so – we need more food.

Note
1. Dertha's letter is dated Wednesday 30 January; the raid on London took place on the night of Monday 28 January. Thirteen Gothas and two Riesenflugzeuge (Giants) took off from Germany, six turned back before reaching England and the rest made landfall at about 8 p.m. and continued to London. Over a hundred British night-fighter sorties were flown, resulting in one Gotha being shot down after being subjected to a co-ordinated attack by two Camels from 40 Squadron RFC, the first victory for night-fighters against a bomber over Britain. On the Tuesday night, another 15 enemy aircraft crossed the Kent and Essex coasts at about 8 p.m.; they returned about 11 p.m.

Harold was now based at General Headquarters (GHQ) which since March 1916 had been located at Montreuil-Sur-Mer, situated conveniently near Channel ports and about half way between London and Paris. In addition to Haig's headquarters at Chateau Beaurepaire ten miles to the southeast of the town, Montreuil could accommodate the departments of GHQ in its military academy and provide billets for the General Staff in the town. The functions of GHQ, apart from determining military strategy, included transportation of supplies and equipment, the management of transportation networks (roads, railways, inland water transport, and docks), agricultural production and forestry, law and order, engineering, medical and veterinary services, personnel, pay, the Church, education, postal service, training, the Inspector of Mines, censorship, ciphers, 'listening' and counter espionage. Days were long and work went on late into the night. The remit of the Military Secretary covered appointments promotions, 'removals' and honours and awards.

Life at Montreuil was monastic with precious little leisure time. A walk on the Ramparts was the chief recreation for the majority of officers. Riding was not a common exercise for horses were scarce. There was an old fosse which had been converted into a hard tennis court and the GHQ Recreation Ground provided a 'lumpy' cricket pitch but judging from Harold's letters, he spent most of his time chained to his desk. He may have managed the occasional day out at Le Touquet to play a round of golf with the Chief and the odd evening in the Officers' Club where once a week there was a guest night and a band. As Frank Fox put it, the laborious life of the 300 or so Monks of Montreuil at GHQ was sober and strenuous but it was hardly dull or tedious.[1]

Twenty-four hours before Harold took over as Military Secretary to General Haig,[2] the morning of 21 March 1918 was ushered in with a thick, white fog, and at dawn a bombardment of massive proportions was opened against the front of the British Fifth and Third Armies. It heralded the beginning of *Kaiserschlacht*, the German spring offensive to bring an end to the war before the United States could transport sufficient manpower across the Atlantic and fully deploy its resources. Bolstered by 50 divisions which had been freed by the Bolshevik government's withdrawal from the war with the Treaty of Brest-Litovsk, there were four concurrent German offensives.

The main effort, *Unternehmen Michael*, was to break through the Allied lines, outflank and defeat the BEF (which held the front from the Somme river to the English Channel). Once that was achieved, it was hoped that the French would

---

1   Fox, Frank ('GSO'), *GHQ (Montreuil -sur-Mer)* (London: Philip Allan & Co., 1920), pp.47-65.
2   *London Gazette Supplement No. 30676*, p.5562, 7 May 1918.

seek armistice terms. The remaining offensives, designed to divert Allied forces from the main offensive, were subsidiary to *Michael*. By the close of the first day, the British had lost 7,512 dead and 10,000 wounded and the German *stosstruppen* had made a number of inroads into Fifth Army's front. After two days Gough's army was in full retreat. As it fell back, many of the isolated redoubts were surrounded and overwhelmed by the follow-up German infantry. The right wing of Third Army became separated from the retreating Fifth Army, and also retreated to avoid being outflanked. On 23 March, in his Special Order of the Day, Haig bluntly told his troops and his political masters in London and Paris that 'we are again at a crisis in the war. The enemy has collected on this front every available division and is aiming at the destruction of the British Army'.[3]

Since becoming Prime Minister in December 1916 after five months as Secretary of State for War, Lloyd George had had difficulty in finding a general he could trust. He had little time for Haig whose leadership he held in disdain and by the end of 1917, he viewed the CIGS, General Sir 'Wully' Robertson, as equally incapable of 'stopping the butchering on the West front'. When criticism of the military management of the war was voiced at the first meeting of the Imperial War Cabinet in March 1917, Lloyd George quickly formed a committee of the Dominion Prime Ministers which also included General Sir Henry Wilson, the British Military Representative on the Supreme War Council, and Lord Alfred Milner, Minister Without Portfolio and a member of the Prime Minister's five-person War Cabinet.[4] His agenda was simple: to replace the civilian and military heads of the navy and army. First out was Sir Edward Carson, First Lord of the Admiralty, in July 1917; Admiral John Jellicoe followed in December. The Army proved a tougher political nut to crack as Milner was 'not yet clearly convinced that a better substitute for Haig could be found'. Robertson, who viewed Lloyd George as a 'real bad 'un' and an 'under-bred swine',[5] and Wilson were also Haig supporters as was Lord Derby, Secretary of State for War.

Kaiserschlacht finally provided Lloyd George the opportunity to act but there was a caveat for there was no way he could remove Haig at this moment of extreme peril. In looking to make 'scapegoats of the generals', Lloyd George swooped on General Sir Hubert Gough, the commander of the Fifth Army which had fallen back in the face of the hurricane of steel unleashed by the Germans. Already his reputation had been tarnished in London by his Fifth Army's performance at the Third Battle of Ypres in late July and early August 1917, when it had come

---

3   TNA WO 256/28
4   Lord Milner assumed the post of Secretary of State for War in April 1918.
5   Woodward, David. *Lloyd George and the Generals* (Newark, Delaware: University of Delaware Press, 1983), p.197

unstuck on the Gheluvelt Plateau and failed to maintain the critical momentum. Given that the unseasonable inclement weather vastly added to his problems, Gough had repeatedly asked Haig to discontinue the offensive. Despite the fact that by this point nearly 70,000 men from some of Britain's best assault divisions had been killed or wounded, Haig refused and the offensive ground on through near impossible conditions of flooding and mud. Any hopes of an early significant breakthrough had been firmly dashed by mid-August 1917. At the time and in hindsight, little of this perceived campaign debacle could be attributed to Gough.

Like a Greek tragedy, the removal of Gough played out in two Acts. Alerted by Milner and Wilson at Beaurepaire on 24 March who both expressed their misgivings about Gough,[6] despite the fact that he had told them that Gough 'had dealt with a most difficult situation very well … and never lost his head', two days later Haig was buttonholed again this time by Lloyd George and Milner at Doullens. After conferring with Wilson, Haig decided to replace him with Rawlinson who at the time was British Permanent Military Representative to the Inter-Allied Supreme War Council at Versailles (previously he had commanded both the Fourth Army and the Second Army in France). Given that the German offensive was far from over, Gough spent much of 27 March with Bertie Watts, his XIX Corps commander, and then with Ivor Maxse whose XVIII Corps was being relieved by the French. It was typical of Gough's style of leadership to go forward to his formations' headquarters and when he returned to his own Headquarters around 5 p.m., he found Harold, whom he had known from Boer War days, waiting for him. 'Not having an idea of what he had come to see me about, I sat him down to some tea. He then asked to see me alone and told me as nicely as he could that the 'Chief' thought that I and my staff must be very tired, so he had decided to put Rawlinson and the staff of the Fourth Army to take command. I was very surprised and I suppose I was very hurt, but beyond saying 'All right', I only asked when Rawlinson would be coming to take over'.[7]

The next 24 hours were frenetic as Gough and Byng's Fifth and Third Armies juggled their resources to halt the German advance; fortuitously XIX Corps and 1st Cavalry Division managed to hold the Stop Line. Gough handed over to Rawlinson at 4.30 p.m. on 28 March. Over dinner the next day, Haig told him that he wanted him out of the line, along with an Army-strength staff, to prepare an East-West line of defence from Amiens to the sea in case the Germans broke through and the BEF had to defend the Channel ports whilst evacuating

6   TNA WO 256/28: Haig Diaries, 24 March 1918.
7   Farrar-Hockley, Anthony, Goughie: The life of General Sir Hubert Gough (London: Hart-Davis, MacGibbon, 1975), pp.308-9

its men to England.[8] Gough duly set up Reserve Army headquarters at Crécy-en-Ponthieu on 2 April. However, with few friends at court, he was politically even more vulnerable for he had clumsily made an enemy of Wilson who was privy to a letter he had written to Sir Clive Wigram, the King's private secretary, in which he called him 'a thorough intriguer' and 'a danger' to the British Army should he be given any power.[9]

Act Two opened on the afternoon of 3 April. It was at the Beauvais conference to discuss French unification of command on the Western Front that Milner informed Wilson that he 'was in favour of removing Gough'.[10] That afternoon, Haig shared a car with 'a thoroughly frightened Lloyd George'[11] who, in expectation of being attacked in the House of Commons for ignoring Robertson's advice not to send troops to the East[12], was looking 'for a scapegoat for the retreat of the Fifth Army' and wanted Gough's head on a charger as an offering to public opinion. Deaf to Haig's analysis that 'fewer men, extended front and increased hostile forces'[13] were the main causes of the retreat of the Fifth Army and that 'with few reserves (on) a very big front entirely without defensible works recently taken over from the French (where) the weight of the enemy's attack fell'[14], Lloyd George informed him that 'Gough must not be employed'.[15] Sensing Lloyd George was a 'cur' and that he could not resist 'a feeling of distrust of him and of his intentions', Haig refused to condemn a general officer unheard and asked for a Cabinet order to that effect; Lord Derby duly issued one the next day, instructing Gough to vacate his command and return home because his troops had 'lost confidence in him'.[16] Haig personally broke the news to Gough and assured him that he would have every chance of defending himself for there would be an enquiry. It was never convened.

8   TNA WO 256/28: Haig Diaries, Friday 29 March 1918.
9   Jeffery, Keith, *Field Marshal Sir Henry Wilson: A Political Soldier* (Oxford, OUP, 2006), pp.188-89
10   Callwell, C.E., *Field-Marshal Sir Henry Wilson: His Life and Diaries*, Vol. 2 (London: Cassell and Company, 1927),p.78.
11   TNA WO 256/29: Haig Diaries, 3 April 1918.
12   By early 1918 there were some 120,000 British troops in the Middle East and Lieutenant General George Milne's British Salonika Force (BSF) eventually numbered over 200,000 soldiers.
13   In a briefing to HM The King at Beaurepaire on 29 March, Haig made it clear that British infantry at the start of the German offensive were 100,000 less than the previous year; that three times as many Germans were on his front than the same time the previous year and that he had extended his line by order of the British government fully one-fifth more than it had been the last autumn thus rendering it dangerously thin.
14   TNA WO 256/29: Haig Diaries, 3 April 1918,
15   Ibid.
16   Ibid.

Ironically, faced by overwhelming odds, Gough had conducted a skilful fighting retreat in extremely difficult circumstances over the last seven days. Whilst suffering terrible losses of men and material and giving up much ground, Fifth Army did not break. Furthermore, Gough's Fifth Army had, after all, taken over a line to which Lloyd George had committed it against his wishes, and he had had no time to build suitable defences. Duff Cooper, who as a young lieutenant had won a DSO with the Grenadier Guards in 1918, concluded that 'in the conduct of this great battle from 21 March to 28 March, it is impossible to prove that Gough, fighting against tremendous odds made a single mistake'.[17] In 1919, Haig informed Edward Beddington, a friend and former staff officer of Gough, that '…after considerable thought I decided that the public at home…demanded a scapegoat, and that the only possible ones were Hubert or me'. He added candidly, 'I was conceited enough to think the Army could not spare me'.[18]

Judging by his letter to Dertha, Harold may well have felt that any reference to what was really happening would be indiscreet.

29 March 1918
GHQ

My own dear one,

I am now firmly installed in the seat of M.S. At one time I was a little doubtful whether I should not go elsewhere. But now Peyton (1) has been promoted and I am here.

I have a very comfortable billet with a good bed and we have a mess about six min away, good food with plenty of bread and butter. I am very strict about my two (small) glasses of port after dinner.

I take a walk every afternoon and hope I shall not get too fat. My leg is quite better and I have given up using the bandages. I dined with the C in C the other night, he was in very good spirits and very nice.

H

PS After the pressure is over I am going to take to learning French. Have you got a good book of French / English conversation you could send me and which I could learn by myself?

Note

1. Later General Sir William Peyton, KCB, KCVO, DSO (1866-1931). He returned to England to command the Reserve Army. He ended the war commanding Harold's old division in the Hundred Days advance through Flanders.

---

17   Cooper, Duff:, *Haig* (London: Faber and Faber, 1936), pp.266-67.
18   LHCMA/KCL: Beddington, Edward: 'My Life', Beddington Papers, pp.173-4.

Judging from Haig's diary, life at GHQ soon returned to normal for on 4 April he 'spent a good part of the morning with the Military Secretary (Ruggles-Brise) over a list of rewards to be published in the King's Birthday Gazette'.

Harold wrote home on 1 June endeavouring to reassure Dertha about the on-going German offensive.

GHQ (France)

My own dear wee one,
You must not be disturbed about the German attack. The Boche with their enormous concentrations are bound to make good at first and we must expect it. The French are in good spirits and quite happy about it. The Boche aeroplanes are rather annoying us at present, they come over every night and all the lights have to be put out and we cannot do any work. They try to drop their bombs on the railway but generally miss it.

There is another Boche aeroplane coming over us again no doubt to see what damage he has done last night.
H

By 1 August, the death knell was sounding on the Kaiser's ambitions. American troops were now on the ground and fighting well under AEF commander General John Pershing. The Australians continued to prove their extraordinary fighting ability and the Australian General, John Monash, was one of the very best (some say the best) Allied commanders. The period from 8 August to the Armistice is referred to as 'The Hundred Days' which included a series of major Allied offensives starting with the Battle of Amiens on 8 August. The Allies had longed for a war of movement and this was the moment as the Germans were pushed back, reversing their earlier gains. The Allies broke through the Hindenburg Line and clocked up victory upon victory. Along the Western Front between 18 July and the Armistice the German military losses were enormous. Over 100,000 dead, nearly 686,000 wounded, almost 386,000 taken prisoner and some 6,700 artillery pieces captured.

Harold's letters to Dertha reflected the progress.

1 Aug 1918
GHQ (France)

My own dear one,
The Boche have had a nasty setback (1) but are not quite finished. At the same time it is quite satisfactory. They have moved up a large part of their reserves and done nothing but take a knock. What is pleasing is that the

Americans have fought so well and found themselves the equal of the Boche troops.

Note

1. On 1 August, French and British divisions under ruthless French General Charles Mangin advanced to a depth of nearly five miles. This ended the Second Battle of the Marne, leaving the front had been shortened by 28 miles. This strategic gain marked the end of a string of German victories and the beginning of the Allied military momentum that would in three months end the war.

2 Sept 1918

I hope that you are satisfied with the British Army again. It has done a very big thing after being badly knocked about in the spring. I think we have taken nearly 50,000 prisoners in the last month and got the Boche on the move in the right direction and I suspect we shall go on pushing him along until we are exhausted. There are two great things which show the actual beginning of the downfall. He is getting quite short of men; he cannot keep his divisions up to strength and his morale is deteriorating. His infantry are rotten, though his machine gunners are first rate.

In September, Haig asked Harold to start planning a fund for disabled officers. The King's Fund for Disabled Officers and Men had been launched in August and, following the King's own donation of £78,000, a widespread appeal to the public for £3,000,000 was underway. This was one of several initiatives, one of which was the Kitchener House for Wounded Officers at 34 Grosvenor Place where Lady Haig was a trustee. As far back as January 1917, lobby groups had been formed to hold the government to account, such as The National Association of Disabled Sailors and Soldiers, The National Federation of Discharged and Demobilized Sailors and Soldiers and the Comrades of the Great War. Organized along trade union lines, they were not fund-raising institutions themselves. It was not until 1921, after Haig had championed the idea of a single large organization to support all the Armed Forces, including officers, that the British Legion came into being.

By mid-October there was a sense of optimism that war might really be about to end.

11 Oct 1918

Everybody is in very good spirits and thinks that, if the Boche is wise, he will make peace.

I hope you approved of Wilson's reply (1). No-one quite knows whether the Germans will accept the fourteen points and evacuate all the occupied territory. If he does, there might be peace in a fortnight. On the other hand he may act like a wild man and make up his mind to do all the damage he can before he surrenders. On the other hand, there is not much about war that he does not know and he must realise the game is up. I met a fellow last night who knows Prince Max of Baden well. Apparently he is one of the best kind of Germans and admires English methods. But it is doubtful if he is a strong enough man to carry the job through.

Note

1. The German message asking for an armistice went out on 4 October. Wilson took his time to agree to the request, sending three diplomatic notes between 8 October and 23 October 1918. On 24 October, Ludendorff issued an army order that called Wilson's third note 'unacceptable' and called on his troops to fight on. On 25 October, Hindenburg and Ludendorff then ignored explicit instructions by the Chancellor Prince Maximilian of Baden and travelled to Berlin to see the Kaiser. Max asked for Ludendorff to be dismissed; Wilhelm II agreed and on 26 October told Ludendorff that he had lost his trust. Ludendorff offered his resignation and Wilhelm II accepted.

Dertha wondered what the Armistice would mean for Harold.

> 2 Nov 1918,
> Bourtree

My Dearest,
Is the Kaiser going to abdicate? What an extraordinary month. You never answered my question as to what would happen to you if peace were declared. Would you have to stop in France while they were demobilising?

I thought my 'pension' business would land me in trouble with the police before long and sure enough here it is – Mr Down sent me to visit the family of a Mrs Fry who had just died. Her husband had lately been killed. The door was opened by a young woman, a lodger (a laundry girl). An aunt had arrived but was out. I asked whether there was any money coming.

Harold was cautious in his reply for rumours abounded.

> 10 Nov 1918

Things have been moving so fast that the whole thing is a sort of rush. We do not yet know what will happen, but the general impression is that the Boche will have to accept our terms. Whether we man our Headquarters or not depends on what Foch says. The latest report is that the Kaiser has really abdicated (1). The armies have made wonderful progress and I hope that by the hour of the armistice we shall be where we started – in Mons. We shall know at 11a.m. tomorrow, and meantime everyone is brim full of hope for the best, especially as Germany seems going the same way as Russia and Austria.

Note

1. On 9 November 1918, having lost the support of the military, and with a revolution underway at home, Kaiser Wilhelm II was forced to abdicate his throne and flee Germany for Holland. Power was handed to a government led by the leader of the left-wing Social Democratic Party, Friedrich Ebert.

11th Nov 1918

We heard last night that the Boche is going to accept our terms. I think and hope that it is alright – so the war is over. Of course, I do not know in the least what is going to happen, but it is an enormous relief to think that there will be no more fighting and we must be more than thankful that everything has come out alright in the end. At times it has been a narrow shave, but we have luckily pulled through. All I look forward to now is living in a little housey with my precious mum.

Harold found an opportunity to visit the battlefields after the Armistice including the town of Metz which the Germans had held until 11 November and Woerth, north of Strasbourg and not far from the German border.

1918 (date unintelligible)
Niederbronn (1)

My darling little woman,

I could not write to you yesterday as we had a long and very cold day. We started at 8am, drove to Weissemburg (2) 18 miles and only got back at 8pm. It is very interesting indeed looking at the battlefields after one has read so much about them. I saw a few German soldiers at Metz, but did not think much of them, they were untidy. Today we have been over the battlefields of Woerth (3). I have seen so many pictures of it that I knew what it looked like before; but all the same I brought a large photograph. There is a large party of German dragoon officers dining here. I never saw such pigs at eating, and every other minute they clink their glasses and drink to one another. I never saw such idiots. We have had a scorching hot day today and I am most thirsty. The cultivated country is very undulating but not so petty as the hills and forests, and driving entails a good deal of

getting out of the carriage and walking – so one comes back pretty tired. We go on Saturday to the Grand Hotel, Metz and I am looking forward to a letter from you and hearing all about your dear little self,
Ever your most loving Harry

Notes
1. Niederbronn Les Bains is situated in the Vosges, ten kilometres from the German border.
2. The two battles of Wissembourg occurred in October and November 1793 respectively. In the first battle, the First Coalition defeated the French Republican Army; the result was reversed in the second battle..
3. Harold is referring to the Franco-Prussian War Battle of Woerth (August 1870) during which the Prussians defeated the French Imperial Army and opened the way through the Vosges to Paris.

It is sobering to reflect that 514 Old Wykehamists were lost in the Great War. Approximately five times this number served in uniform and many others served in scientific, medical and diplomatic roles .

Amongst Bramston's boys who fell were:

- Lieutenant Gilbert Hammond, Kings Own Scottish Borderers
- Captain John Cunliffe, Manchester Regiment
- Lieutenant Herbert May, Kings Royal Rifle Corps
- Corporal Peter Smith, Royal Flying Corps
- Lieutenant Campbell Crabbe, Grenadier Guards
- 2nd Lieutenant Guy Morgan, Royal Welsh Fusiliers
- Pte Henry Ruddock, Canadian Infantry
- Lieutenant Wilfred Niel, 11th Bn. Royal Fusiliers
- Lieutenant Philip Wilson, Cameron Highlanders
- Captain Colin Gordon, Royal Fusiliers
- Brigadier Richard Greenfield, Royal Inniskilling Fusiliers and General Staff
- Lieutenant Gilbert Talbot, Rifle Brigade
- Captain John Hardcastle, Oxfordshire and Buckinghamshire Regiment
- Lieutenant George FitzGeorge–Hamilton, 1st Bn Grenadier Guards
- 2nd Lieutenant Alastair Murray, Cameron Highlanders
- Captain George Gilroy, Royal Highlanders
- Major Henry Howard, 19th Earl of Suffolk, Royal Field Artillery
- Captain Matthew Buckle, Royal West Kent Regiment

All the above were younger than Harold save Matthew Buckle who was born in 1869. Two (Crabbe and FitzGeorge-Hamilton) were Grenadiers and may have been known to Harold. FitzGeorge-Hamilton served with the 1st Battalion and was killed in action on 18 May 1918. Crabbe was killed on 27th September 1915 whilst serving with the 3rd Battalion.

Harold returned to London in time for Haig's 'London Home Coming' on 19 December. Haig and his party arrived at Dover on a Belgian hospital ship, the *Jan Breydel*, escorted by two destroyers. Following a civic welcome, they travelled to the metropolis by train to be received at Charing Cross by a Grenadier Guard guard of honour, after which Field Marshal The Duke of Connaught, the King's representative, and Lloyd George welcomed them. From there, in five open Royal carriages, their procession, cheered by crowds along the route, passed by Trafalgar Square, proceeded down Pall Mall before turning up St James's Street and then along Piccadilly to Hyde Park Corner and on to Buckingham Palace via Constitution Hill. Sitting in the fourth carriage with General Horne,[19] Lieutenant General Fowler[20] and Major General Davidson, what a glorious day it must have been for Harold. The King gave a lunch party for his generals at the Palace; to the relief of all present, there were no speeches for it was a family occasion for the father of the nation to thank his senior soldiers[21].

Early January 1919 brought the good news of Hamish's return.

Hessle Mount, Hessle, E Yorks (1)

My Dearest,

Hamish has arrived. I nearly missed him as the boat was earlier than they said. He has gone to Ripon for the night then London for a few days where I shall stay with him. He looks very thin and very tired but the latter may be accounted for by their spending two nights on board. They were so uncomfortable that they hardly slept. I think you had better still write to Hythe as I shall probably be back there at the beginning of the week. Got rather a heavy cold – your nasty one I think.

Dee

Note
1.   Hessle Mount was the home of Oswald Sanderson's family.

Harold's duties still necessitated him being in France and he took the opportunity to visit Kruisek, the scene of such bitter fighting at the start of the war.

---

19   General Henry Horne, 1st Baron Horne, GCB, KCMG (1861 – 1929).
20   Lieutenant General Sir John Fowler, KCB, KCMG, DSO (1864 – 1939)
21   *The Times*, 20 December 1918.

14 Jan 1919

I am still horribly busy. The worst part is that everyone including all our clerks are beginning to worry to get away and one must keep them quiet. I had to go to a dinner on Saturday at Lille. On the way back I visited Kruisek where we fought in October 1914. I could not recognise the place. There was not a single vestige of the big farm that I slept in or of the other houses or woods. The bricks seem all to have disappeared. I think they must all have been used for roads. The country looks awful. The fields are nothing but shell holes full of water. The whole country, including Ypres, is a desert.

The Armistice brought with it a strange sense of uncertainty for Harold as he approached his 55th year.

19 March 1919
General Headquarters, British Army in France

My dearest Flory,
Thank you so much for your nice letter and wishes.
    We are very busy here and I expect to get away during the middle of April. Our show will take a lot of winding up.
    I expect we shall be very comfortable in our little flat, but I do not know in the least what I am going to do in the future. I am afraid that at the moment it looks like unemployment.
Best wishes to all,
Your very affectionate Harold

To that uncertainty was added some disappointing news from the War Office.

4 September 1919
War Office, Cornwall House, Stanford Street

Sir,
With reference to War Office Medical Board. In reply to your letter I am directed to acquaint you that your claim to a wound pension has been carefully considered, but as the effects of your wounds are not now regarded as very severe you are not entitled under Section X of the Pay warrant to a wound pension.
I am, Sir
Your obedient servant
J.G. Ashleg
For the assistant financial secretary

On 30 January 1920, Harold received a letter from the War Office informing him that the Army Council had almost completed selection of Major-Generals and that they had reluctantly come to the decision that there was no possibility of offering him any further employment before the date on which his retirement became compulsory. Early retirement on full pension with effect from 9th March 1920 must have left Harold with mixed emotions.

12

Final Years

It is unsurprising that a man of Harold's background, compassion and ability was to make one more major and lasting contribution to the lives and well-being of serving soldiers and veterans. On his return to England, Earl Haig had dedicated his time to the plight of former soldiers of all ranks. Lady Haig had been active throughout the war in devising various initiatives such as the Kitchener House at 34 Grosvenor Place which offered social and educational services for wounded officers and St. Mark's Court in St John's Wood which provided twelve flats for officers' widows and dependants. She also headed a fund for temporary aid to officers whose claims to pensions were still under review or whose gratuities had not come through. However, as the National Relief Fund committee put it in July 1919, they had not yet been able to take action in regard to ex-officers 'owing to the difficulty of finding a suitable organization competent and willing to undertake the work'. This was the problem Haig now applied himself to.

Although two of the three societies for ex-serviceman admitted officers to their membership, their work was dominated by the multiplicity of problems facing the enormous numbers of other ranks. Earl Haig and General Sir William Mackinnon set about persuading the various officers' societies which numbered nearly fifty to come together under one umbrella, the Officers' Association. In a visit to Manchester in January 1920 when he received the Freedom of the City, Haig stressed that none of them could afford to forget the obligations that the Great War had left them with. It would be many years before those obligations were discharged. 'So long as there remained in our midst a single man blinded, crippled, or disabled in that great struggle for our national freedom, our obligation to help and care for him would remain'. He singled out the case of ex-officers and pointed out that although 'the great mass of pre-war officers had some private resources, small, perhaps, in addition to their Army pay and pension, the vast majority of the men who had officered our National Armies during the war had no private resources at all. Their case was all the harder...and the most difficult part of the general ex-Service question and required the attention of generous and patriotic men and women'.

On 30 January 1920, under the chairmanship of the Lord Mayor of London, Haig, together with Earl Beatty and Sir Hugh Trenchard, launched the Officers Association at the Mansion House. Its aims were twofold - first, the protection of the interests and the promotion of the welfare of all who had at any time held a commission in His Majesty's Forces, and secondly, the relief of distress among them. Haig did not mince his words, highlighting the fact that 20,000 ex-officers were unemployed and 33,000 were maimed or otherwise incapacitated and trying to eke out an existence, in many cases with wife and children, on an average pension of £50 a year. He then took the government to task for its want of generosity as evidenced by the second Report of the Parliamentary Committee on Pensions. Why out of the 15,000 children of disabled officers, did only 2,000 receive the maintenance grant of £24 a year? And in the case of the £50 a year allowance to wives of disabled officers, did those gathered know that this only applied to an ex-officer with 100% disability and if his disability was 30%, the allowance was reduced to £15 a year?[1]

In front of a financially astute audience, he then outlined the forecast of expenditure for the next year. £70,000 was earmarked for disabled officers and a further £100,000 to continue the payments of the King's Fund to disabled officers which had been discontinued as part of the restructuring of officer charities. Another £150,000 was needed for the officers' family fund and £50,000 for the employment and resettlement branch. Whilst not a King's ransom, it was still a very significant amount of money. Soon after the launch, he launched an appeal for funds, phrased as 'an obligation from the country for between two and three million pounds to make provision for the employment of ex-officers and for the sustenance and education of wives and children of those who had been killed and disabled, and who did not have the financial means to do it themselves'. The government contributed £100,000 from the National Relief Fund ('The Prince of Wales's Fund') which had been set up in August 1914[2] to help support the wives and dependants of soldiers and sailors and those made unemployed due to the war. The War Office's United Services Fund, chaired by General Lord Byng, also made a contribution.

The Association started work in February 1920 with Harold as the General Secretary and some 26,000 ex-officers eventually joined with over 100 provincial branches being established. In November 1920, the Association reached an agreement with the Appointments Department of the Ministry of Labour that

1   *The Times*, 31 January 1920.
2   By September 1914, it had raised £2.3 million.

the work of finding appointments for ex-officers would be done solely by the Appointments Department so that the Officers' Association could concentrate on its other activities of relief work. It would however remain involved with a representative on each District Headquarters Office to interview hardship cases, disburse small sums of money in cases of immediate necessity, and receive complaints on all matters. Furthermore, a military member would be appointed by the Officers' Association to each panel of business men who interviewed applicants regarding appointments[3].

Haig favoured yet greater unity and the British Legion was founded in 1921. Six Officers Association representatives sat on its National Executive committee with the Association handing over its Appeals Department and its Great War Remembrance League subscription list (established by Earl Haig). The Association also made a cash donation to support the administrative costs of set-up. In return, it received a share of funds raised by the Legion which contributed to its operating costs. As a result, the Officers' Association was granted its own Royal Charter and renamed 'The Officers' Benevolent Department of the British Legion'. This was not universally popular but was necessary given the different regulations applying to ex-officers and the disbursement of that funds had been donated specifically for ex-officers. Harold remained General Secretary of the department until his death. In 'Keeping Faith, The History of the Royal British Legion', Brian Harding writes that 'he (Harold) was a man of great personal charm as well as genuinely sympathetic towards the problems of ex-officers'.

In *The Grenadier Guards in the Great War of 1914-1918*, author Lieutenant Colonel the Rt. Hon. Sir Frederick Ponsonby refers to the 'generosity of an officer and his wife' who in 1918 started sending wives and children on annual seaside holidays. Although not named, the officer and his wife were Harold and Dertha. Following his death in 1927, the officers of the Regiment subscribed to the Ruggles-Brise Holiday Homes Fund to perpetuate Harold's memory. His old friend and fellow Grenadier officer, Brigadier General Frankie Lloyd, who had now reverted to his substantive rank, acted as treasurer of the fund. An impressive sum was raised, equivalent to nearly £70,000 today. A large number of letters from subscribers showing their esteem for Harold were bound in a leather folder, inscribed with the Regimental Cypher, and handed to Dertha. With the approval of the Regimental Trustees the sum was invested and the Ruggles-Brise Holiday Home Fund was established, the income being used for the maintenance of the married families at the holiday home. The home selected was that of Mrs M. Hopkins of 15, Stanpit, Christchurch, Hampshire.

---

3   *Hansard* <https://hansard.parliament.uk/Commons/1920-11-10/debates>

Harold was the epitome of a soldier, officer and gentleman. He was courageous, successful, loving, caring and respected greatly by those of all ranks who knew him and served with him. Today Harold would be described as having a 'glittering career' but whereas such success can give rise to arrogance, aloofness and pomposity, in Harold we find warmth, humility, generosity and selflessness. This was a man who served his country and his fellow soldiers in two wars, nearly died in doing so and continued to serve veterans and their families until his untimely death.

Only three potential criticisms of Harold have been identified during the research for this book. The first is that in the fighting near Kruisek. Trenches had been dug on forward slopes, a criticism that can be applied more widely to 7th Division. In the face of a rapidly advancing enemy, Harold's men had been thrown into the first line of defence and were severely limited in their opportunity to pick text book ground in which to dig shallow trenches. As it was, they spent the whole of the 20 October improving the line. Any observation about the location of trenches has to be put in that context.

The second criticism relates to Harold's time as Commandant at Hythe. Tim Travers in his book *The Killing Ground* suggests that Harold 'dragged his feet in suggesting reasons why the anti-aircraft machine-gun should not be developed'. He never objected to this role for the Vickers MK I; what he pointed out was that the tripod, which weighed in at fifty pounds, needed to be lighter in order for the infantry to make the role feasible.

The third relates to Harold's role in the court martial of Private Francis Murray, a Gordon Highlander, in September 1916. Murray, in a drunken state, fired at some unarmed soldiers causing wounds from which one died. Harold convened the court martial and Murray was charged with murder and an alternative of manslaughter. Further charges included shooting with murderous intent and wounding. The proceedings are covered in detail by Julian Putkowski and Mark Dunning in *Murderous Tommies*. Murray was sentenced to death but with a strong recommendation for mercy based on the influence of drink and previous good conduct. Harold took a different view and recommended the sentence of death be carried out. Major General Henry Hudson endorsed that recommendation, General Sir Richard Haking recommended execution and Haig concurred. Murray was shot on 1 October. The authors criticise how the proceedings were managed, pointing to the failure to correctly apply the Manual of Military Law in respect of drunkenness and an erroneous statement by Harold that that Murray intended to murder an officer. Ninety years after their deaths, 306 of the 346 soldiers who were executed for military offences during World War I were granted posthumous pardons from the Ministry of Defence. These soldiers were executed during hostilities for breaches of military discipline that included desertion, cowardice, quitting their posts, striking a Superior Officer, sleeping at their post, and casting away their arms. The remaining group of 40 soldiers including Murray were not granted a pardon because the nature of their crimes included murder and mutiny.

On the afternoon of Sunday 27 June 1920, Harold was invited to the dedication service of the Finchingfield War Memorial[4]. Designed by the popular watercolourist 61-year-old Arthur Legge RBA[5] who had retired in 1918 to Cabbaches, a medieval village house, the memorial stone, surmounted by a cross, contained a bronze plate on which the names of 27 village men were displayed. With an average age of 27, the youngest being 19 and the eldest 38, they represented a broad spectrum of rural life from farm workers, grooms, thatchers, stockmen, and silk dyers to the gardener of Spains Hall. Nine left wives and children bereft of their breadwinner; three families each mourned the loss of two sons. The tragic loss of such stalwarts in remote village communities was replicated all over the country and to this day the deep scar of worthy lives so abruptly ended can been seen on similar memorials.

By the time Harold arrived, a large crowd had gathered on the village green with many families having walked or cycled from outlying hamlets and farms. After he had inspected some 80 demobilized soldiers lined up on the green, the dedication service began with the hymn *For All The Saints*. The Reverend Chester, a Congregational pastor, then offered prayers before Harold unveiled the memorial. In his address, he spoke of the valour of the fallen men of Finchingfield and the undying memories they had left behind; it was fitting that they would be forever remembered by the memorial erected by the village. The hymn *Peace, Perfect Peace* was followed by dedicatory prayers read by the vicar, the Reverend Jordan, and then buglers from the Boy Scouts sounded *The Last Post* echoing Wilfred Owen's immortal line 'bugles calling for them from sad shires'.[6] The ceremony ended with the placing of flowers by the mourning relatives. It was a far cry from the celebrations staged by the village on Harold's return from the Boer War some twenty years previously.

Harold remained a keen sportsman in retirement and it was after a game of real tennis that he fell ill.

June 1927

On Saturday 18 June, he played a very hard game of real tennis at Lords and then went to look on at the cricket in the cold. I was away for the weekend. I came back on Tuesday, it was luncheon time, and found him

4   *Chelmsford Chronicle,* 2 July 1920; and *Haverhill Echo* 3 July 1920.
5   Legge was also the art instructor at West Ham Municipal College where one of his students was Essex-born Helen Jacobs, the well-known children's book illustrator.
6   Owen, Wilfred, 'Anthem for Doomed Youth' (1917).

very unwell. I tried to get him to stay in and see a doctor but it was no use. He said he must go to a meeting. He dozed a good deal that evening but his temperature was not much raised and he did not have a really bad night. On Wednesday morning he said he felt a little better. His temperature was 99 degrees. He said it was absolutely necessary for him to go to a British Legion meeting at 12 a.m. but he would be back at 1p.m. and sit by the fire for the rest of the day. I had arranged to go to Wimbledon with some friends and he made me go, but I secretly made up my mind to come back at 2 p.m. I was having luncheon not far away at 1 o'clock when I was rung up to say that he had been brought home in a state of collapse. I was back in a very short time and found him lying in his chair complaining about his leg and knee and evidently dreadfully ill. His temperature was 104. I got him to bed and after a little difficulty I got hold of a first rate doctor. He took a grave view at once. In half an hour we had two excellent nurses, a consultant sent for and everything possible being done. A clot in the lung complicated by an acute attack of pneumonia.

All Thursday he held his own but fighting for breath. On Friday his temperature came down. He insisted on my bringing the wireless and make it play because he thought the nurses would like it. 'It was so dull for them.' When he was a little wandering and was given champagne he thought he was at dinner and said the doctor must be helped first so the latter had to pretend to drink it. In the afternoon he had an attack of heart failure. He rallied – then had another in the evening and did not get through.

He told me only the other day that he did not fear death but his only fear was at losing his great bodily and mental vigour and _that_ he never did. He wanted to go first and said something told him it would not be long. I answered I was sure he would live to be very old. He said _no_ and that he had been so happy it almost frightened him to think there could ever be any unhappiness for either of us.

His Majesty dispatched a telegram to Dertha.

I am shocked to hear of the death of General Ruggles-Brise whose friendship I have valued for forty years since the days we were at Bermuda together. I offer you my heartfelt sympathy in your great sorrow. George R.I.

A service for Harold was held in the Guards' Chapel, Wellington Barracks on Tuesday 28th June. The service included the hymns *Onward Christian Soldiers, Souls Of Men Why Will Ye Scatter* and *Abide With Me.* There were two readings – Psalm

121 and the Wisdom of Solomon, Chapter III Verses 1 to 9. Later that day Harold was buried in the family plot in the graveyard of the Fourteenth Century Church of St. John the Baptist at Finchingfield. With views of an ancient patchwork of arable farmland in every direction, how appropriate that Verse 6 reads 'and in the time of their visitation they shall shine and run to and fro like sparks among the stubble'. Amongst the floral tributes were two wreaths of Flanders poppies, one from the British Legion and the other from Field Marshall Earl Haig. The first was inscribed 'In memory of a true-hearted friend of the ex-serviceman' and the latter carried the words 'In loving memory of my old friend at Oxford and comrade in war'. The hillmen and gillies of the Forest of Blair Atholl sent a wreath of Scottish heather that was tied with tartan and bore the words 'With respectful sympathy and warm remembrance of a true sportsman'.

The Times of 27 June published a correspondence concerning Harold's work for ex-servicemen:

His colleagues in that work feel that by his untimely death they have lost a true friend whose devotion to duty, sound judgement and warm heart were ever at their service.......and many an ex-Serviceman sorrows for the death of one who gave him a helping hand when he was down.

The *Guards Magazine* of summer 1927 remembered him as 'a soldier who was as distinguished as he was modest ... Altogether admirable as he was through the long years of fighting, his post-war services were no less valuable, for with heart and brain, he devoted himself to the care of soldiers on whom the war had left its cruel marks – and his place as Secretary of the Officers' Association will, perhaps, not easily be filled.'

Harold's grave bears the well-known and lovely words from the Song of Solomon: 'Until the morning breaks and then shadows flee away'. Inside Finchingfield Church there is a memorial plaque that concludes:

BELOVED OF ALL

'I have fought a good fight – I have finished my course'

Dertha survived Harold by a decade, dying aged 71 years at Vence in Southeastern France on 28 December 1937. Her funeral took place privately at Blair Castle on 6 January 1938. Draped with a plaid of Atholl tartan, her coffin was carried to the family's burial ground in the woods by relays of estate hillmen and uniformed members of the Blair Atholl curling club. Her cortege was preceded by four pipers of the Atholl Highlanders and after the coffin had been lowered, Piper Irvine played the dirge *A Finger Lost*. Among the pall bearers were her brothers, the Duke of Atholl ('Bardie') and Lord James Stewart-Murray ('Haimish') and her nephews, John Ruggles-Brise, representing her brother-in-law Archie, and Sir

Edward Ruggles-Brise[7]. It is in some ways sad that Harold and Dertha should have been buried so far apart but they each rest in places that were very special to them and where their family roots run deep. In every other respect they were, and remain, inseparable.

Harold and Dertha did not have children and thus it is here that their story comes to an end. Harold was an outstanding soldier and attained one of the highest ranks in the British Army. He was courageous, loyal, generous and warm-hearted. A man of bearing, a man of wisdom, a man of sincerity, a man of charm and warmth and a man of kindness and gentleness who served his country and fellow men for almost his entire life. He achieved this with the profound love, support and friendship of a remarkable lady, his wife Dertha. Those who search for the epitome of a soldier and a gentleman need look no further than Major-General Sir Harold Goodeve Ruggles-Brise, Knight Commander of the Order of St Michael and St George, Companion of the Order of the Bath, Member of the Royal Victorian Order, Mentioned in Despatches (10 times), Commander of the Order of Leopold, Commander of the Legion of Honour, and Croix de Guerre of both France and Belgium.

7   *The Dundee Courier*, 7 January 1938.

Appendix I: The Ruggles-Brise Family

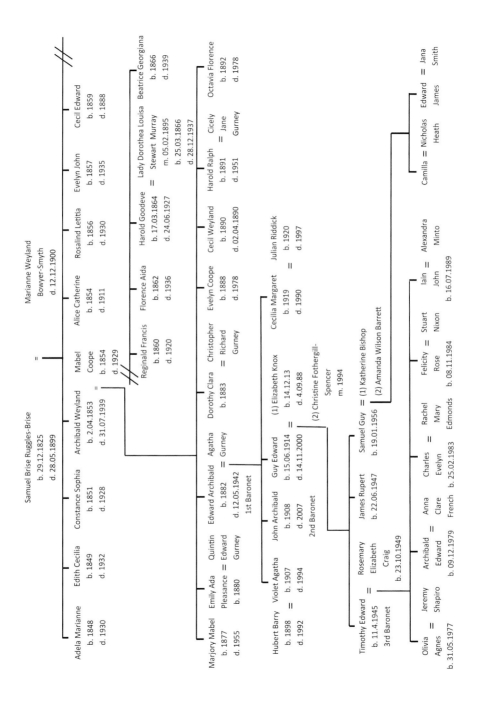

259

Appendix II: The Atholl Family

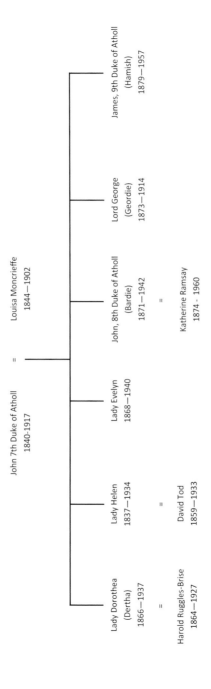

John 7th Duke of Atholl
1840-1917

=

Louisa Moncrieffe
1844—1902

Lady Dorothea
(Dertha)
1866—1937

=

Harold Ruggles-Brise
1864—1927

Lady Helen
1837—1934

=

David Tod
1859—1933

Lady Evelyn
1868—1940

John, 8th Duke of Atholl
(Bardie)
1871—1942

=

Katherine Ramsay
1874 - 1960

Lord George
(Geordie)
1873—1914

James, 9th Duke of Atholl
(Hamish)
1879—1957

Appendix III

Order of Battle 7th Division, Ypres 1914

G.O.C Major-General T. Capper

Divisional Cavalry:	Northumberland Hussars
Divisional Cyclist Company	
Royal Artillery:	Brigadier-General H.K. Jackson
	14th Brigade Royal Horse Artillery
	22nd Brigade Royal Field Artillery
	35th Brigade Royal Field Artillery
	3rd Heavy Brigade Royal Garrison Artillery
Divisional Ammunition Column	
Royal Engineers:	54th Field Company R.E.
	55th Field Company R.E.
	Divisional Signal Company
20th Infantry Brigade:	Brigadier General H. Ruggles-Brise
	1st Battalion Grenadier Guards
	2nd Battalion Scots Guards
	2nd Battalion the Border Regiment
	2nd Battalion the Gordon Highlanders
21st Infantry Brigade:	Brigadier General H.E. Watts
	2nd Battalion the Bedfordshire Regiment
	2nd Battalion the Yorkshire Regiment
	2nd Battalion the Royal Scots Fusiliers
	2nd Battalion the Wiltshire Regiment
22nd Infantry Brigade:	Brigadier General S.T.B Lawford
	2nd Battalion the Queen's
	2nd Battalion the Royal Warwickshire Regiment
	1st Battalion the Royal Welsh Fusiliers
	1st Battalion the South Staffordshire Regiment
Army Service Corps:	7th Divisional Train
Royal Army Medical Corps:	21st, 22nd and 23rd Field Ambulances

Appendix IV

Order of Battle 20th Infantry Brigade, Ypres 1914

Brigadier-General H. Ruggles-Brise
Brigade Major: Major A.B.E. Cator (Scots Guards)
Staff Captain: Captain B.N. Brooke (Grenadier Guards)
1st Battalion Grenadier Guards: Lieutenant-Colonel M. Earle
2nd Battalion Scots Guards: Lieutenant-Colonel R.G.I. Bolton
2nd Battalion Border Regiment: Lieutenant-Colonel L.I. Wood
2nd Battalion Gordon Highlanders: Lieutenant-Colonel H.P. Uniacke

Appendix V

Order of Battle 40th (Bantam) Division, 1915-1916

G.O.C. Major-General H.G. Ruggles-Brise

119th Brigade ('Welsh Bantam Brigade'):
19th Battalion the Royal Welsh Fusiliers
12th Battalion the South Wales Borderers
17th Battalion the Welsh Regiment
18th Battalion the Welsh Regiment
119th Machine Gun Company
119th Trench Mortar Company

120th Brigade:
11th Battalion the King's Own Royal Lancaster Regiment
13th Battalion the Cameronians (absorbed in 14th Highland Light Infantry in February 1916)
14th Battalion the Highland Light Infantry
13th Battalion the East Surrey Regiment
14th Battalion the Argyll and Sutherland Highlanders
12th Battalion the South Lancashire Regiment (absorbed into 11th King's Own)
120th Machine Gun Company
120th trench Mortar Battery

121st Brigade:
12th Battalion the Suffolk Regiment
13th Battalion the Yorkshire Regiment ('Green Howards')
18th Battalion the Sherwood Foresters (merged with 13th Yorkshires in April 1916)
22nd Battalion the Middlesex Regiment (disbanded April 1916)
20th Battalion the Middlesex Regiment
21st Battalion the Middlesex Regiment
121st Machine Gun Company
121st Trench Mortar Company

Divisional Troops: 12th Battalion the Yorkshire Regiment (pioneers)
Divisional Mounted troops: 'A' Squadron the Royal Wiltshire Yeomanry
Divisional Artillery: 178th (Howitzer) Brigade, RFA
      81st Brigade, RFA
      85th Brigade, RFA
      88th Brigade, RFA
      40th Divisional ammunition Column, RFA
      V.40 Heavy Trench Mortar Battery, RFA
      X.40, Y.40 and Z.40 Medium Mortar Batteries, RFA
Royal Engineers: 224th and 229th Field Companies
      231st Company
      40th Divisional Signals Company
Royal Army Medical Corps: 135th, 136th and 137th Field Ambulances
      83rd Sanitary Section
Other Divisional Troops:40th Divisional Train, Army Service Corps
      51st Mobile Veterinary Section
      40th Divisional Motor Ambulance Workshop

Appendix VI

Zandvoorde Military Cemetery Burials

The dead of 20th Brigade can be found in a number of the cemeteries within the former Ypres Salient. The greatest concentration is to be found in Zandvoorde Military Cemetery, close to the scene of the bitter and bloody fighting of late October and early November 1914. In this one cemetery are the graves of the gallant men who gave their all in halting the enemy tide. These were and remain Harold's men and a few hours in this burial ground brings home the scale of the sacrifice made by this one brigade over a few days fighting. Here you will find 21 men of 1st Grenadier Guards (listed below), 22 of 2nd Border Regiment, 10 of 2nd Scots Guards and 13 of 2nd Gordon Highlanders. All fell between 20 October and 7 November 1914. On the Menin Gate are found the names of nearly 55,000 men who have no known grave and amongst their number are the missing of 20th Brigade.

Private Arthur Bacon d. 26-10-14
Private A Bond d. 26-10-14
Private Henry Edward Thomas Bullen d. 26-10-14
Private WH Bush d. 26-10-14
Private George William Coles d. 26-10-14
Private P Dash d. 29-10-14
Private J Elson d. 29-10-14
Private Reginald Charles Hamer d. 26-10-14
Private C Halfpenny d. 26-10-14
Lance Sergeant WC Hiles d. 26-10-14
Private A. Ingram d.2 9-10-14
Drummer Harold Alfred Jowett d. 26-10-14
Private A Kearns d. 7-11-14
Private Albert King d. 26-10-14
Lance Corporal George Gordon Oliver d.29-10-14
Corporal JW Pickering d. 7-11-14
Guardsman Robert Henry Smith d. 20-10-14
Major Humphrey St. Leger Stucley d. 29-10-14
Lieutenant Philip Van Neck d. 26-10-14
Private Thomas Wainwright d. 29-10-14
Private H Williams d. 7-11-14

Appendix VII

Serving Their Country

This volume has centred on the life of a remarkable career soldier whilst making mention of his nephews **Edward Ruggles-Brise** who was created a Baronet in 1935, **Evelyn Ruggles-Brise** and **Ralph Ruggles-Brise** who also served with distinction during the Great War.

Commander **Hubert Barry** RN born in 1898 married Sir Edward's eldest daughter Violet and served as a Midshipman on HMS *Albermale*, playing deck hockey with the future George V1. He was subsequently transferred to HMS *Malaya* and had a narrow escape at the Battle of Jutland when one of the gun turrets he was sending ammunition up to took a direct hit. He lost a shipmate and escaped with only a broken nose. After Jutland he wanted to transfer to the Royal Flying Corps but was dissuaded by his family. However to their consternation he became a submariner. On one occasion whilst on patrol in the North Sea they surfaced in thick fog to recharge the ship's batteries only to find themselves amongst a fleet of German minesweepers disguised as fishing trawlers. They were spotted and dived and most fortuitously came to rest in a depression in the sea bed. For 24 hours the Germans dragged the sea with depth charges attached to nets. However, they had set the depth charges too high so no contact was made and no explosions took place. Afterwards he is reported to have said 'it was somewhat tense!' He served in the Second World War in a shore-based capacity.

More recently subsequent generations have served and continue to serve with distinction and I believe Harold would be most approving of their inclusion in his story.

Sir Timothy's father, Captain **Guy Ruggles-Brise** TD, DL was born on 15 June 1914. Guy attended Eton and later joined 104th (Essex Yeomanry) Field Brigade Royal Artillery. In 1940 he transferred to No 7 Army Commando for training in Scotland and departed for North Africa in the rank of Captain, having married only one month before. Guy was captured during a raid on Bardia in 1941 and was inspected by Rommel before being handed over to the Italians. He was held in a camp near Padula before being transferred to a camp near Bologna and then Vincigliata Castle where a number of high-ranking British prisoners were held. He, along with Lieutenant Daniel Knox 6th Earl of Ranfurly, served as ADCs to the Generals.

Guy was released along with his fellow prisoners and an American pilot following the Italian Armistice in September 1943. He spent many months 'on the run' in the Apennines and on one occasion was given shelter in the house of some partisans who hid him in their loft for two days whilst the Germans used the house as their HQ searching for escaped POWs. They probably saved his life at great risk to themselves. On one occasion he was with Major General Michael Gambier-Parry who told him that he was going his own way and that it was his Silver Wedding Anniversary. Guy produced his silver hip flask and gave it to the General with the words 'Michael, please take this as a present to you and your wife'. The General made it home via the Vatican dressed as a nun! Many years later in the mid-1970s after the General and his wife had died, their daughter found the flask, remembered the story and returned it to Guy. It is a treasured item within the family's memorabilia.

Guy eventually reached the coast, putting to sea in a badly leaking boat. He along with others were rescued by a friendly Italian vessel and landed at Ancona. Shortly afterwards he was sailing up the Clyde to be reunited with his wife in May 1944 after a separation of three and a half years. After the war Guy had a distinguished career in the City and was appointed a Deputy Lieutenant and served as High Sheriff of Essex 1967-1968. He died on 14 November 2000 aged 86 years. Two excellent books recall the epic escape story *To War with Whitaker* by The Countess of Ranfurly, a cousin of Guy and Sir John, which includes the Earl of Ranfurly's personal account of the daring escape. Guy was in the same party although they split up and re-grouped as necessary. The second is *Guerrilla in Striped Pants: A U. S. Diplomat Joins the Italian Resistance* by Walter W. Orebaugh, an American diplomat who joined the escape party in which Guy was described as being 'rather impatient!'   1

The Monte San Martino Trust was established in 1989 by Keith Killby, himself an escaped prisoner, to provide financial support to the descendants of the Italian Partisans who so bravely helped Allied POWs to escape capture. Over £3 million has been raised which enables around 40 students to come to the UK annually to learn English.

Sir Timothy's uncle, Colonel Sir **John Ruggles-Brise**, Bt, CB, OBE, TD, OStJ, was the eldest son of Sir Edward and Guy's older brother. Sir John was born on 13 June 1908, also attended Eton and before the war worked on a family farm in Canada before pursuing a successful career in the City of London. He joined the Territorial Army in 1938 and on the outbreak of war he enlisted as a gunner in the 54th Anti-Aircraft Regiment. He was subsequently commissioned and commanded an anti-aircraft battery near London during the blitz. In 1942 he took command of 180th Heavy Anti Aircraft Regiment based in Scotland before deployment with his unit to Plymouth prior to the D-Day invasion. Sir

John continued to serve with the TA after the war and was awarded the Territorial Declaration (TD) as well as receiving the Military OBE and being awarded the rank of Honorary Colonel. He served as Lord Lieutenant of Essex (1958-1978) and was honoured by becoming a Companion of the Order of the Bath in 1958. He died on 20 February 2007.

Cecilia Ruggles-Brise, youngest daughter of Sir Edward and sister of Guy and Sir John served in the Women's Auxiliary Air force 1941-44 with the rank of Section Officer. She was born 1919 and died in 1991. She married Captain **Julian Riddick** (1920-1997) who commissioned into the Royal Artillery engaged in an anti-aircraft capacity in the UK.

Their daughter **Elspeth Riddick** married Sergeant **Philip Shirtcliff** who as a National Serviceman joined the Royal Ulster Rifles in January 1953 for his initial training and was later transferred to the Royal Army Education Corps for further training until May. He was then kitted out to go to Korea but at the last moment the Government changed its mind and he was deployed to Egypt as part of the Middle East Land Forces and sent to the Suez Canal Zone where he taught soldiers to read and write with a little military and political history and desert map reading. He was mostly attached to 58 Car Company, Royal Army Service Corps, who supplied drivers and cars to officers in Fayed. He remained there until December 1954 when he was de-mobbed.

Philip and Elspeth's son Lieutenant **Justin Shirtcliff** RN attended the Britannia Royal Naval College in 2014 and commissioned as a Midshipman in July 2015. He started as Officer of the Watch on Type 23 Frigate HMS *Richmond* just prior to promotion to Sub Lieutenant. Justin subsequently conducted further navigation training before becoming the Navigating Officer of the Mine Countermeasures (MCM) Squadron 2, Crew 6 where he navigated HMS *Hurworth*, HMS *Ledbury* and HMS *Cattistock* during which time he was promoted to full Lieutenant. This role included a six month tour in the Arabian Gulf on Operation KIPION followed by a three month tour conducting historic ordnance disposal under Standing NATO MCM Group 1. Following this Justin became the Operations Officer of HMS *Tyne* where he helped in planning for the maritime security element of the 2017 G7 Summit at Carbis Bay shadowing Russian warships in the Channel, and continued operations throughout the period of the Covid period. He resigned his commission in 2022 to become Deputy Harbour Master of the Bristol Port Company.

Alethea Ruggles-Brise was the daughter of Harold Ralph and Cicely served in the East African Women's Territorial Army/ First Aid Nursing Yeomanry (FANY) in Kenya from 1943. She was married to Ernest Waller and died in 2012.

Another Uncle of Sir Timothy (brother of his mother Elizabeth) was Colonel Sir **Bryce Knox** KCVO, MC and Bar, TD, OStJ. Bryce was born on 4 April

1916 and educated at Stow. He read Geography then land management at Cambridge before joining the Ayrshire Yeomanry. With the 152nd (Ayrshire Yeomanry) Field RA he served on Orkney before his regiment became part of 6th Armoured Division and took part in the landings in North Africa. He fought in the battle of Kasserine Pass in Tunisia and took part in the final drive on Tunis. At Hammamet he led the capture and took the surrender of some elite German soldiers. He saw further action in Italy and won the Military Cross in July 1944 under heavy shelling and fire at Arezzo and a bar to his MC three months later at Monte Battaglia when on both occasions the Ayrshire Yeomanry were in support of the 3rd Battalion Grenadier Guards. During the advance into Austria, he led the liberation of British POWs imprisoned at Villach. Sir Bryce commanded the Ayrshire Yeomanry from 1953 until 1956 and was its Honorary Colonel 1967-1971. He was Lord Lieutenant for Ayrshire and Arran (1974-91) and a member of the Queen's Bodyguard for Scotland (Royal Company of Archers) .He died on 22 November 2003 aged 87.

Lieutenant Thomas **Oliver Ruggles-Brise** was born on 18 November 1922, the younger son of Captain Evelyn Ruggles-Brise and cousin of Guy and Sir John. Oliver, as he was known, was commissioned into 2nd Armoured Battalion, Grenadier Guards and was killed aged 21 in action at Cagny rear Caen on 18 July 1944 when his tank was shelled. He was last seen to get out of the tank but his body was never found in spite of extensive searches. He is commemorated on the Memorials at Bayeux in Normandy, Eton and in the church of St John the Baptist at Finchingfield, Essex.

Oliver's elder brother **Stephen Ruggles-Brise** served in the Rifle Brigade and Royal Army Ordinance Corps in the Second World War. He was deployed to Palestine and Egypt and died unmarried in 1977.

Oliver and Stephen's sister **Jane Ruggles-Brise** married **Anthony Birley**. From 1944-45, she worked as the principal secretary to Colonel Maurice Buckmaster of F Section SOE, which was responsible for running agents in Occupied France and fostering resistance against the Germans. She had a lucky escape when she was thrown off her bicycle on her way to work when passing the Guards Chapel when it was hit by a flying bomb on 18 June 1944. She died in 2010. Her husband was commissioned into the Royal Artillery in July 1941 and saw active service in North Africa and Italy being wounded in March 1944. He died in 2006.

Stephen Pym was the son of Octavia Ruggles-Brise, Sir Edward's youngest sister and Francis Guy Pym who emigrated to Canada after the First World War. He served throughout the Second World War as a pilot in the RAF as his father had done in Royal Flying Corps in the First World War. He died in 2014.

Hubert and Violet's eldest son **William Barry** served his National Service in the Kings Royal Rifle Corps, commissioning into Royal Green Jackets in 1956.

He was deployed to Libya visiting Dena (Cyrenaica) harbour, the battlefield at El Mechilli, shooting at Cyrene Pigeon Hole and the USAF base in Tripoli. His regiment were requested to provide extras for Richard Attenborough's 1958 film *Sea of Sand* in which he played a truck driver! He died in 2022.

Their eldest daughter Rosemary Barry married Captain **Alastair Leslie** TD who served his National Service in the Royal Scots Fusiliers. Commissioned in 1953, he deployed to Malaya in 1954-55. He continued to serve in the Territorial Army until 1962 .

Their son Second Lieutenant **David Leslie** commissioned into the 1st Battalion, Scots Guard in December 1987 having attended the Brigade Squad and undertaken the last six month course at Sandhurst. He completed the Platoon Commander's Battle Course and training in Canada. Following the Battalion's last two months at Elizabeth Barracks he spent the remainder of his career in BOAR and on an emergency four and a half month tour in Northern Ireland. He was given the important task of commanding the Mortar Platoon which was responsible for providing the Battalion's Quick Reaction Force. His platoon attended every major incident in the Battalion's area all of which passed very smoothly. Tragically he died in a car crash in 1989, aged 22. He is remembered as a well-liked, intelligent, mature and resourceful officer, respected for his leadership qualities both by his Guardsmen and fellow officers.

Rosemary and Alastair's grandson Lieutenant **Lochlan de Klee** commissioned into the Coldstream Guards in August 2021 and was deployed to the Falkland Islands, and to Kenya for training.   His ceremonial duties have included carrying the State Colours at the last State Opening of Parliament in the late Queen's reign, attended her Lying-in-State vigil, and carrying the King's Colour of the Coldstream Guards from Westminster Abbey to Buckingham Palace at HM King Charles III's Coronation. His ancestor John Leslie, Duke of Rothes, carried the Sword of State at Scone Palace for the coronation of Charles II in 1651.

Major **The Lord Glenarthur** DL is married to their younger daughter Susan. Simon attended Mons Officer Cadet School from February to July 1963 and was commissioned into 10th Royal Hussars (Prince of Wales's Own). He served as a Troop Leader in Germany and in UK before the Regiment was posted to Aden in September 1964. In Aden, he served as an Armoured Reconnaissance Troop Leader 'up-country' in forward bases during the infiltration of Aden by dissidents who sought the withdrawal of UK from Aden. For four months, he was seconded as one of two ADCs to the British High Commissioner. He subsequently returned to Regimental duty as a Troop Leader at Salala in Oman; and at Sharjah in the then Trucial States, before returning to the West Aden Protectorate close to the border with Yemen.

On returning to the British Army of the Rhine in late 1965, Simon continued to serve as a Troop Leader in the Armoured Reconnaissance role, and, following his Signal Officers course, was appointed Regimental Signals Officer. In 1968, he attended the School of Army Aviation and on receiving his 'wings' in May 1969 was immediately posted to Northern Ireland to join the Air Squadron of the 17th/21st Lancers as 'the troubles' began to develop. After just over two years, he was posted back to his Regiment at Tidworth, which had now amalgamated with the 11th Hussars (Prince Albert's Own) to become Adjutant of the Royal Hussars (Prince of Wales's Own). In 1973, he returned to flying in command of the Air Squadron of the 16th/ 5th Lancers, and subsequently that of 1st Royal Tank Regiment, with deployments on exercises to Kenya, Germany and Belize.

Simon retired from the Regular Army in October 1975 in the rank of Major, and subsequently spent four years as a Territorial Army Volunteer Reserve officer in the Royal Armoured Corps Reserve Pool of Officers, remaining as a Royal Hussar. He was a member of The Queen's Bodyguard for Scotland (Royal Company of Archers) from 1985-2016; Honorary Colonel of 306 Hospital Support Medical Regiment(Volunteers) from 2001 to 2011; and Honorary Air Commodore of 612 (County of Aberdeen) Squadron, Royal Auxiliary Air Force from 2004-2014.

Lady Ruggles-Brise's uncle Colonel **Thomas Craig** CBE, OBE(Mil), TD, DL OStJ. LLD was commissioned into the 6th Battalion The Cameronians (Scottish Rifles) in 1927. In 1938 he was promoted to Major OC HQ company and in 1942 attended the Senior Staff College, Camberley. He was subsequently appointed Divisional Assistant Adjutant and Quarter Master General of the 52nd Division. He was awarded the Territorial Declaration in 1943.

In November 1944, he was considered largely responsible for the swift replacement lost kit following Op MALLARD, the night crossing of the heavily mined Sloe channel and mudflats between the Dutch islands of Zuid–Beveland and Walcheren. In 1945 he was Mentioned in Despatches and awarded an OBE (Military). In 1949 The King of Norway awarded him The Liberty Cross in recognition of the 52nd Division's involvement in the planning for and liberation of Norway as part of Force 134 under Op APOSTLE. From 1947-1965 he was Honorary Colonel of the 124 Field Regiment (Engineers) and 6/7th Battalion Cameronians.

Following the War he was Chairman of the Colville Group, Motherwell; Deputy Governor of the Bank of Scotland; a director of The British Steel Corporation as well as President of the Iron and Steel Institute following in his father's (Sir John Craig) footsteps for which he was awarded a CBE. He died in 1994.

Major **Charles Ruggles-Brise**, younger son of Sir Timothy and Lady Ruggles-Brise, was born on 25 February 1983. Commissioned into 1st The Queen's Dragoon Guards in December 2007, Charlie was deployed as a Formation Reconnaissance

Troop Leader to Afghanistan in October 2008 on Op HERRICK 9, Garmsir District, Southern Helmand. He was subsequently deployed back to Helmand as Second in Command of the Brigade Reconnaissance Force on Op HERRICK 15 in October 2011. On return to the UK he was ADC to the Defence Senior Advisor to the Middle East. In April 2013 Charlie was appointed Adjutant, 1st The Queen's Dragoon Guards, and held that appointment for just over two years before being selected for promotion and attending the Intermediate Command and Staff Course (Land) at Shrivenham. In May 2016 he was appointed Military Assistant to the Army's Chief Information Officer based at Army HQ Andover and subsequently commanded A Squadron 1st The Queen's Dragoon Guards from 2018-2020. He currently holds his second staff appointment in the Ministry of Defence.

Charlie's father-in-law Flight Lieutenant **John Edmonds**, born in 1944, was commissioned into the RAF in 1968 and trained as a navigator on C-130 Hercules. Having completed advanced training, he was immediately posted to No 47 Squadron. His early career was spent circumnavigating the globe, conducting high altitude freefall parachuting and displays before being selected to work with Special Forces. In 1976 he deployed to Malta as the Maritime Briefing Officer, returning two years later to join No 24 Squadron flying Hercules once again in a variety of global operations. On April 4 1982, he was one of the first to deploy in support of British efforts to recapture the Falkland Islands, a conflict that would define much of his career as RAF transport and tanker operations continued well after victory was assured. In 1983 he moved to No 70 Squadron and was tasked with advancing low level flying techniques across the force. In 1984 he flew regular sorties on Op BUSHEL, delivering famine relief via low level drops and landings in Ethiopia. Twelve years in Germany followed including postings to RAF Laarbruch as Mission Planning Officer for Tornado Bombers, RAF Wildenwrath as Station Navigator Officer and then Squadron Leader Operations during the first Gulf War before a final appointment as Operations Officer at RAF Bruggen. He finished his 34 years career with 10 Squadron, operating VC10s in their VIP transport roles. John retired in 2002 and died in 2022.

Bibliography

I. Primary Source Documents

The National Archives of the United Kingdom (TNA)
WO 32/9089:
WO 76/2:
WO 95/1650/1:
WO 95/1657/3:
WO 105/18:
WO 105/7:
WO 140/13:
WO 163/16:
WO 163/17:
WO 163/20:
WO 180/253:
WO 256/28:
WO 256/29:

National Army Museum
No. 8002-40: Ruggles-Brise Maps and Documents

II. Published Sources

Allinson, Sidney, *The Bantams* (Barnsley: Pen & Sword, 2009).

Applin, Captain R.V.K., *Machine Guns Tactics* (London: Hugh Rees Ltd, 1910).

Atkinson, C.T., *The Seventh Division 1914-1918* (Uckfield: Naval & Military Press reprint of 1927 edition).

Barrie, Alexander, *War Underground: The Tunnellers of the Great War* (Staplehurst: Spellmount: 2000).

Becke, Major A.F., *Order of Battle Divisions, Part 3 B, New Army Divisions (30–41); & 63rd (R.N.) Division* (London: HMSO, 1945).

Beckett, Ian F.W., *Ypres: The First Battle* (London: Pearson Longman, 2006).

Bond, Brian & Cave, Nigel (eds.), *Haig: A Re-Appraisal 80 Years On* (Barnsley: Pen & Sword, 1999).

Carver, Field Marshal Lord: *The National Army Museum Book of The Boer War* (London: Pan Books, 2000).

Callwell, C.E, *Field-Marshal Sir Henry Wilson: His Life and Diaries* (London: Cassell and Company, 1927).

Cave, Nigel and Sheldon, Jack, *Ypres 1914: The Menin Road* (Barnsley: Pen & Sword, 2019).

Colvile, Major-General Sir H.E., *The Work of the Ninth Division* (London: Edward Arnold, , 1901).

Colyer, David G., *Bygone Kent*, Vol. 11, No. 11 (Smittingbourne: Meresborough Books, 1990).

Conan Doyle, Sir Arthur, *The Great Boer War* (Driffield: Leonaur, 2010).

Cooper, Duff, *Haig* (London: Faber & Faber, 1936).

Corns, Cathryn and Hughes-Wilson, John, *Blindfolded and Alone* (London: Cassell, 2005).

Crozier, Brigadier-General F.P., A *Brass Hat In No Man's Land* (London: Jonathan Cape, 1937).

Davies, Frank & Maddocks, Graham, *Bloody Red Tabs* (London: Leo Cooper, 1995).

Easdown, Martin and Genth, *Thomas: A Glint In The Sky* (Barnsley: Pen & Sword, 2004).

Edmonds, Brig-General J.E. (ed.): *Military Operations France and Belgium 1914*, Vol. II (London: Macmillan & Co., 1925).

Farrar-Hockley, Anthony, *Death of an Army* (London: Arthur Barker, 1967).

Farrar-Hockley, Anthony, *Goughie: The Life of Gen Sir Hubert Gough* (London: Hart-Davis, MacGibbon, 1975).

Farwell, Byron, *The Great Boer War* (Barnsley: Pen & Sword, 2009).

Forester, C.S., *The General* (London: Michael Joseph, 1958).

Fox, Frank ('GSO'), *GHQ (Montreuil-sur-Mer)* (London: Philip Allan & Co., 1920).

Freeman, Edith, *A Family Story: The Ruggles of Spains Hall* (Sudsbury: Don Fraser Print, , 1993).

Fremont-Barnes, Gregory, *The Boer War* (Oxford: Osprey Publishing, 2013).

George, Michael and George, Christine, *Dover & Folkestone During The Great War* (Barnsley: Pen & Sword, 2008).

Gleichen, Maj-Gen Lord Edward, *A Guardsman's Memories* (Edinburgh: William Blackwood & Sons, 1932).

Gough, Hubert, *The Fifth Army* (London: Hodder & Stoughton, 1931).

Hamilton, Lord Ernest W.: *The First Seven Divisions* (London: Hurst & Blackett, 1916).

Hanning, Henry: *The British Grenadiers* (Barnsley: Pen & Sword, 2006).

Harding, Brian, *Keeping Faith: The History of The Royal British Legion* (London: Leo Cooper, 2001).

Hesketh-Pritchard, Major H., *Sniping in France: Winning the Sniping War in the Trenches* (Barnsley: Pen & Sword, 2014).

Holt, Major and Mrs, *Definitive Battlefield Guide to Ypres Salient & Passchendaele* (Barnsley: Pen & Sword, 2017).

Jeffery, Keith, *Field Marshal Sir Henry Wilson: A Political Soldier* (Oxford: OUP, 2006).

Jones, Spencer, *From Boer War to World War: Tactical Reform of the British Army, 1902-1914* (Norman, Oklahoma: University of Oklahoma Press, 2013).

Keegan, John: *The First World War* (London: Hutchinson, 1999).

Kennedy, John: *With the Immortal 7th Division* (London: Hodder & Stoughton, 1916).

Launcey, James, *Blair Castle* (Atholl Estates, 2013).

LoCicero, M., Mahoney, R. and Mitchell, S. (eds.), *A Military Transformed? Adaptation and Innovation in the British Military, 1792-1945* (Solihull: Helion & Company, 2014).

Lowry, Edward P., *With the Guard's Brigade During the Boer War* (Driffield: Leonaur, 2009).

Maurice, Maj Gen Sir Frederick, and Grant, Captain Maurice, *Official History of the War in South Africa 1899-1902*, Vols. 1-4 (London: Hurst and Blackwell, London, 1906-1910).

Messenger, Charles, *Broken Sword: The Tumultuous Life of General Frank Crozier* (Barnsley: Pen & Sword, 2013).

Mitchinson, K.W., *Villers-Plouich* (Barnsley: Pen & Sword, 1999).

Murphy, David, *Breaking Point of the French Army: The Nivelle Offensive of 1917* (Barnsley: Pen & Sword, 2015).

Nicolson, Harold, *King George V* (London: Book Club Associates, 1969).

Oldham, Peter, *The Hindenburg Line* (Barnsley: Pen & Sword, 2000).

Packenham, Thomas, *The Boer War* (London: Weidenfeld & Nicolson, 1980).

Pienaar, Philip, *With Steyn and De Wet* (London: Methuen, 1902).

Ponsonby, Lieutenant-Colonel the Rt Hon Sir Frederick, *The Grenadier Guards in the Great War*, Vol. 1 (London: Macmillan & Co., 1929).

Putkowski, Julian and Dunning, Mark, *Murderous Tommies* (Barnsley: Pen & Sword, 2012).

Putkowski, Julian and Sykes, Julian: *Shot At Dawn* (Barnsley: Pen & Sword, 2007).

Radley, Kenneth, *On the Dangerous Edge: British and Canadian Trench Raiding on the Western Front 1914-1918* (Warwick: Helion & Co., 2018).

Reed, Paul, *Walking Arras* (Barnsley: Pen & Sword, 2007).

Ridley, Jane: *George V* (London: Chatto & Windus, 2021).

Robertson, Sylvia and Young, *Patricia: Daughter of Atholl* (Atholl Publishing, 2007).

Ruggles-Brise, Major H., The *Official Records of the Guards Brigade in South Africa*, (London: Keliher & Co., 1904).

Schwink, Otto, *Ypres 1914* (Driffield: Leonaur, 2012).

Sheffield, Gary and Todman, Dan (eds.), *Command and Control on the Western Front* (Staplehurst: Spellmount, 2007).

Sheffield, Gary, *The Chief: Douglas Haig and the British Army* (London: Arum Press, 2011).

Sheffield, Gary and Bourne, John (eds.): *Douglas Haig: War Diaries and Letters 1914-18* (London: Weidenfeld and Nicolson, 2005).

Simkins, Peter, *The Guards* (Peterborough: Jarrold Publishing, 2007).

Stevens, F.T., *Complete History of the War in South Africa 1899-1902* (London: W. Nicholson & Son, 1903).

Terraine, John, *Douglas Haig: The Educated Soldier* (London: Hutchinson, 1963).

The Times History of the War in South Africa, Vols. 1-7 (London: S. Low, Marston & Co., 1900).

Travers, Tim: *The Killing Ground* (London: Allen & Unwin,1987).

Van Emden, Richard: *The Soldier's War* (London: Bloomsbury, 2009).

White, C.M., *Gotha Summer: The German daytime air raids on England, May to August 1917* (London: Robert Hale, 1986).

Whitton, Lieutenant-Colonel F.E., *History of The 40th Division* (Uckfield: Naval & Military Press reprint of 1926 edition).

Wilson, Jean Moorcroft, *Isaac Rosenberg: The Making of a Great War Poet* (London: Phoenix, 2008).

Woodward, David, *Lloyd George and the Generals* (Newark, Delaware: University of Delaware Press, 198).

Wright, Thomas, *The History and Topography of the County of Essex* (London: George Virtue, 1831).

Unpublished Sources
LHCMA/KCL: Beddington, Edward: 'My Life', Beddington Papers.

Index